HEAD TO HEAD

Oliver Hill

Published by **Dolman Scott Ltd**

Copyright ©**Oliver Hill 2014**

All rights reserved. No part of this publication may be reproduced, stored in a retrieval system, or transmitted in any form or by any means, electronic, mechanical, photocopy, recording or otherwise, without prior written permission of the copyright owner. Nor can it be circulated in any form of binding or cover other than that in which it is published and without similar condition including this condition being imposed on a subsequent purchaser

ISBN 978-1-909204-48-5

Dolman Scott
www.dolmanscott.co.uk

DEDICATION

This book is dedicated to my wife Dominique, without whose unstinting support and dedication none of which is chronicled could have been achieved. My feelings are best expressed in the words of Shakespeare:

When in disgrace with fortune and men's eyes,

I all alone beweep my outcast state,

And trouble deaf heaven with my bootless cries,

And look upon myself, and curse my fate,

Wishing me like to one more rich in hope,

Featured like him, like him with friends possest,

Desiring this man's art, and that man's scope,

With what I most enjoy contented least;

Yet in those thoughts myself almost despising,

Happily I think on thee: and then my state.

Like to the Lark at break of day arising

From sullen earth, sings at Heaven's gate;

For thy sweet love rememb'red such wealth brings,

That when I scorn to change my state with kings.

CONTENTS

DEDICATION	iii
PREFACE	1
NOR IRON BARS	2
REBEL WITH A CAUSE	8
THE EARLY YEARS	15
RHODESIA	24
RHODESIA – THE STRUGGLE BEGINS	36
THE ELEPHANT FEAST	46
SLEEPING WITH THE ENEMY	60
EXIT AMERICANS	89
SABLE COMPLETION	93
TA – TOBACCO AUCTIONS	108
TOYS R US	121
PERTAMINA	131
LONDON	147
PERTAMINA PART II	152
FINANCE	165
THE RESERVE BANK	179
DIVERTISSEMENTS	186
SWAZILAND – THE PAPER TIGER	197
SWAZILAND – THE REAL FIGHT BEGINS	228
IN WITH A BANG	233
MORE BANG	244
TOVEX	249
PHASE II	272
STRATALOC AND KEVLAR	278
INTO THE BLEACH	283
LLOYDS	287
REVOLUTION	291
FINANCE WEEK	299
RIDING HIGH	309
FARMER HILL	339

PREFACE

In Johannesburg, South Africa, on 24th July 1939, Robert Oliver Hill was born.

No-one realised at that time that a few decades later this boy, now a man, would revolutionise the way business was done in South Africa and its neighbouring countries.

This book is a "must read" for entrepreneurs all over the world. It teaches and inspires how one can succeed even against the most formidable opposition. A real-life story told candidly and truthfully.

Likewise, it should be a "must read" for those in the business world who become complacent in their existing positions of power.

It was a pleasant, educational, and humbling experience for me to have had the honour of associating with Oliver, who possessed such unusual talent. He could converse with a miner in the deepest shaft, or with the Chairman of the Board of the largest companies in the world. He could quickly comprehend the aspects of complex technology, was a wizard at developing financial strategies, demonstrated outstanding marketing skills, and was a genius at discovering the weakest part of his competitor's armour.

I hope you will find this book helpful and inspirational in your endeavours.

Robert Oliver Hill will always be in my fondest memories.

Ward N. Kissel, Jr
Licensing Manager (retired)
E. I. Du Pont de Nemours, Wilmington, Delaware

NOR IRON BARS

Clunk. The cell door of Brixton prison slammed shut. At long last the South African Reserve Bank had got me where they wanted me. And they would stop at nothing to haul me back to South Africa for a kangaroo court hearing. As a senior official said to one of my lawyers, "We know he's guilty. Whatever evidence we have to produce to convict him, we will."

Dominique outside Brixton

As Philip Clarke (the managing director of our fertiliser company and of Triomf Fertilisers) said to me: "You are obsessed with legality. I can tell you that you have driven a cart and horses through their precious system, and, regardless of the legalities, the South African Reserve Bank is going to cut your legs off at the knees. They will do whatever it takes to do that."

What aggravated the Reserve Bank even more was that my legal team had butchered them in the Supreme Court and they had been ordered to return my family's assets. When they appealed the judgement, the Appeal Court had ruled that they had no right *ab initio* to seize them. This, of course, opened the door to a massive damages claim and made them even more determined to nail me. When they knew that I was to go to America for an arbitration hearing, they initiated an extradition request to the USA, with whom they had an extradition agreement. I got to hear about it and left the USA; but, as there was an arrest warrant outstanding, I asked my US lawyer to investigate. He got a copy of the indictment supposedly issued in May 1993. The only indictment for which we had a copy was issued for Exchange Control breaches before May 1993. This later indictment made no mention of Exchange Control, which, of course, does not amount to a crime in any of the civilised countries of the world. The affidavit, issued by the Clerk of the Court, accompanying the indictment had very peculiar wording. So I asked Oshy Tugendhaft, my lawyer, to investigate the court record in Johannesburg. At first the Clerk denied that there was such an indictment, but inspection of his record book found that an indictment was entered on 31st December 1993, but supposedly dated May. Clearly a back-dated indictment had been issued, but, because of the consecutive numbering system and the chronological sequence, it was not possible to insert an indictment with the date of May to satisfy US legal requirements.

For the USA it was a requirement that the indictment be issued within 5 years of the supposed crime as there was a statute of limitations.

Clearly, the indictment issued to the American authorities had been back-dated and the records in South Africa falsified in order to comply with US law. Presented with this evidence, the US authorities vacated the arrest warrant and I travelled freely to the USA.

Once South Africa re-entered the Commonwealth, the Reserve Bank made a further effort, as South Africa was now party to the Commonwealth Extradition arrangements. This allowed them to have an arrest warrant issued by the British authorities, and they then had three months to bring their case before the magistrate. In the meantime you cooled your heels in prison. To be incarcerated in a Victorian prison (Brixton), with all that entailed, was a stressful experience. Such was the sense of humour of the system that, as a white South African, it was considered appropriate to house me with a black African from Nigeria. Eventually it backfired, as from being very hostile we became friends and I was instrumental in getting his case dismissed. Eventually, all the foreign blacks in Brixton took to consulting me, as none of them could afford a lawyer. I was then moved in with a 22-stone armed robber, Graham, who took to being my protector. When one of the British blacks decided that it was time to attack me, Graham leaned on him as he was standing against the balcony and crushed the breath out of him, muttering in his ear to lay off me or he might just fall off the balcony. He laid off me and I was not bothered thereafter.

Unfortunately, the policy of the British Government was not sympathetic to white South Africans.

I, of course, made an application for bail. To the horror of my lawyers, I was not allowed to attend the Court hearing and nor could I communicate with them, either in person or by phone, as I was only allowed two minutes on the phone. In spite of having top barrister Charlie Falconer (later Lord Falconer and Lord Chancellor under Labour), bail was denied.

The matter then went before the Magistrate. Under English Law it was necessary to prove someone had suffered actual prejudice. The only prejudice which could be asserted in reality was that a Government is entitled to have its laws obeyed. As the only crime which in reality could be asserted was that of Exchange Control violations (not a crime in England), a new prejudice had to be found. This was found by the SA Government asserting a loss of R130 million to the South African Treasury. As Oshy, my lawyer, had come to England for the hearing as a witness, we were pretty confident that he would be able to shoot down this blatant lie. But at the behest of the barrister for South Africa, one Michael Birnbaum, I was prohibited from bringing any evidence at all to the court. So, of course, that accusation stood. Oshy would have been able to testify that it was all a pack of lies and that factually no-one had suffered any loss. Three years later, in another case, the House of Lords ruled that it was a basic right to bring evidence in one's own defence and in the case in question, the plaintiff was set free immediately. So I had been unlawfully incarcerated in Brixton for three years.

But before this case came up we attacked the Attorney General in South Africa, and brought a case against him, demanding an indictment and asking the Court to declare the Reserve Bank powers to be unconstitutional. In Court he asserted his right to try me for whatever he wanted. But he had given assurances to the British Home Secretary that I would only be tried on the basis of the case before the English Courts. Even the supine courts in South Africa would have held him to that. So he agreed to withdraw from the case, provided I settled with the Reserve Bank. I made the settlement with the Reserve Bank, which would allow me to return to South Africa without fear of them then hounding me for Exchange Control.

Even though I had been obsessed with my legal rights and thought I would be able to fight them off, I was too tired to get into another long legal wrangle. The settlement was secret at the behest of the Minister of Finance. One of the conditions was that all members of my family and all companies associated with me had to agree not to make any claim for damages against the SA Government, the Department of Finance and the Reserve Bank, and that the agreement with the Treasury was to be kept secret. I assume, therefore, that I can be sued for this revelation. On the other hand, Mark Shuttleworth has proved that many of the Reserve Bank powers used against me are totally unconstitutional. I had brought a case against the Attorney General asserting that many of these powers were both *ultra vires* and unconstitutional. In the Shuttleworth case this was, in fact, what the Constitutional Court had ruled. No wonder the Attorney General forced me into a settlement with the Reserve Bank; they faced a monumental claim for damages!

Sitting in that miserable hellhole of Brixton, I could contemplate the incredible duplicity of the SA Government and the Reserve Bank. I also thought back to a dark and stormy night in South Africa when I was called out to hear that there had been an explosion at our Bronkhorstspruit explosives plant. I rushed out there to find there had been an explosion and five staff members were missing. We collected some of their remains in fertiliser sacks. The explosives mix house had been destroyed. At midnight I sat down with Phil Smart (the factory manager) and his deputy, Ray Gibbison, to hold a conference. Everyone was distraught. It was one of the most traumatic experiences of my life. I was asked: "What next?"

I said: "Tomorrow morning we will bury our dead. In the afternoon we will start with a new mix house and you guys have three weeks to complete it." They did.

I then got a letter from the wife of Johan van Aswegen, our dead production manager. His funeral had been traumatic. Her letter was a profound shock. She said she was not bitter about Johan's death, because he had died as a very happy man pursuing "Oliver Hill's Dream". She was thankful for the many happy years he had spent with my team.

People like this are worth their weight in diamonds – as was underlined when Sasol bought the explosives company, and told me that they would only keep the top management for a month or two as they wanted to install the "SASOL way". In fact, they took my two top men over to run the whole explosives business! No greater compliment could have been paid; my team were amongst the most motivated and capable people one could find.

We found incontrovertible evidence of the sabotage of the plant and evidence as to who had been responsible. This was all produced at the inquiry. The people we had lost had been murdered.

It was an open secret that those stalwarts of human rights, Generals Pinochet and Franco, were the two bastions of South Africa's arms supplies. The evidence pointed directly to Spain. However, it was not politically convenient to follow this line of inquiry and the matter was never pursued.

It is true that I turned the South African chemical industry upside down, but this was by introducing new products and processes which rendered many of the plants obsolete. This upset the cosy, but powerful, cartel.

On the other hand, we didn't commit murder.

REBEL WITH A CAUSE

After twenty turbulent years in business in what have to be some of the most momentous years in the history of my country, and after having been tried and condemned by the press as a criminal, I feel that it is time to place on record my side of the story. It is one of the great ironies that the days of the white man making history in Africa are rapidly drawing to a close, and the vicarious pleasure which the petty officials of the Afrikaner Establishment have derived from vilifying me are as nothing in the grand sweep of history.

Nevertheless, the impact of a small group of people has been profound, and it will compound the South African tragedy if the effects of the wild excesses of Afrikaner Nationalism are parodied by their successors in title, the African National Congress. The experiences I have undergone are a microcosm of the attitudes, mores and prejudices of my countrymen.

I am an Afrikaner. Although my name is English, the blood flowing in my veins is almost entirely of Afrikaner origin. Being English speaking with such a heritage makes me a traitor in the eyes of Afrikanerdom. The Afrikaners have throughout their history been rebellious against what they have seen as officious authority, except in the last century. In this century, the power of groupthink has forced a conformity upon Afrikanerdom, all too evident in their appointments to the Courts, to the increase of legislation by fiat, to the pressures to "be a good South African" which means a kind of slavish chauvinism, reinforced by the laager mentality into which we have been driven by a world which does not understand us. Anyone who lifted his voice against this mainstream of thought was branded a traitor to the volk.ast.

My Afrikaner forebears have had a long history of being rebels. My upbringing by a mother, Dora Kotze, who cherished the ideals of democracy and Liberalism all her life made me receptive to the ideas to which I have been exposed to in my education outside South Africa. My mother's family, the Kotzes, throughout our long history in South Africa, have been vilified by the establishment for their strongly held views. When today one reads of the issues for which they were vilified, it hardly seems credible.

Both her grandfathers were dominees. The one, the Reverend D.P.Faure, decided to become a minister and went off to Leiden in Holland to study theology. On his return to Cape Town he was invited to preach in the Groote Kerk. His sermon, although one carefully calculated to be mild, was greeted in stunned silence by the congregation. No-one came to the vestry after the sermon, so in the end, to save them the embarrassment of having to go home without their coats and hats, he left quietly. A violent campaign was waged against him by the Moderator of the Dutch Reformed Church, the Reverend Andrew Murray, who preached a sermon on the basis of Chapter 13 of Deuteronomy, calling for Faure to be put to death by stoning. It seems a harsh punishment for a man who held the heretical views that it was possible to believe in Charles Darwin's recently published Origin of the Species and God at the same time! And was not afraid to say so! The upshot was that he was forced by his followers to found the Free Protestant Church in Cape Town as the Dutch Reformed Church closed its ranks in horror against his heresies.

The other grandfather, the Reverend J.J.Kotze was one of the leaders of the liberal movement in the Dutch Reformed Church, together with the Reverend Thomas Francois Burgers (later to become President of the Orange River Republic) For denying the existence of a personal devil, and the sinlessness of Christ, he and Burgers were suspended by the Church Synod. Although they sued and won in the Supreme Court and were reinstated, the vituperative campaign against them never ceased. In these days we laugh at the death sentence passed upon Salman Rushdie by the Ayatollah Khomenei, but in our own history we have little to be proud of. Whilst our nation has always produced independent thinkers, the Establishment has tended to react with extreme violence towards them.

The brother of the Reverend Kotze was the famous Chief Justice (later Sir John Kotze) of the Transvaal Republic. As one of the country's most highly regarded jurists in Roman-Dutch law he had a difficult row to hoe. The President of the Republic, the redoubtable Paul Kruger, knew what he wanted. He was usually able to force his views through a compliant Volksraad, and was one of the earlier dictators of our society.

Sir John had earlier taken the view that the Volksraad was sovereign, and could do as it pleased. Accordingly he took the view that the Courts had no power to test the laws of the Volksraad against the Grondwet (the Constitution). However, after many years on the bench, and having been profoundly influenced by the American Constitution, he came to the view that the High Court existed as, inter alia, the Guardian of the rights of citizens against the arbitrary exercise of power by the Volksraad. Accordingly, when a fairly insignificant case came up, he changed his earlier view, and declared that the law passed by the Volksraad was in conflict with the Grondwet, and gave judgement accordingly. One of his fellow judges ducked the issue by deciding that the Volksraad could not have intended to make the legislation retrospective (something from which our current rulers do not shrink!) But Sir John came out fairly and squarely on the main issue. And he took the position that the independence of the judiciary was one of the hallmarks of a civilised state, and that that this independence served as the citizen's bulwark against a state which was only too anxious to arbitrarily deprive citizens of their rights.

Kotze was a lone voice in the wilderness. Kruger reacted with ferocity and demanded that the judges all sign an oath relinquishing any pretension to the "testing right", which he described as an "abomination". All the judges except Sir John eventually complied and thus became lackeys of the State. Kruger thereupon summarily fired Sir John, an act which again was remarkable for its complete lawlessness and the supine reaction of the populace, who in any event had their eyes upon the much more momentous events unfolding as the Boer War loomed.

In the end, Sir John had the last laugh as he ended his days as a much loved and respected judge of the Appeal Court of the Union.

But the leopard has not changed his spots. The totalitarian tendencies present in my Afrikaner brethren are all still there. It is their accepted norm to pass retroactive legislation, and to empower Ministers to make regulations which effectively remove the law making function from Parliament and place it in the hands of bureaucrats. These bureaucrats are then also vested with a quasi-judicial function. Even the rubber stamp for the Nationalists that Parliament was for 40 years is an embarrassment. The attitude is that cabinet ministers are somehow endowed with all-seeing, all-knowing powers; they do not need the inconvenience of courts to scrutinize them, they never make mistakes ! (This was asserted to my lawyers by Dr Lombard, the then Deputy Governor of the Reserve Bank).

My grandfather, Sir Robert Kotze, was one of South Africa's greatest unsung technocrats. With his far-sighted vision of the mining industry, he installed a tax system, which has remained unchanged in principle for nearly a hundred years. He took the then unfashionable view that the riches of the earth belonged to all the people, subject to a proper system of incentives for private enterprise to seek, find and recover those riches. Long before environmentalists became fashionable in the rest of the world, he set about creating environmental laws in the mining industry, as well as safety laws, which even to this day are a model. He was responsible for the creation of Eskom, which he modelled on the Tennessee Valley Authority.

He ran foul of a minister who decided that it was his prerogative to appoint the staff of the Department of Mines. As the minister had decided to appoint an unqualified person as an Inspector of Mines, against my grandfather's advice, Kotze resigned. He thereupon was invited to stand for Parliament by Smuts where he served with distinction for a decade. He also was invited by Ernest Oppenheimer onto the boards of De Beers and AE & CI, quite an irony in view of my latter history.

And the even greater irony is that he was invited to join those boards to bring some respectability to as ruthless a bunch of robber barons ever to grace the South African business scene!

So my family became very Establishment over time.

The peculiar thing about the South African business structure, which was heavily weighted by its gold mining and diamond mining background, is that these activities needed no marketing. Gold was sold at a fixed price to the Americans, and diamonds were sold through a cartel. The normal disciplines of a capitalist society, in which the market is the all driving force, were almost entirely lacking. The people who rose to the top in the system were just politicians, who knew how to climb up through the bureaucracies which inevitably developed. And as the mining houses got control of the industrial base of the country, they followed the same philosophy of rigged markets, because they simply didn't understand what a market based capitalist system was about.

This cosy world looked down upon the people who actually sold goods for a living. It was somehow not quite acceptable to be associated with people "in trade". The highest social class was made up of people who sold gold for a living because there was no competition - definitely a job for gentlemen! It was anticipated that I would do the normal thing expected as a scion of such a system; go to the best private school in the country, get a decent degree at a South African university, finished off by a post graduate degree at Oxford or Cambridge. The final step would be to join a mining house, and march up the ladder within the establishment, and never, but never, rock the boat, or question the system.

Well, my mother was something of a maverick and she and my father decided that perhaps I was not entirely cut out to be a conformist member of that little world.

I went to Wits where among other subjects I had the rare privilege of majoring in applied mathematics. This little class had daily exposure to Arthur Bleksley. Bleksley was an inspiring person, and although regarded with awe by all his students he was a very approachable man and never belittled students. I went to him with a zany idea which, if it worked, would enable one to overcome the second law of thermodynamics.

I explained that I wanted to use a funnel to capture gas molecules and allow them to accumulate in a vessel which would then become pressurised. The gas could them be let out to generate power and would drop in temperature. Bleksley listened and said to me, "Well if I were catching tennis balls I know which end of the funnel I would use. But both of us know that you can't overcome the second law of thermodynamics. Let's work it out."

The simple answer in the end is that for every molecular path you can postulate from the funnel end you can postulate for the tight end so that equal numbers of molecules have to go through from each end and it has nothing to do with the geometry of the collector. But I wasn't ridiculed, which is one of the reasons students loved this inspiring man.

After getting a first class honours degree on chemistry at Wits, my family came to the conclusion that I was, horror of horrors, a commercially orientated individual, with an extremely rebellious attitude towards authority, and that perhaps the American way of looking at life was a more appropriate for me. I was therefore persuaded by my father that perhaps I should look at trying for the Harvard Business School instead of Oxbridge or the London School of Economics. I thought this was a great idea and decided that I was going to Harvard !

Utilizing the last leverage of being in the Establishment, Charlie Engelhard, the Platinum King, gave me a job in America at his company in New Jersey, and there I duly arrived in the spring of 1962. I worked in the research and development division of Engelhard Industries whilst waiting to see whether I had been accepted at Harvard. We had sailed for America under the assumption that I would be accepted. Part of it was arrogance, part was just the assumption that failure to be accepted was not possible. I had written a test called the GMAT, which was used as one of the factors determining your acceptance or otherwise. In this test, which had no upper limit score, I got a score of 49. The upper 10% score was greater than 39. The upper 1% was greater than 42. So I assumed that I had to have a score somewhere near number one out of the ten thousand who wrote that year, and therefore that I would be accepted.

Well I was, so off to Harvard we went.

THE EARLY YEARS

Having gone to America to work for Charlie Engelhard, the legendary boss of Engelhard Industries, before hopefully being accepted at Harvard, I started in the Research and Development Department. My boss was a Doctor Straschil, an Austrian who had walked back to Austria from Stalingrad and then emigrated to the USA. I had to pass his little test on thermodynamics before I was allowed to work in the gas labs. We were there concerned with the catalytic treatment of gas streams for pollution control and for catalysis of gas reactions.

The big deal was the idea that, with new California legislation to control exhaust gases from cars, there would be massive demand for platinum and the race was on to develop catalytic converters. For this, unlimited funds were made available. I learnt a great deal about the business.

Finally, I was advised that Harvard had accepted me. My wife Dominique and I had to prepare to move there.

For young impressionable students to go to Harvard in 1962 was like being hit by the revelation of St Paul on the road to Damascus. Kennedy was president and his vigour and vision had a dazzling impact on us. One of my colleagues at Engelhard later explained it as follows: First, he said, Kennedy "had class". Secondly, one must understand the difference between Roosevelt, Johnson and Kennedy.

- Roosevelt came to power on the promise of "a chicken in every pot!"
- Johnson came to power on the promise of "two chickens in every pot!"
- Kennedy came to power on the promise of "a man on the moon".

The Kennedy vision of America and everything he stood for made America and what the Americans stood for an exciting vision of the future world order. We went through the Cuban missile crisis sitting in our car in the snow listening to Kennedy and wondering whether we should drive off to our friends' cottage in Vermont. Boston, with its electronics industries, would clearly be a prime target for a Russian hydrogen bomb.

The adroit handling of this and many other revelations showed us democracy at work. And, of course, we were in the cradle of the Kennedy administration at Harvard. One of our professors at the Business School told us proudly that the school now had more than 50% Republicans, as "all the lousy Democrats have gone to Camelot!"

When we were there it was said to us that we would never again sit in the same room as 95 other persons with as much brain and ability as those present. They pointed out that for the 670 places on offer there were 20,000 applicants. That the process of selection meant that prospective employers who used to recruit at Harvard every year from the graduating class knew that Harvard had already selected from the brightest and best in the business world, that salaries were at least double what you might expect elsewhere and that this, of course, fuelled the desire to become a Harvard graduate.

I have to mention that the case method of instruction means that no-one is lecturing you. There are no right and wrong answers. After studying and discussing a thousand cases over the two years, you develop your own business philosophy. And you have the continuous input from a lot of hyper-intelligent people who really make you think! Your work week is at least 70 hours. Only at exam times can you relax, because there is nothing for which to swot!

So, apart from the dazzling feel of being young, in America, in the Kennedy administration, input from Harvard stimulated me in a way in which I have never ever since been exposed. In the words of Wordsworth: " Bliss was it in that dawn to be alive. To be young was very heaven."

And working at Engelhard Industries during the summer at American Platinum and Silver Works, I gained a great insight into the workings of large-scale dealing with precious metals as a newly half-qualified industrial engineer putting into practice all the lessons learned by wading through all the production cases at Harvard.

I finally graduated with four distinctions.

After graduation, I spent a year in the marketing department of Engelhard Industries. One of the more interesting things we did was marketing ferrochrome. Back in South Africa, my father had been instrumental in supporting Micky Bleloch to make low-carbon ferrochrome from Transvaal ore. Rand Mines built the first plant out at Middelburg to produce the stuff. Because of the low chrome/iron ratio, their product had only 55% chrome compared to the more normal 67% from Rhodesian ore. We tried convincing the steel companies that they were getting all that beautiful low-carbon iron for free! Even in America that took some selling. Today, of course, South Africa dominates the world in ferrochromium and all from Transvaal ore. But it was tough to get there initially.

South Africans generally are very risk averse. I was asked to do a marketing study for Rand Mines on the market in the United States for acid-grade fluorspar, as they were contemplating buying a mine and producing 60,000 tons a year. I enthusiastically set about it. The *Engineering and Mining Journal* provided me with all the data required and I discovered that basically three companies were responsible for 80% of consumption – Essex Chemical, Du Pont and Allied Chemical. I quickly arranged appointments with all three and got a commitment from each for 20,000 tons per year at the *E&MJ*-posted price – 60,000 tons sold, and having done the whole thing in ten days I was pretty chuffed with myself and sent off a report.

The reply from Rand Mines in South Africa was that as they had to risk the money they expected at least a three-month investigation and couldn't believe anything done so quickly could be for real. I explained that currently the buyers were in the hands of Mexico and Italy (not very reliable suppliers) and that they were more than happy to place a quarter to a third of their business with another supplier. Bang went one fluorspar mine. It shows the mindset of the big mining houses at the time.

Being close to Charlie Engelhard and an Oxford friend of my father's, Herbert (Woody) Woodman, who was president of a large chemical company, we were privileged to enjoy some of the fleshpots. Charlie had a four-bedroom flat in the Waldorf Towers, filled with Monets, Renoirs and Cezannes, at which we were able to marvel, as well as Woody's flat on Park Avenue, so we spent many happy weekends in New York. Then Charlie asked us to do a favour for the erstwhile owner of Interwoven Socks and Fleischman liquors. John Mettler was a very down-to-earth guy who spent his summer farming in British Columbia, and wanted someone to look after his estate in New Jersey. So we had two happy summers in North Branch, New Jersey, in a fabulous house.

When the Woodies visited, Jean Woodman gasped. She said to us: "Do you realise you are living in a museum of George Washingtoniana!" At least five hundred items in the house either belonged to him or were associated with him. Jean said that the house was a treasure trove worth many millions of dollars – all collected by John Mettler's father, the sock baron of America. The Mettler estate was only a mile from a funny little railroad which ran a commuter service to Newark, where I worked, so it was easy to get to work every day.

All good things come to an end, however, and it was time to come home. Dominique and I had got married and gone to America with four suitcases, but we now had three shipping tons. We also had a daughter born in America and very little money to get home. To finish off at Harvard I had borrowed a couple of thousand dollars from Engelhard. So I owed that as well.

I had been corresponding with a family acquaintance, John Hahn, about what I might do when, and if, I returned to SA. John was a great entrepreneur who had an engineering company and had started in the electrolytic manganese business from uranium plant effluents. He then entered the ferrochrome business using Rhodesian ore. He was in partnership with General Mining and was chafing under the dead hand of bureaucracy. He suggested that we start a company. He would give me a salary of R200 per month and a car and initially 40% of the company with an option for R10 for another 10% after five years. To live on that with a now pregnant wife and a daughter didn't exactly look like a hell of a deal. But my father agreed to finance our home, which was in Johannesburg's Vivian Estate and where gum trees blocked his view, on condition he could cut down the gum trees. So for R14,000 we were the happy owners of the forester's cottage on the Sachsenwald Estate, now Forest Town and Saxonwold. Incidentally, the two empty stands on the estate sold for R14,500 each, so our house was considered to be worth − R500.

To return home I had been pulling some strings, as we got to know Anitajean Galantucci, Charlie Engelhard's secretary, rather well. He was planning to go to South Africa in his plane − the *Platinum Plover*. This was a 60-seat turboprop Convair converted for 20 passengers. Very comfortable, and in those days one of the few private airliners around. Anyway, Charlie had just bought into a company in South Africa and he wanted to install one of his own people to "strengthen the management". He asked what I wanted and I said R10,000 a year plus perks. No problem. It was an American salary.

The bosses of RMB Alloys also wanted me at a good local mining house on a salary of R150/month. So did Syfrets, the investment and banking house, at the same magnificent salary. So John's R200 was not out of line with SA salaries, actually.

Anyway, with a free ride for myself, wife, daughter and three tons of luggage, I agreed to meet with the boss of the company Charlie had acquired. Well, his attitude was that he did not have anything for me to do and it was clear that I was viewed as Charlie's spy planted on him. So I told him that I certainly didn't want a job with nothing to do and I was just seeing him at the request of Mr Engelhard. If there was nothing to do, I would cheerfully duck on it. At once he became warm and friendly and we parted the best of friends. But the shit hit the fan in Engelhard Industries. Charlie was mightily upset.

So I took up with John Hahn and National Process Industries was born in May of 1966.

Being hot off the press, so to speak, in the platinum business, the project with which I first became concerned was in Rustenburg, northwest of Johannesburg. John had negotiated a chrome deal with Edward Molotlegi, who was chief of the Bafokeng tribe. The tribe owned some 17,000 hectares of land at Rustenburg. Edward had agreed with John that he could negotiate for the platinum rights. So I was out to Rustenburg twice a week for some months. I worked out a deal with Chief Edward. He would get a down payment of R6,000, which would enable the tribe to buy a tractor and plough, and would enjoy a royalty of 12.5% of profits from mining, refining and marketing.

I had put this in as I had insight to the deal Charlie had done with Rand Mines. What he had charged them for refining and marketing was obscene and the company had made a staggering amount of money out of them when I was in America. I did not want to chisel the tribe, and thought that 12.5 % was fair (later, we discovered that the going rate from the mining houses was 2.9%). Anyway, we worked out a very nice deal and it was necessary to go out and raise money. From my time in America I knew that Union Carbide, who were John's partners in ferrochrome, used some 400,000 ounces a year of palladium. So it was logical to talk to the Union Carbide metals division and the boss thereof duly arrived in South Africa.

I took him out to Rustenburg and showed him the set-up .We even walked down an old incline shaft sunk in 1929. I showed him the Merensky reef, the main platinum-bearing horizon, and told him that there was a resource of probably 150 million ounces of platinum, 60 million ounces of palladium, 14 million ounces of rhodium and a million tons of nickel. The value was many billions of dollars.

He asked me: "How is it conceivable that this could be available for R6,000 down and 12.5% of profits? Why hadn't one of the great mining houses snapped it up? There must be a catch."

I explained to him that the conventional wisdom in South Africa was that if you didn't have a deal with Johnson Matthey or Engelhard, you couldn't sell your platinum. You had to have a marketing deal. His response was that that was crap. Union Carbide bought hundreds of thousands of ounces of palladium from Russia every year and the Russians sold all the platinum they wanted to into the market. My proposition was absurd and there had to be a very deep-seated catch to the whole thing. So Union Carbide turned it down. The rest is, of course, history. Two Johannesburg stockbrokers – Anderson and Wilson – picked up my contract, paid the R6,000, and Impala Platinum was born.

Syd Newman, then in charge of Rand Mines, told me much later how Anderson and Wilson had hawked the project all over town without any takers. When they came back to Syd (who was constrained by his Engelhard/Anglo deal), he advised them to go to Union Corp and put in a good word for them. Many multi-millionaires were created as a result.

Some time later, when my father was a consultant to President Mangope of Bophututswana, he came to me with a problem. The Bophututswana Government was deriving very little revenue from

Impala Plats. He asked me to look at the books and I discovered that what General Mining (the new owners of Union Corp) were doing was to apportion the profits between the refinery in Springs (in South Africa) and the mine in Bophututswana. They did this on the basis of the capital employed in each place. However, the capital in the mine was written off as a wasting asset, and the refinery was written up each year to its replacement value. That meant that the lion's share of the profit was taxed in South Africa at an industrial rate, whilst at the mine it was taxed at the precious metals rate (much, much higher). In addition, the tribe no longer got a share of the refining profit.

I said to my father: "Why, General Mining is swindling the tribe and the Bophututswana Government of the profit share that they are entitled to." My father, being of the old school, was shocked and said that General Mining would never stoop to stealing from the tribe who were entitled to their profit share and tax. But, in fact, General Mining waltzed off with hundreds of millions by this means. Having worked in the share valuation department at Rand Mines and been exposed to the way taxes were manipulated to pay as little as possible, I took that comment with a sack of salt.

We then turned our attention to other platinum projects in the area. One of the tribes we talked to was the Bapo Bo Mogale tribe, represented by their chief, Fred Mogale. Fred fell for our offer hook, line and sinker. After the obligatory meetings with the Tribal Council and much haggling, they accepted. The signing was set for the next week. As we parted, Fred said to me that they had another contract but it was not serious and meant nothing. I said I'd better take a look at it anyway.

Well, it was our old friend Tiny Rowland, the Lonrho mogul. The Lonrho contract was the most one-sided I had ever seen. No minimums, no programme and an everlasting right in favour of Lonrho. I regretfully told Fred that he was tied up hands and feet forever and had no out. Tiny could sit on those rights for 50 years and he could do nothing about it. And all that for a miserable 2.9%! Now, of course, it's Western Platinum/Lonmin.

The final throw we had was with George Abdinor, who was involved with Rowland in mines in Rhodesia. George wanted to get into platinum. There was a farm which, while under the Bafokeng, was Native Trust land and not owned by the tribe. It therefore fell under the Minister for Native Affairs. On approach, he in turn passed the buck to the Department of Mines for a recommendation. Their recommendation was unequivocal. It should go to us.

But by then Union Corp was in full swing with the Bafokeng. One of their directors was a certain Dr Holloway, one of the top Broeders (the secret Afrikaaner business "club") in the country. The minister got the message loud and clear. It goes to Union Corp.

So that was the end of our foray into platinum.

Time to go fishing! Incidentally, with Syd Newman. September 1966.

RHODESIA

Rhodesia is where it all began. I had returned from the USA with one aim really, and that was to catch a marlin at Bazaruto Island off the coast of Mozambique. September 1966 therefore found me on nearby Paradise Island with a boat chartered for two weeks, with this objective in mind.

The season had started early, fortunately, as usually the marlin came at the end of September, whilst the sailfish arrived at the end of August. In those days, although the management and administration of the hotel was unbelievably bad, the atmosphere was magic. With a dozen boats plying the waters, seeking marlin and other denizens of those warm waters, the evenings in the pub were full of fun and camaraderie, and we did no little damage to the green wines of Portugal, which flowed copiously all night. Two characters from Rhodesia, Lofty and Cecil, farmers from Umtali, were particular favourites of ours, and we spent happy hours solving the problems of Africa, and talking about the day's fishing, the fury and cunning of marlin and any other subject on earth.

The common wisdom was that one in three marlin that struck were hooked, and one in three marlin that were hooked were landed. The sight of these huge fish all lit up in silver and purple, slashing away at the baits and teasers, and, if hooked, tailwalking away at high speed, was pretty adrenaline pumping. Anyway, after an hour-long fight, I landed my first marlin, a small striped specimen of 250lbs.

It was during one of those evenings that I started talking about the fertiliser ring, and how I had an idea to make fertiliser more cheaply. I had come back to South Africa believing that the South African fertiliser ring was engaged in ripping off the farmers in any way that it could. This was, of course, music to any farmer's ears and Lofty told me that the Rhodesian Government was asking for proposals to establish a fertiliser factory, and that he thought that the deadline was at the end of the month in Salisbury.

Having caught my marlin, I returned to Johannesburg and told John about it. We went to see Mr John Gaunt, the Rhodesian representative in Johannesburg, who confirmed that there was indeed a tender out for proposals to manufacture fertiliser in Rhodesia. However, the closing date was at the end of the month.

Gaunt arranged a meeting for us with the Minister, George Rudland, for the next day, and we flew off to Rhodesia. It was immediately apparent that there was to be only one proposal, and that was by the cartel who had the market sewn up in Rhodesia: AE and CI and Fisons. Rudland agreed that he would extend the date by one month, and we could submit a proposal, if we could do so, by the end of September.

I actually knew virtually nothing about the manufacture of nitrogenous fertiliser. Like all science students, I knew about Haber and Bosch, and that ammonia was made from hydrogen and nitrogen. Nitrogen was easy enough to get from the air. But hydrogen?

The Rhodesian Government had suggested two possible sources of hydrogen. The first was from naphtha from the new oil refinery at Umtali, and the second was from coke-oven gas at Risco, the iron and steel company. It was obvious that this was going to be a long haul, and because John Hahn was a member of the Rand Club, he took advantage of reciprocity with the Salisbury Club, where for the magnificent sum of £2 you could get bed and breakfast.

Having the advantage of knowing virtually nothing about ammonia manufacture, I approached the ammonia problem with no preconceived ideas – a great advantage. All I knew was the basic chemistry of ammonia, which required nitrogen and hydrogen. Everyone knows that the nitrogen comes out of the air. You must find a source of hydrogen. I knew that Sasol in South Africa made its hydrogen by the gasification of coal. I also knew that hydrogen was made for margarine factories by the electrolysis of water. So, apart from the sources suggested by the Rhodesian Government, here were two further possibilities. At the meeting, Rudland granted a month's extension for proposals.

I went into the library at the Salisbury Club, and immersed myself in the books about Rhodesia, the local financial news, and in fact anything I could lay my hands on to learn about the structure of the country and its whole economic foundation. One of the very interesting factors which became immediately apparent was the rather advanced state of electrical power development. The Kariba Dam had been built to supply the needs of both Rhodesia and Zambia, and, in order to make it economic, a very high voltage distribution system, far in advance of anything in South Africa, had been built, linking the Kariba Dam from the Zaire system to as far south as Bulawayo. All the thermal power stations had been closed, and were just maintained for standby purposes, and there was a large surplus of water available which had to be spilled every year through the dam. This surplus power was essentially free. Further, it became apparent that the system, especially in Rhodesia, had a very high daily peak, and for most of the rest of the day it languished at a very low level. So the capacity was unused at these times, but, and this was the important part, the power corporation charged virtually nothing for the actual power used, only for the maximum demand established at any time during the whole year! As Rhodesia effectively paid for the "peak", anyone who could use the valley was essentially entitled to its power for free.

The idea of free power seemed to me to be a promising avenue to follow as a possible source of hydrogen. Naphtha from the new

Umtali refinery was another source being put forward. Naturally, the Umtali council was promoting it heavily. However, there was strong political pressure to have a wholly indigenous source of feedstock. It was believed, rightly as it turned out, that if Rhodesia declared UDI, the refinery would close, being unable to import crude oil, and bang would go the ammonia plant. So naphtha was discarded as a source at a very early date.

Brief investigations into coal gasification showed it to be relatively uneconomic on such a small scale. The two routes which seemed to me, therefore, to hold promise were coke-oven gas and water electrolysis.

The coke-oven gas in question came from Risco, the iron and steel company. This gas had a hydrogen component which could readily be extracted via a nitrogen wash process. There was sufficient to make 150 tons per day of ammonia. If more was needed, then both the carbon monoxide and the methane in the gas would have to have been brought into play, increasing the size and complexity of the plant immeasurably. So, if the economics of an electrolysis plant could be made favourable, this seemed to be the most promising route.

The more I investigated the alternative, and the power circumstances in Rhodesia, the more I liked electrolysis. Not only was the process clean, simple and direct, but it seemed that it could fill a valuable role in the overall power structure of the country. Also, Risco was in the process of going to oxygen steel-making, and would need a very large supply of oxygen, so there would be a ready market for the by-product oxygen from the electrolysis plant.

Now it was just a question of economics.

I returned to Johannesburg, and John got hold of a friend of his, Gerry Caplette, who was the boss of the local Air Liquide subsidiary. Air Liquide were in the fertiliser business in France, and they sent a man out from France to help us put together a technical proposal.

Through a local margarine firm who used electrolytic hydrogen to make margarine, we went into the business of making hydrogen by electrolysis of water. Everything hinged on the price of power.

So it was back to Rhodesia to try to find out power costs. The local Electricity Supply Corporation (ESC) bought its power from the Central African Power Corporation (CAPCO), which owned the Kariba Dam and the high-voltage distribution system in Rhodesia and Zambia. They bought power under a two-part tariff, the base part being power at the cost of their thermal stations (now closed) and the increase at a figure of £9 16s 6d per kw per year plus .025 pence per unit (basically free!). So, if one did not create excess maximum demand, one should essentially get free power.

What I therefore proposed was to use the coke-oven gas from Risco in a gas turbine power station which would generate peak power, and to use power from the system at off-peak times. In this way, and by load shedding at the peak as well, it was logical that we would be paid by the ESC, and get our 120 MW of power to boot. This then was put in our proposal.

It created a firestorm! The ESC were shouting that we had not contributed to the development of the system and why should we benefit from it? So we decided to go direct to the power corporation and buy the power at the Sherwood substation busbars (Sherwood was CAPCO's main midlands substation). Willie Black, the power corporation's operations manager, was appalled, as it upset all the cosy little relationships they had built up. But we created up a big political head of steam, especially as we pointed out that the off-peak power availability was in effect an asset of Rhodesia's and by doing it the way the CAPCO and the ESC wanted, we would be giving half the benefit to Zambia. This was out politically.

Finally, after months of acrimony, I got together with John Magowan, the head of the ESC, and we reached a compromise that I felt we could live with. At the end of the day, the power that was going to be used was literally being pissed down the river by spilling, so that whatever we paid was a net profit to the two countries. Magowan made sure that the lion's share of that profit stayed in Rhodesia.

But this is to run ahead. We put in a formal proposal that the project should be done by the electrolysis of water, and the consortium of the fertiliser companies proposed a coke-oven gas project. Most eyes in Rhodesia were fixed upon the political horizon at the time, as UDI was looming. In a fit of pique, the opposition warned Ian Smith that if the country declared UDI he couldn't have a fertiliser factory. We grabbed that and said that it would only encourage us, as they would have showed that they weren't prepared to be pushed around by the establishment! We also amassed a team of Rhodesians who worked like beavers: Fred Newton, the mayor of Que Que, who was fighting for the plant to go there; Vic Hurley, a prominent local tobacco farmer; C. G. Tracey, a prominent farmer involved in the Rhodesian Promotion Council – all joined in with gusto demanding an independent outfit.

The price of nitrogenous fertiliser in the country was astronomical. It was run by the same cosy little cartel which operated in South Africa. The unholy alliance of AECI and Fisona. At first, they poo-poo-ed the whole concept of the project, and pointed out, quite correctly, that we were not exactly an outfit of substance. The whole electrolysis concept was derided as an old and outdated process. All of this was true; but, in the circumstances of Rhodesia, it made sense. We also noted that whoever made the fertiliser, marketing would be done by the ring, who would charge whatever they wanted. We therefore got a change in the ground rules from Government that meant that anyone who could buy in wholesale quantities could buy at the price agreed with Government directly from the factory. Wholesale quantity was defined as a minimum of one truck per month every month of the year. The ring went berserk over this proposal, but the Rhodesian Front Government had come to power on a basic anti-establishment platform, and the howls of anguish from the ring only served to confirm to the politicians that the course that they were adopting was the correct one.

Once the proposals were in, after much lobbying and discussion, the Government decided to adopt our proposal. But, with the intense pressure from the ring, they announced that both parties were to be given an opportunity to make proposals on the basis of electrolysis. We howled that this was totally unfair and demanded a meeting with Ian Smith, the Prime Minister. He told us bluntly that the Anglo-American Corporation was far too powerful for him to appear to be taking sides against them, but that he recognised that we had a case in equity. What suggestion could we make?

I pointed out to Smith that we had prepared our proposal from scratch and delivered it in full within 30 days. It seemed to me fair therefore that if our little outfit could do that, the vast resources of Anglo would be able to make short work of it, and that the Government should give each party thirty days to submit their final proposals based upon electrolysis. This seemed eminently reasonable to Ian Smith and he proceeded accordingly.

What we had banked upon then happened. For the first three weeks, the Anglo group argued with the Government that the idea was ridiculous and uneconomic. They did no work on the proposal. When they were finally told that there would be no change and no delay, it was far too late for them and all they were able to do was submit a memorandum which castigated the decision and refused to participate. The project, because of the sanctions situation, then went underground.

This was great. We had a project, but one which was going to cost the then astronomical sum of £13,000,000. In today's terms, more like $400,000,000. How the hell to do this with only R6,000 in the bank was the great problem.

Enter Herb Hamilton and Cordell Hull. Hamilton was one of the great entrepreneurs of the chemical construction industry who had started life as a scrap dealer dismantling wartime nitric acid plants in the USA. Instead of selling them for scrap, he sold them to industrial customers, and, once this source dried up, took a licence from Du Pont to build new ones. He became the first man in the world to build standardised plants. He had only two nitric acid plants. They were 180 ton/day and 350 ton/day. Anything ordered below 180 ton/day was serviced with the 180-ton plant and anything above that with the 350-ton plant. He had persuaded Thyssen of Germany and Brown Boveri of Switzerland to build the long delivery equipment for him and to finance it so that Hamilton could offer a plant on a six-month delivery, whereas his competition needed at least 24 months because of the long delivery equipment.

Hamilton had sold a 180-ton plant to AECI in 1957, and John Hahn had got the contract to erect it. So John was put on an aeroplane to Cincinnati to go and see Herb and he came back with the offer from Hamilton to do the whole project as a joint venture. Cordell Hull, Herb's right-hand man, was dispatched to South Africa to work out the details.

We had a memorable meeting with Ian Smith. He told Cordell Hull that, as far as he was concerned, we were the favourite and his personal money was on us; but, making reference to the last Durban July in South Africa, when Sea Cottage, the favourite, got a bullet in the backside, being favourite did not necessarily make one a winner. After the meeting, Cordell Hull said to us, "When the judge of the race tells which horse his money is on, we will back that horse." So they came on board.

The Rhodesian Government wanted a 60,000-tonne-per-year nitrogen plant. All the offers were based upon this size of plant. This implied twin nitric acid plants of 215 tonnes per day capacity each. The capacity sought by the Government was predicated upon a linear rate of growth in the market. In fact, the market was growing at a compound rate, and, if the price was to be halved, as was required by the Government, it was reasonable to suspect that what was really needed was a 90,000-tonne-per-year plant. This implied twin nitric acid plants of 320 tonnes per day each.

It did not actually matter what the capacity specified was, because the plants Hamilton had in stock were two 350-tonne-per-day plants, although at the altitude of Que Que, their outputs would be only 330 tonnes per day each. We had reached agreement with the Government on the price for the whole complex, which had been exhaustively checked by their consulting engineers as being a competitive price. Now we wanted to talk them into increasing the capacity (which was what they were going to get anyway), and justifying a price increase for the plants based upon the well-known scale-up formula. This was finally agreed, and we achieved a fabulous price for the plants, as the entire increase went to our bottom line, except for a small increase in the licence fee payable to Hamilton by virtue of the increased capacity. The first phase of the project was sold for £6,500,000. After a huge struggle with the Rhodesian Government, the Treasury had agreed to the Government issuing its guarantee up to an amount of £3,800,000 on the paper to be issued by Sable. We estimated a profit of £1,500,000 on the project, and, in the short term we could use up to £700,000 of financing given by Thyssen and Brown Boveri. But we were still short of about £500,000. Finally, the Government agreed to the go-ahead on the premise that when we got going we would be able to raise finance from the Rhodesian private sector. So we were issued shares in Sable and, in turn, the money for the shares was used to pay ourselves the down payments and other progress payments on the plant. This did not give us any actual money, but it was agreed that progress payments could be made from the Government guaranteed funds as the equipment arrived on site. To the surprise of the Government, the two nitric acid plants were in Rhodesia within six weeks of the final agreement being signed, and we were able to issue Sable promissory notes, surreptitiously guaranteed by the Rhodesian Government, but for the outside world, for a mere 1%, by the Standard Bank of South Africa, by virtue of the special arrangements agreed to by the Reserve Bank of South Africa.

The next problem we faced was that of a construction site. We had various issues to consider. We had to build the power lines from Sherwood switching station to the plant. We had also promised an oxygen pipeline to Risco, which was south of Que Que. Although the maximum length of line had not been specified, the Government wanted the maximum revenue to reduce the fertiliser price. As I had demanded some flexibility, this was achieved by specifying the maximum volume of the pipeline. The longer it was, the smaller the allowable diameter. Then a Mr Garmany from local government pitched up and said that his department was not going to allow it to be so far from Que Que and that we had to build a town to service the company.

So we thought a nice piece of ground north of Que Que would be ideal. It turned out to be on a farm called the Sebakwe Block.

The really good news was that this was owned by Lonrho. We approached Tiny Rowland to buy 500 acres from him. He thought an appropriate price was £1,000 an acre. This was definitely not in the budget.

So our farming friends approached Rowland to buy the whole Sebakwe Block on the grounds that having a fertiliser factory on the doorstep meant that reject fertiliser could be bought and used to fertilise the veld and set up a cattle-fattening proposition. They offered one pound an acre. Rowland said he would consider it if they bought the Sherwood Block off him in the same transaction. The Sebakwe Block was 18,500 acres and the Sherwood Block was 40,000 acres. We sent the boys back to protest that their budget would not run that high, but at ten shillings an acre they could look at it. Tiny then countered with twelve shillings and sixpence an acre and offering that Lonrho would finance £20,000 of the price over seven years at

5% per annum. At the last minute he decided to excise 2,500 acres abutting the town, saying it would be needed for the fertiliser factory which was going next to the town. So, as John put it, we had bought an ox for less than the price of a steak, and could select our own cut. Lonrho has never sold the 2,500 acres held out. Not many folks put one over Tiny.

We were then approached by the biggest construction firm in South Africa: Roberts Construction. Charles Skeen, one of the craftiest and ablest construction bosses in South Africa, was out looking for work, and was prepared to buy it in the most imaginative way he could think of. We needed, apart from the concrete chucking skills, amounting to no more than 10% of the job, a lot of work to be done in South Africa because that was what we had agreed with the Reserve Bank to get their co-operation. Roberts knew absolute zero about building petrochemical plants, but wanted to get into the business. So we gave them a contract and placed six American engineers in their offices, and engineered and built the whole of Sable from there. This was the first time that a South African company was involved in the totality of the design of such plants from the ground up, and was a great step forward for all concerned. Roberts brought to the table one other ingredient – confidence. They took up shares in Sable to the tune of £200,000 (which, of course, they made in their profit!) with the agreement that we would buy them back after three years, and subject to an "engineering fee" equal to the interest on their money. Roberts also taught us a thing or two about financing. They had the attitude that all suppliers and subcontractors knew that they would eventually be paid by Roberts. That meant that all these lesser beings would whistle for their money – usually for up to nine months. This, of course, was of dramatic assistance in building the plant, as we all knew that when we approached completion we were short of at least £300,000!

When all is said and done, Sable has to be one of the finest achievements ever in the field of petrochemical construction in Southern Africa. We signed the final agreement with the Rhodesian Government in early December 1967 and we produced our first prills of ammonium nitrate on 20th April 1969. Sixteen months on a greenfield site from bush to an operating plant – at that time, twice the size of anything else in South Africa. To this day no-one else in South Africa has ever come close. It must be remembered that a complex that size would in today's money cost around $400 million and a normal good construction time would be 30 months. Well under time and under budget – that was Sable. This, of course, helped because we could get into production quickly, even before the last of the creditors had to be paid.

RHODESIA – THE STRUGGLE BEGINS

Sable started up on 20th April 1969. We were committed in terms of our contract with the Government to build the ammonia plant and bring it on-stream within three years from date of signature. With all the problems, it became apparent that until we had resolved the financing of stage one, we could not get on with the ammonia plant. Our financing plan called for us to import ammonia for 20 months, which would create a cash flow which, together with the funds we hoped people would lend us, would be sufficient to go ahead with the ammonia plant. These kinds of plans never work out that way.

In another chapter I have explained the trials and tribulations of Mozambique regarding the building of the ammonia terminal. All that we had to build it with was a loan I had got the Standard Bank there to give us to cover local costs of R300,000. The tank itself was one of Hamilton's shelf items which was owned by GATX, and financed by Banker's Trust. Cordell induced us to sign notes in favour of Banker's Trust to pay for the plates, and we just bought the rest of the equipment on the hope that somehow we would find the money to pay for the goods after they had arrived.

To add to our woes, Risco, the iron and steel company, now wanted to get into the oxygen steel-making business. We would not have oxygen available from the electrolysis process for years, and they wanted it now – or, they threatened, they would build their own air plant. The economics of Sable in the long term absolutely demanded an outlet for the oxygen produced, so we had a hell of a time trying to find a way to buy the needed air plant which was to be part of our ammonia plant, without any money whatsoever. We needed another £750,000 to build the plant, and we had to find a way to build a high-pressure oxygen line from Sable to Risco, a distance of 17 miles. This was something which had never been attempted in South Africa. The cost was thought by many to be prohibitive, and, indeed, on the basis of overseas experience, we had been given figures of about one million pounds per mile! I had gone into it, and as is usual in these matters, the bulk of the cost was associated with the rights of way and security costs, as these lines can be highly dangerous in built-up areas, where they can catch fire with the concentrated oxygen. (In fact, the line turned out to cost only £600,000 in the end!) At this juncture, however, we did not have it and had very few prospects of getting it. That is, until I had a phone call from Beau Sutherland.

Beau Sutherland was the boss of Afrox, the local subsidiary of British Oxygen. He was well known for his business acumen and his inimitable sense of humour. Out of the blue, whilst wrestling with the problem, I had a call from him. His inquiry was blunt and to the point. "I hear you are going to have some oxygen in Rhodesia. If you are, it clearly is something of which we must take cognisance." I told him that indeed we were. When he asked me about the quantities and I replied to him that we would have some 550 tons per day of gas and 15 tons of liquid, you could hear a pin drop. Rhodesia's demand for oxygen was four tons per day. An immediate meeting with Beau, his technical director Hoffie, and myself was called for. I had frantically asked Gerry Caplette, the boss of the local Air Liquide subsidiary, to give me some guidelines. He told me that the oxygen was worth about 70 cents per 1,000 cubic feet, but in the circumstances he would go as high as R1.20 to keep us out of the market. He also told me to forget about the oxyacetylene business, as the cost of entry in terms of bottles and transport was enormous, and Afrox had thousands of written-off bottles with which we could never compete. Apart from the fact, of course, that we had no money to even contemplate such a venture.

The whole affair now became a cliffhanger. Risco was demanding an immediate answer from the Rhodesian Government. The pressure was enormous as the establishment wanted Sable to be an unmitigated failure and so get plenty of egg on the faces of the Rhodesian Front, so that the Front would have to go back to the ring, cap in hand. Rhodox (the British Oxygen subsidiary in Rhodesia) was put under the same pressure and was told that the whole project was just a boondoggle. However, Beau took the precaution of sending Hoffie with me to visit the plant under construction, and came to the conclusion that the Rhodesian Front had too much political capital riding on the success of Sable to allow the ring to sabotage it. We desperately needed allies from the establishment part of Rhodesia which had closed ranks against us. We also needed to find finance for the pipeline on acceptable terms. So I went in trepidation to the meeting with Beau and Hoffie.

Beau didn't beat about the bush. He wanted to know what our gas production possibilities were. When I told him, he said he was prepared to buy the lot. I told him I couldn't sell him the gas, which had to go to Risco, as we had a formula with the Rhodesian Government whereby gas sales would be used to reduce the price of fertiliser on an agreed basis. We might be prepared to sell the liquid instead of marketing it though. It was implied that Air Liquide might be willing to set up shop in Rhodesia. Beau said he would buy the gas and asked the price. I told him I knew nothing about oxygen and surely he should make us an offer. In his typical fashion, he said he wasn't prepared to bugger about – R1.20 per thousand was his price! I said "sold!", and that was the end of the liquid oxygen discussions. We then got onto the question of transporting the gas from Sable to Risco. I told Beau that we were able to offer a contract to a company at an annual contract price of 20% of the capital cost of the pipeline to do the job.

This would be deductible in Sable's hands against the credit which had to go to the price of fertiliser.

Beau then got even craftier. He said that Afrox would put up £100 to form a company and would borrow the cost of the pipeline from Rhodox, who were putting their money into the Building Society at 2.5%, as they were banned from paying dividends to Britain. He would pay them 3% and get a 10-year loan. We got down to some serious horse-trading and it was finally agreed that we would form a joint company called Gas Pipelines, which would have a capital of £300, of which we would have £100 and Beau would borrow £600,000 from Rhodox at 3% to finance the line. The company would receive an annual revenue, which after operating costs of about £5,000 per year would show a profit of £97,000 per year. With tax allowances, there would be no tax for some years, and a quite spectacular return to the shareholders.

With his typical sense of humour, Beau went off to his next board meeting at Rhodox. At that meeting, he mentioned that he had found that Sable was to produce 550 tons per day of oxygen, and had anyone in Rhodox thought about the consequences for their business. When the shocked Rhodox board asked for details, Beau chuckled and announced that Afrox had contracted to buy the lot and was going to distribute it. He had also contracted to build a pipeline and had the rights to distribute gas in the industrial township by pipeline. He would graciously allow Rhodox to provide him with £600,000 at 3% to do this. Finally, of course, the Rhodox board insisted that they take the Afrox deal for itself. All this was agreed to within the space of a week.

The result of all the wranglings was that I was able to put a deal on the table for the Rhodesian Government whereby they were able to insist that Risco bought its oxygen from Sable. And we had gained a valuable ally from the establishment in Rhodesia in the form of Campbell Coppen, the Chairman of Rhodox, but, more importantly, also Chairman of the Central African Merchant Bank. Now we had a friendly establishment merchant banker on board.

We now had to build the air plant. There were two companies fighting tooth and nail to get the business. The problem was that we had no money. Our Government guarantee was fully taken up with the rest of the project. So we had Linde of Germany beating down the door, as well as Air Liquide. Both companies were offering finance – but, of course, predicated on our being able to offer a South African bank guarantee. Of that we had no chance. However, the competition became fiercer and fiercer, and we told both of them that the finance offers had to be on the standing of little old NPI with its R100 of share capital. Finally, Air Liquide took the bait and gave us the financing direct to NPI with just the personal sureties of John and myself. We now had not only the air plant financed, but the first step of the ammonia plant was in place.

The next problem was that we wanted to import the ammonia needs of the plant for the first two years. The railways did not have the rolling stock, and they told us in South Africa that whilst the SAR would consider it, it had to go through the normal budget procedure. This meant that the earliest that we could contemplate getting rolling stock would be at least two and a half years away. We would have to buy our own, and we would have to get the Railway System to accept privately owned stock on the railways. From the SAR the answer was a flat "No". From Rhodesia Railways the answer was that they would, if instructed to by Government. So now we had to try to get the stock financed. We found a local manufacturer, one George Ware of Morewear Industries, who built the things, who was willing to build them and finance them on the basis that the tank cars were paid for over the first 18 months as a charge to the cost of fertiliser. Since we were looking at a million-pound contract for the tank cars, the Government had a total fit when this proposition was put to them. They stepped in with their petrol-smuggling organisation, Genta, and made Genta buy the tank cars and charge one pound per ton for the use of them for transport. So we finally solved the ammonia transport problem.

To complicate matters, John Hahn had a little engineering company called Vector Equipment Company. He insisted that George Ware give him the contract for the construction of the vessels.

John always approached whatever he tackled with enormous energy and enthusiasm, if without the attention to detail which is often necessary. He rose early every morning at about 5.30 and rushed out to Vector and if he could have built the things with pure energy, he would have done so. He scorned the use of a jig to build the tank cars on, but just "welded 'em up". He had bought an automatic welding machine to weld the barrels, but for some reason the welds were all being rejected on X-ray. John demanded that George Ware drop the X-ray requirement! It was pointed out that this was a code requirement which no-one could relax, and that perhaps, as the welds were all failing, it was even more important that the welds be X-rayed. The programme was falling catastrophically behind, as we needed the 86 tank cars available by mid-April, and at John's production rate it would be Christmas before they were all finished.

When the first six came off the line, a great sigh of relief went up. Off to Cape Town they went to fetch their first load of ammonia from Fedmis. Next morning at 6am I had a phone call at home from the Chief Operations Manager of the SAR, who informed me in a total fury that my six tank cars had derailed at Kroonstad and had blocked the main line to Cape Town for 12 hours and he was holding us responsible for the entire cost of the blockage. Our tank cars were now banned from the SAR system until the problem was solved! As an insight to the functioning of the bureaucracy, he commented, "Thank God they were approved by the Chief Mechanical Manager – Workshops!"

The problem turned out to be that by not building the tank cars on a jig, the chassis of the tank cars was twisted. Being pressure vessels, they were rigid, and so, on going around a corner, the side friction clearances caught up and forced the bogeys of the tank car to carry on straight, and thus to derail on bends. So now we had some thirty to forty tank cars in various stages of construction which would all have to have their carriages cut off and rewelded on a concrete jig. And the automatic welder was not working properly, so that rejects were still coming off the line and fouling up the whole production process.

This affair led to one of the sayings of the NPI Group which is engraved in stone to those who went through the mill with me. "When all else fails, try reading the instruction manual." John had been at tank car building for the best part of five months, 12 to 16 hours per day, without success. Finally, I picked up the instruction manual for the automatic welder and said: "Let's just start from the beginning."

The first passage I read out was along the lines of: "Take a coil of 3/16-inch wire and place in the machine." The reaction of the operator was: "No, we use 1/8-inch wire." I said: "Well, just try what the manual says." He tried it, it worked, there was not a single reject thereafter, and production roared ahead!

At last we seemed to be getting the act together. Somehow we had managed to finance all kinds of things that we had never thought we would have to and knew we never had the money to do. The plant was coming together at a rate of knots, the terminal was going up, the tank cars were financed, an oxygen pipeline was under construction, the air plant was going up. The only problem was that, as we got to the end, the shortage of money was now manifest. Fortunately, we had the well-heeled Roberts Construction as our major creditor, who by now were some six months in arrears in their payments and they were becoming restive. We must secure finance.

As we reached production day, the Government called a meeting of the ring to discuss the distribution of the fertiliser from Sable. The ring told the Government that they were not interested, as they still considered that the Government should not go ahead with the project. When they were told that the project was actually starting production in the next week, they nearly expired. Sable had been built whilst they were still fondly imagining that the Government were cogitating about the project.

When they heard about the requirement that anyone would have access to the factory who could buy in wholesale lots, they nearly went mad. We found that the flexibility of the banks suddenly clammed up. No indulgences. Pressure from subcontractors. Pressure from Roberts, who told us from whence it came. They were going to break us. We had to raise a sum of £1,500,000 to meet our creditors. And even though the plant had started up, we could not get ammonia from Iran, on which all our economics were based. We had to buy outside, and the cost left us with no profit on the price we were getting (which was half the existing price). No way was the Government going to let go on this political football. It was sacrosanct. We were operating on the bones of our arses generating no cash flow, and with the creditors out there becoming restive. We had to have finance.

We decided to open negotiations with the ring. The leader of the ring, by common consent, was Evan Campbell, Chairman of Standard Bank, Chairman of Fisons, a former High Commissioner in London, and a formidable adversary. John coined the nickname for him of "The Walrus", by which name he has gone down in Sable history. AECI provided William van der Bijl and Michael White. This merry gang used the tactic of trying to find out just how bust we were, and knew that by stringing us out, our position would get worse by the day, and we would finally be delivered to them on a plate. It was a hell of a poker game and only we knew just how bad a hand we really had. They had us by the balls and they knew it. They just wanted to eke the maximum political capital out of it without driving the Government to come to our rescue, which of course was, in their minds, always a possibility. Little did they know of the total ineptitude of the Government, who actually just hoped we would somehow survive. The Treasury was strutting around with a lot of "I told you so's" and no way were they coming up with a penny.

Due to the severe effect this would have on the oxygen deal with Rhodox, I decided that, as the pipeline was by now half built, and Rhodox was in up to their necks, I would go and see Campbell Coppen, with whom I had established an excellent relationship through Gas Pipelines Board, on which we both sat. I knew that Rhodox was sitting on a vast stockpile of cash which, because of sanctions, they could not pay out to British Oxygen. The return on this cash stockpile was derisory. Maybe Rhodox could find a formula to come into Sable in some way, although this was not their real field of endeavour. Nothing ventured, nothing gained. I talked to Campbell, who voiced just that sentiment. He was, however, concerned about their oxygen investment, and he did not go along with the idea of trying to plaster Ian Smith's face with as much egg as possible. He cogitated. The Walrus pressed harder. Effectively he was saying: "Hand over the company to us and maybe we will let you go away empty-handed if you are lucky."

On one of the most climactic days of my life, we were assembled in Salisbury. We had a meeting scheduled for 3 o'clock with the Walrus, when he was going to tell us the price of salvation. Not a pleasant prospect. At 10 o'clock we had a meeting scheduled with Campbell Coppen. At that meeting he offered us R3,500,000 in financing, with the carried option for Rhodox to take control of Sable in the future on an agreed basis. We accepted and signed their offer on the spot.

Champagne had all but disappeared from Rhodesia, but Meikles rose to the occasion and we indulged for lunch. I now know what it must be like to be reprieved as the tumbril reaches the foot of the guillotine. Now for the meeting with the Walrus, at which he was expecting to savour his triumph over us.

We sat down quietly, and as John was the elder, and for a 26-year-old to put in the knife was thought to be rather pushing it, John quietly thanked the Walrus for the meeting which we were now merely attending as a matter of courtesy to tell them that we had received an offer for 50% of Sable and that we had accepted. We thanked them for their time and effort and suggested that we would have to do business another time.

The Walrus went berserk. He picked up the phone to the Minister and told him that it was outrageous and he would not stand for it in any way. He was coming over right away and the Minister should please cancel all appointments and see him immediately.

Well, there was much shrieking and wailing and eventually, to get peace, Rhodox agreed to form a holding company in which the ring could have 49%, called Chemical and Gas Holdings. Rhodox's various options would go there, so that eventually CGH would acquire control of Sable. So now Sable was fully financed and the money flowed to enable us to get on with building the ammonia plant. Or so we thought.

One of the things which soon reared its ugly head was getting enough ammonia to the plant. I, as the youngest, was given the job.

The ammonia was railed from the terminal in Lourenço Marques to Sable. We had got the tank car fleet on the basis of the Government estimates of the requirements of the country. Well, with the price being halved and, because of sanctions, more maize and cotton were planted, the demand was actually the full capacity of the plant — something the Government did not expect for 10 years.

Later, I will explain in detail how I managed to do the loaves and fishes effort that meant we were able to nearly double our production.

THE ELEPHANT FEAST

Mozambique was the cradle from which the business enterprises, which set us on the road, were largely spawned.

After we started Phase 1 of the plant in Rhodesia, in terms of the business plan, it was necessary to bring ammonia in by sea for the first 18 months, or to import from whatever source we could. We explored many options. One thing became clear, however. Whatever we did, we would have to set up an import terminal in Mozambique, as there were neither the logistics nor the capacity to supply our ammonia needs in Southern Africa.

Our partner in this endeavour, Herb Hamilton of C&I Girdler Corporation, was one of those unique business geniuses who, however, had fallen for that oldest of all beliefs: that all of us who become successful believe that we are infallible, and because we have thought of an idea, it must, by definition, be a good idea. Herb had persuaded his various suppliers that he was the greatest salesman in the world, which, as he sold them this idea, was quite close to the truth. His idea was that he could sell plants, and he could sell more of them if he could offer his customers a quick delivery. If they would build the critical components, and finance them for stock, he could ensure both a cheap price and a rapid delivery, which would scupper his competition.

Hamilton, in order to be able to come up with the goods quickly, had components in stock of various plants, nitric acid and ammonia.

In ammonia he had developed the idea of a packaged plant, all prefabricated, which could be delivered instantly. They were called Ammopacs. He had persuaded Thyssen of Germany to build two of these and to hold them in stock. Unfortunately, these did not prove to be as wonderful as he had envisaged, and they were becoming something of a white elephant. Thyssen were bleating to get rid of the things, and Herb couldn't sell them.

Enter Cordell Hull, and the "New Idea". Why not erect the ammonia plants in Mozambique and supply Sable from the Ammopacs, as well as importing ammonia? We approached Bulhosa, the oil mogul of Mozambique, with our idea. Cordell negotiated a package, whereby he would supply finance for the Ammopacs (from a reluctant Thyssen, who would have little choice in the matter anyway), and Bulhosa would finance the power plants from Brown Boveri. Cordell would finance the tank plates, with Bulhosa financing the rest of the requirements. The cash flow indicated that we could pay off the plants in two years.

The deal was scheduled to go ahead, and we immediately set about construction. Bulhosa set aside a portion of land belonging to him, and started to construct the foundation for the ammonia tank. The tank, which was in stock, was shipped out to Bulhosa.

The foundation for an ammonia storage tank at atmospheric pressure is a complicated affair, because of the low temperatures involved. There are a variety of designs possible, all expensive. After soil tests and time estimates, we opted for a specialised ring wall with crushed stone and various layers of compacted fill, capped by foam glass blocks. We got a local contractor to work, as we had to receive ammonia by 1st May 1969. This gave us, in September 1968, just eight months to build the whole terminal, so we could not afford to waste a second. As soon as the contractor gave us a price, we gave him the job.

Meanwhile, back at the ranch, Cordell was having heavy sledging with Bulhosa. Finally, when Bulhosa found out that Hamilton had bounced a promissory note due to Brown Boveri, he cancelled the whole deal.

Now we had a half-built foundation on Bulhosa's land, a tank on the water, and no basis for a deal to supply ammonia to the plant well under construction in Rhodesia, with the full financial catastrophe that implied! We had to find an alternative.

One of the most charismatic characters in Portugal at that time was Antonio Champalimaud. Reputedly the richest man in Portugal, and married to a De Mello (the Blue Bloods of Portugal), he was the steel and cement baron of the country. Champalimaud had just outflanked his great rival, the CUF Group, by getting an "alvara" to build a fertiliser factory next door to his cement works called Quimica Geral. He was in need of a supply of ammonia for this factory, and he represented one alternative. His factory manager, Campos, when he heard that we were planning to build an import terminal, became determined to get it built in his plant. The other alternative, of course, was to use Bulhosa himself.

Bulhosa was said to have made his fortune by supplying the Axis powers with oil for their submarines during the war. (Certainly, Mozambique was full of dubious characters, such as Count Werner von Alvensleben, who had been a prominent early member of the SS and who surfaced in Mozambique just before the war.) We met with Bulhosa in Portugal, and he decided to allow us to build the terminal, entirely financed by ourselves, with the proviso that we should give him the option to buy the terminal at the end of five years, at depreciated value. His agreement stipulated that the depreciation rate should be a straight line over five years! With this agreement, we would have had to have given him back the whole thing at the end of five years, gratis.

We felt that this was not a good deal, and that Bulhosa was trying to exploit us to the limit. We were also scared that he would use his land-owning position to put the screws on us when the factory started up.

With time being as short as it was, we had to make a deal quickly. Campos told us that Champalimaud was only available on his safari concession, where he was entertaining the French Foreign Minister to a spot of shooting. We would have to go there if we wanted to make a deal.

We flew to Beira, and then picked up the local air taxi, which flew around the Zambezi valley. After a series of quick stops at funny little strips, we set off for Champalimaud's concession. Champalimaud's set-up was a measure of the style of the Portuguese empire of the time! He had acquired 500,000 hectares from the Government as a safari concession, which he used for his personal shooting box. The only stipulation was that at least two people had to buy licences every year. The concession was a hell of a place to find. It was the time of the year when the veld was set on fire by the locals, and visibility was about 300 metres at best. Our pilot flew at 200 feet over the bush looking for landmarks. It was nearly dusk when he suddenly, out of the gloom, chanced upon the small bush strip.

Antonio met us, and a quick conference ensued. The pilot said he had to leave within 10 minutes. He could return in the morning. Antonio said that if we didn't mind roughing it, we could spend the night. This seemed to be the best thing under the circumstances, so we stayed on.

There was due to be an elephant feast that night as Antonio had shot an elephant the day before, which was lying in a clearing adjacent to the camp, blown up like a miniature barrage balloon. Antonio's idea of roughing it was a camp that would put most modern safari camps to shame. We lacked only air conditioning.

In an hour we knocked together a deal. He would get all the alvaras (licences) needed. His statement to me was: "I am Champalimaud. Champalimaud builds first and is given his alvaras afterwards!" We could get a five-year lease on a piece of ground within his fertiliser plant. Champalimaud would supply all utilities at cost, including cooling water, and in exchange we would supply him at a fixed price of

$53 per ton for five years, with a maximum of 45,000 tons of ammonia. At the end of the five years we would either, at our option, sell him the terminal for $400,000, or give a free 50% share of the terminal company to him, or we could remove the whole establishment. (This last option was tossed in at the last moment, as no-one believed that it was possible to do so).

Champalimaud threw in one final condition. Our tank plates had been imported by Bulhosa, and were at that very moment in seven railway trucks on their way to the refinery. We would have to achieve the diversion of the trucks from out of the refinery to his site, and their unloading, or pay a penalty of $100,000 to him. This was because he would have shown his hand in going to war with Bulhosa, and he would undoubtedly be screwed by Bulhosa, if Bulhosa ended up with the terminal.

After negotiations, we repaired to the boma, and a sumptuous dinner of various delicacies. We had with us a young American lawyer, John Macdonald, of definite left-wing views, who Cordell had sent along to help with the drafting of the agreement. After dinner we were to have the ceremonial start to the elephant feast. This eventually began at 11pm.

It certainly is one of the most dramatic and primeval scenes I have ever witnessed. Ever since morning the locals had been gathering, and had set up circles of small cooking fires around the elephant. They had been supplied with liberal amounts of cheap wine in 44-gallon barrels, and had perhaps 50 or 60 marimba players going at it like the clappers. By the time it was 11pm, all concerned were as high as kites, and the sight and sounds of the marimbas, the flickering firelight, and air of suppressed excitement, created an atmosphere that would have been the envy of Hollywood.

Antonio climbed up the elephant, accompanied by the local chief, with a spear which dwarfed him. This was plunged into the elephant's stomach, accompanied by cheers from the crowd. A vast eruption of gas and rotten stomach contents showered out, drenching Antonio and those of the mob that had ventured too close.

This was the signal for the feast to begin, and a horde descended on the elephant, and started to cut it up, carrying meat to the fires, accompanied by a crescendo of sound from the marimbas. I noticed that the chief had the choice cut of the elephant's penis. I suppose it was believed to give one increased sexual powers! The feasting carried on well into the small hours.

In the morning we were up very early to get things under way. John Macdonald, the young American lawyer, was found at the remnants of the previous night's festivities. All that was left of the elephant was a large rib cage, in the middle of which was a huge pile of dung, soaked in blood. On top of the pile sat three piccanins, picking off the remnants of meat, and eating it raw. John was nearly throwing up, and he turned to me and said: "For the first time I believe that one man, one vote is not the solution in Africa!"

We arrived back in Lourenço Marques at noon, and went into a huddle with Cecil Lindsay, the local Rennies boss in LM. (Rennies were our local clearing agents and were very effective in Mozambique.) We were battling with the question of how we could get the railway trucks out of Bulhosa's yard, into Quimica Geral (Antonio Champalimaud's company), and offloaded. Cecil undertook to divert the trucks through his CFM connections, and to truck over a steam crane to do the offloading the next day. The trucks would be moved that night after everyone had gone home. We reckoned that once the plates were offloaded, Bulhosa could do nothing; but as they had been imported, and consigned to the refinery, if they were still in the railway trucks he might be able to get the trucks sent back.

It was in the early hours of the morning that we got the steam crane operative and were frantically offloading the plates. Fortunately, the "mañana" attitude played into our hands, and it was not until the day after that someone from the refinery came looking for the trucks. By then we had already unloaded six of the seven, and were busy with the last. They were given some mumbo-jumbo about temporary storage, and referred to Lisbon. We completed the unloading later that day.

I then went to visit the contractor who was just completing the foundation for the tank. He very proudly showed me over the site, where the final layer of compaction was being completed, and told me he would hand over that afternoon. I asked him what his price would be for another one, identical, and whether he could start that day. He looked at me as if I was quite mad, but gave the same price as the foundation that he had already completed, and his crew downed tools, and headed for Quimica Geral, where they started digging that very afternoon. It was now late November, and we had to be in business by 1st May – a task that was all but impossible.

We put the contractor onto 24-hour-a-day working, and he completed the foundation in less than a month. Although the concrete was not cured, we started erection of the tank immediately. As we were doing in Rhodesia, we worked the crews until the close on 23rd December. At that point Bulhosa struck.

On the morning of the 24th, we were served with a court order, an injunction prohibiting us from any further construction work using Bulhosa's plates. The return date, which we could not anticipate, was at the end of March, as the Court was closed for three months. It seemed as if Bulhosa had us by the throat.

Our lawyer, Sergio Espadas, was a friend of the judge, so he took off to the judge's house to discuss the matter with him. He pointed out to the judge that we had already half-built the tank, and would never agree to pull it down and build it with Bulhosa. In the circumstances, all that Bulhosa could have would be a claim for damages. In the circumstances the judge agreed that if we gave a bank guarantee for 250,000 dollars, we could have the injunction lifted.

I rushed back to Johannesburg and, with the usual NPI financial juggling, managed to put the guarantee together. On 28th December we re-commenced construction, as the workers returned from their Christmas break.

At last all seemed to be fair set, and we got the tank up six strakes by the end of January, by dint of 24-hour working. Then we had a tropical storm. The tank was at its most vulnerable point in the whole construction. We had built the walls, but neither the compression ring nor the roof. The wind blew in the side of the tank down to the third strake. Two of the plates were so badly damaged that they were considered unusable. These were cut out, and we started looking for replacement plates. The steel of the plates was so-called "charpy steel". This is a special low-temperature steel. It was not made in SA, and we could not find any plates of the right size and thickness anywhere.

We went into deep consultation with engineers and metallurgists. We wondered whether re-rolling the plates would make them usable. Eventually, it was decided that we could and Lloyds (the inspectors of the tank) were prepared to allow it, provided that we normalised the plates after re-working and did not work them after normalising. The plates went off to Johannesburg, whilst we repaired the rest of the tank and started on the roof. The plates were re-rolled and normalised. They came out of the furnace looking like giant potato chips! We tried again, and again our "potato chips" came out of the oven. Then the metallurgists said that we could not go on forever with this process as we would destroy the grain structure. In desperation we re-rolled the plates, and put them into the oven, sandwiched between two three-inch plates, topped by a couple of 5-ton ingots. They came out usable.

At least with the protection of Antonio Champalimaud we were sheltered from the bureaucracy. I believe that we needed no less than

500 different alvaras to get the show going. Antonio told me that he would never take any bullshit. "Do first, and apply for alvaras afterwards" was his motto. In the feudal structure of the Portugal of the time, it gave the Portuguese barons an almost unassailable advantage over all others. The only alvara he failed to get us was one to pump water out of the sea to test the tank! The official who had this particular power held us up for three days!

With Bulhosa's plan to scupper us having gone awry, Cordell Hull was able to settle the matter amicably, without any payment. Bulhosa even agreed to pay for the foundation, on the grounds that if we paid for it, he would be beholden to let us use it.

The construction proved to be another nightmare, however. We had decided to adopt a radical solution to the insulation of the tank. The conventional method was to strap sheets of styrofoam on the tank, and then encase it in aluminium wrapping. A local contractor in South Africa persuaded us that he could do a better job by spraying the whole tank with polyurethane foam. This idea attracted us, and we gave him a contract. He had promised to do the job in half the time we estimated that the conventional process would take. The small print in the agreement, however, allowed him to stop work if the wind exceeded a certain level. Also, most of the material we had ordered had a finite shelf life, and with the storm damage delay, some of it would be time-expired if we had any further delays. We decided to do a kind of bastard arrangement, whereby we made up a lot of blocks of foam, which we glued to the tank, and then foamed between the blocks. By this means we were able to do the insulation in six weeks, with no delays for weather.

Despite these measures, however, we missed the date of 1st May. Sable started up on 21st April, and I had bought ammonia in South Africa to get going, but it was too expensive for us. I had signed a contract with Iran at $48 per ton CIF, and the SA ammonia was R40 per ton FOR plant, at the time $56. With the additional railage, it was prohibitively expensive. It was urgent to get imported ammonia rolling. Cordell, therefore, committed to a starter cargo in a vessel called the Gas Lion. She sailed from the US Gulf in early May 1969, and was due at the end of the month. At a demurrage rate of $6,500 per day, we could not afford any delays.

We seemed to be beset by difficulties. We were not allowed to weld on the oil jetty for four hours before any vessel arrived, and had to remove all our equipment whilst tankers were tied up at the jetty. We had to rely on the window periods we enjoyed for a couple of hours, when we had all our welders working frantically whilst the next tanker was on its way to dock. Our construction foreman, a German ex-Navy man, asked me for a U-boat to get rid of the tankers!

With the best will in the world, we found that we would not be able to receive a cargo before 6th June. This left us faced with a bill of $39,000 before we even started, and there was much gloom in the offices as we contemplated this disaster. The Rhodesian Government reckoned that all demurrage costs were for our account, not the consumers'. I still remember sitting around the table with Cordell in a fit of the glooms, when my secretary brought a telex from the master of the Gas Lion. The telex said that he regretted to inform us that owing to unexpected heavy weather he had been forced to moderate his speed, and now could not arrive before 6th June.

This gave rise to one of the Cordellisms. He said: "I told you guys that it's a lot better to be born lucky than smart."

Fortunately for us, being on the site of Quimica Geral we were able to commission the tank with ammonia from Quimica Geral. This is a highly delicate affair, as first the air has to be purged out of the tank. As ammonia gas is lighter than air, it is introduced at the top of the tank, and it forces the air downwards, where it is vented, until the air has largely been removed. There is, of course, an interface of air and ammonia where the two are mixed, and this, of course, is an explosive hazard, so the exercise is not without its tension during the process. All the engineers were threatened with the most dire consequences if they blew it.

The next operation is to cool down the tank from ambient to minus 33 degrees centigrade. Hamilton had built a tank in Denmark two years before, with a similar time problem. His engineers cooled the tank down in less than 24 hours, instead of the three days considered safe. The tank during this process contracts by about 30 centimetres, and must be free to move inwards. The tank cracked, and the whole fertiliser season was lost for the time it took to repair. We were on edge the whole time in case the time pressures made someone do something silly, which would create a huge setback.

It must be remembered that at that time in South Africa, no-one really believed that ammonia could be shipped by sea in tankers. At the time of commissioning of the tank, AECI were dismissing the rumours of an ammonia terminal as the far-fetched ravings of lunatics. None of us really knew anything about it, but we had heard dire stories of cracked tanks, tanks where the roofs had been sucked in by the compressors, and other horror stories. None of these happened to us. We invented our own unique piece of contractor's folklore for the ammonia business.

We were actually ready for the *Gas Lion* when she arrived. I was in Johannesburg, and the C&I Girdler engineer in charge of the project, Allan Jewell, was in Lourenço Marques. The ship tied up, and we expected to get the good news a few hours later. Instead, we got a frantic telex to say that there had been a great catastrophe – the discharge could not be done. We were told that the design was up the spout, and there were a variety of other problems, all of which meant that we had a terminal at one end and a ship at $6,500 a day at the other, and we couldn't get the stuff from one to the other.

At this point I got in my old reliable, David Leith. David had been with AECI for 37 years, and I had taken him on when he retired. He gave me ten years of outstanding service, mostly because he had forgotten more about ammonia and its derivatives than most people knew. We sat down and pieced together what we thought had happened, and decided to take the plane down to Mozambique first thing in the morning. Cordell was on the phone from the USA that evening as the Captain had complained to Gazocean, the carriers, that he was unable to discharge the cargo. Cordell put a man on a plane, sans visa, that night, as did Gazocean. Everyone was in a hell of a state.

When David and I got down to Lourenço Marques, we found everyone shell-shocked. The story we got out of them was as follows. They had coupled up the stainless hoses from the ship to the pipeline. Allan Jewell was very concerned about the design of the line, which, I am told, was a very ingenious piece of design, as there could be no anchor points for the line, and it had expansion joints in it, which in turn would be stressed by the pumping forces. No-one had ever done it before, and he wanted someone to assure him that the design was safe, in view of the experience. David was pretty sure that it was, but Allan Jewell was unconvinced. What they had done with the ship was a masterpiece. Having coupled up the hoses, they opened up every valve on the line, so that there was unrestricted flow from the pump discharge to the tank. The line and hoses were at ambient temperature. They then started the pump!

With practically no head, the pump threw quite a few tons of liquid ammonia into the hot system at minus 33 degrees. All witnesses agreed that the results were spectacular. The pipeline was a 10-inch line running along the jetty for about 400 metres, whence it took a right-angle bend into the trench. The heat of the hoses and line caused a large slug of ammonia to evaporate, and it gasified instantly, driving the liquid slug along the line at a spectacular speed. When it hit the bend, the line jumped about a metre into the air. All the spectators on the dock jumped into the sea, thinking their last days were on them. The safety valves on the tank blew with a roar heard a mile away, and a huge cloud of ammonia was blasted into the atmosphere. The line then started to jump up and down on the jetty. The pump was finally shut down and all the valves were hastily closed.

The commissioning team were so shaken that all they could do was compose a telex to us and pack it in. In the morning, they plucked up a little courage. Cordell had been on the phone, threatening murder and mayhem if they didn't pump out the ship; so in the morning, before we arrived, they went down and decided to open the valve to allow reduction of the pressure in the line, which had built up in the night. Clearly, the line now contained a lot of liquid, which was now hot. As soon as they released the pressure, the ammonia boiled. Whilst the line didn't dance quite as much as before, the results were clearly unnerving, as when we arrived we found a crew too shocked to do anything.

In the end we pumped the ship out without any problems, and the line has given 20 years of sterling service, without the slightest bit of trouble. We had had one hell of a week, though, and wrote a new chapter of how not to pump out an ammonia ship!

Gazocean had sent out an engineer, one Giovannini, to help. Allan Jewell took him out and showed him the line and explained his problem with the engineering. Giovannini took one look at it and said: "It's a Rolls Royce. You should see some of the crap I am expected to use. I'll pump out the ship in 15 hours. No problem." He clearly didn't have the foggiest idea of the engineering problem Allan was talking about. In the end, the standard procedure was to start the pumps on bypass and just crack the valve to the line so as to allow a dribble of ammonia into the line to gradually cool it down. This took the best part of six hours before pumping could start in earnest. Years later, when the Iranians had cracked their tank, I asked them when I was in Shahpur what had happened. No-one knew, but they told me that they had commissioned their tank from a tanker. I figured that it would take at least a day to purge the tank and another two to cool it down before the ship could discharge its cargo. So I asked them about it. Mr Giovannini had come out to do it. The whole job was done in two days. I chose not to share with the Iranians my view of Giovannini's attitude, as the damages claim against Gazocean would have been in the millions and would have created many strains on the various relationships.

And, of course, when I built our new terminal I put in a gas return line which I used to pre-cool the line prior to the arrival of the ship, so we never had any further problems with pumping out ships.

Thus ended the beginning of our business in Mozambique.

SLEEPING WITH THE ENEMY

At last our troubles were over. Sable was a fully financed outfit and we were well on our way to making the necessary arrangements to build the ammonia plant. Production was coming out of the plant, and we were optimistically thinking ahead to the future. But life is rarely so uncomplicated. The greatest trials were yet to come. The Board of Sable was reconstituted. It is difficult to remember all the Board members at the time. Campbell Coppen, chairman of Rhodox (the Coppenter) was the chairman, Evan Campbell (the Walrus) was there from Fisons, as were William van der Byl and Wapenaar from AECI. We had to run the company with a not-disinterested audience.

NPI as contractors had a sweetheart contract to build the plant. However, under the close supervision of the Government's consulting engineers we did have contractual matters to meet. The most important of these was the "performance test". Prosaically, it was contractually the way in which you had to show in a 48-hour production run that the plant met its guarantees with respect to capacity, utility and feedstock consumption and product specifications. Both our nitric acid plants sailed through their performance tests, but the ammonium nitrate plant was playing up.

Hamilton employed a part-Native American called Cecil Lashlee, who was his technical troubleshooter. Cecil was one of those people who really make industry tick. He and I spent hours while we laid out the plant and the flow of materials through the plant. I sat at the feet of the master and picked his brains as clean as I could. He was no doubt one of the world experts on nitrogen production. Now that the ammonium nitrate plant was clearly not performing up to spec, nobody wanted to present the plant for its performance test.

Cecil contended that we had finally come up against the bottleneck problem. Every plant C&I Girdler had designed had always exceeded by at least 25% its capacity guarantee. So they kept down-sizing and Cecil figured that we had finally reached the limit of down-sizing. Coupled to this, Hamilton had brought in some changes. To keep the height of the prill tower down, air is blown up the tower to give the proper residence time for the prills to solidify. This was done with induced draught fans at the top of the tower. Brilliant idea. Save cost on the tower by shifting the weight of the fans to the bottom and put one forced draught fan there. With eight fans at the top, it was possible to fine-tune the airflow up the tower. With one volcanic fan at the bottom, regulation was very difficult.

We also had a super-sophisticated shaker conveyor at the tower base to convey the prills to the cooler. The trouble was that the springs lasted little more than a day in ammonium nitrate service due to stress corrosion cracking. So that had to go. Then Hamilton had also abandoned the shower header array at the top of the tower and put one big prill pot in its place. The effect of this was that the concentrated column of descending prills swept the air downwards and the peripheral air accelerated upwards. Because the residence time was not enough, the prills failed to solidify wholly, so we created shattered prills which were swept up out of the tower and sprayed the whole countryside with fine ammonium nitrate. It settles on everything and because of its hygroscopicity it caused the insulators on the adjacent power lines to flash over, etc, etc. What a mess! Fortunately, in South Africa we had some ventilation experts who worked out a solution. Eventually, the plant passed its test, but it had cost a lot. Not to mention the down time.

To add to our woes, John chose to air these problems at board meetings, accusing Herb Hamilton of stuffing up the plant and virtually admitting that we were contractually at fault. The Board wasn't interested. The contractor was part of a joint venture and they looked to us to solve the problems.

It took three long months to solve the problems and forever after we had a vigilant bunch of directors watching us.

As the construction of Sable gathered momentum, and as our financial plan began to take shape, it was clear to me, at least, that we would be involved with imported ammonia for much longer than anyone believed. We couldn't raise the finance to finish off Sable in Phase One, let alone go on with Phase Two. Also, things had started to get hot for our American partners.

The United States had started to tighten sanctions against Rhodesia. Where previously the Americans had been prominent in being the effective controllers of the company, as the sanctions started to bite they began to take a back seat, usually trying to use us as front men. Previously they had assumed full responsibility, contractually, for the supply of ammonia at a fixed price. Now they started to duck and dive as the sanctions began to look serious, but, more importantly, as their ability to meet their contractual commitments started to look increasingly difficult.

It had been decided by them that we would use Iran as our major source of ammonia, where a joint venture between Allied Chemical and the National Iranian Petrochemical Company (NPC) was to begin production at about the time we would be starting up. I travelled to Iran with Dave Patterson of IDI (Hamilton's Bahamas company), where we met with Macdonald, the Managing Director of Shahpur Chemical. He and his marketing manager, Mr Phillipe Angostures, met with us, and Mac explained that Shahpur, because of the American involvement, could not deal with us. NPC would, however, buy ammonia from

Shahpur, and, as Iran was not observing sanctions against Rhodesia, the National Petrochemical Company would sell us the ammonia. Mr Angostures was given the task of dealing with us as he was French and had no personal problem in helping to execute the contract. A Mr Shahrokshahi was given the task of being the official contact man, assisted by Ardeshir Molavi.

We sat down to some days of carpet trading with the Iranians, and finally agreed with them on a two-and-a-half-year contract with a minimum off-take of 60,000 tons per year at a price of $48 per tonne delivered Lourenço Marques. Mr Mostofi, the Chairman of NPC, signed for the Iranians, and I took the contract to Liechtenstein, where the Americans had set up a lot of front companies to do the buying. So far, all in the garden seemed to be lovely.

Shahpur Chemical told us that they would not be able to supply us before about July or August, so Dave Patterson and Hamilton made a deal with Mississippi Chemical in the USA to buy two cargoes from the USA to kick off the project. This arrangement caused us a lot of trauma, as the price was a few dollars more than the contract price of $48. At this point Cordell Hull intervened with a *force majeure* claim. The Rhodesian Government wanted him to deliver at the agreed price of $48, which couldn't be done, and Cordell had absolutely no intention of putting one plugged nickel into Rhodesia. So he tried to have his cake and eat it. On the one hand, he didn't want to have to live up to his commitment, but he still wanted to share in the profits of the terminal. We therefore found ourselves with a partner who couldn't perform, but was still sitting there hungrily eyeing the huge profits that we expected to make out of the terminal as the ammonia flow from Iran built up.

The first cargo was arranged in the *Gas Lion*. In order to get permission to export the cargo from the USA, a certificate had to be supplied to state that it would not be sent to Rhodesia. As the youngest, I was elected to provide the letter, bearing in mind the possible consequences of making such a false statement to the US authorities. I thought about it long and hard, and finally drafted what I thought would be an acceptable letter. The letter read:

"This is to confirm that the good ship *Gas Lion* will by no means be diverted to Rhodesia."

As this was a technical impossibility, as Rhodesia was landlocked, and as no mention of the cargo was made in the letter, although the impression was conveyed that the cargo would not go to Rhodesia, it was clear that no actual untruth had been stated.

In due course, the *Gas Lion* arrived, and, as I have outlined, with many trials and tribulations, was discharged. The second ship was booked shortly thereafter, being the *Isfonn*. In a short time, we had 18,000 tonnes of ammonia, and all seemed to be going well.

Then the blow fell. Our manager in Lourenço Marques told us that the US Consul in Lourenço Marques had requested permission to visit the terminal the next day to inspect the American cargoes, and to make inquiries as to the destination of the cargo. There was a monumental panic. We, of course, phoned Cordell and told him that the US authorities were nosing around about the cargoes, and that the US Consul had suggested that there was no way that Mozambique could consume such quantities of ammonia, and that the US was aware that a large plant was scheduled to start up in Rhodesia shortly.

This news fell like a bomb on Cordell. He immediately set about covering all the tracks left in the sand by the Americans. We also agreed that it would be foolish in the extreme to buy yet another cargo from the US. I told Cordell that I would personally go to Lourenço Marques in the morning early, and deal with the Consul by showing him that all the ammonia was still in the tank. It was clear, though, that we would have to find another source until the Iranians came to light.

At 5am the next morning, I took off for Lourenço Marques. I had formulated a quick plan by close cross-examination of Allan Jewell, the project engineer, after ascertaining that the gauge on the tank was a long metal tape connected to a float in the tank. There was a means of adjusting the zero, and there was also a lock at the top of the tank, quite inaccessible, whereby the gauge could be locked into place. After hasty meetings, we decided that the best plan would be to play very dumb, and not let the US Consul meet anyone senior, let alone give him the impression that someone had rushed down from Johannesburg merely to conduct him around the terminal. We decided to rather leave him in the hands of a clearly junior employee, who in all innocence would show him the terminal, not forgetting, in passing, to proudly show him the tank gauge.

He fell for this hook, line and sinker. When shown the gauge, he asked the worker how to calculate the amount in the tank. He was asked to write down the reading, and, in the office, the worker gave him the chart converting gauge readings to tonnes. Surprise, surprise! 18,000 tonnes! As we had already dispatched over 10,000 tonnes to Rhodesia, we were quite pleased with our loaves and fishes effort. Unfortunately, we now had a gauge which was quite *hors de combat* due to all the fiddling and we had great difficulty in ascertaining the quantities in the tank for ever after.

Our shenanigans had the desired effect, however, and the US Consul got off our backs for the time being. It was not until the Americans filed documents in court, which opened up the whole affair, that the matter was raised again.

We were now left with a very real problem. Our American partners were the great experts in ammonia, and they were all paralysed with terror. Someone had to get ammonia, and had to get it quickly. I found myself spending a great deal of time travelling to Iran. The plant at Shahpur was always just going to start up, but next week. Although they were committed to a CIF basis, we knew that there were no ships available in the Persian Gulf, and that when they finally got going, it would take at least 60 days before we smelt a drop of the stuff. We were on the hunt yet again.

Enter Gazocean.

If there is anyone on earth who could be said to be the father of shipping liquefied gases by tanker, that man would have to be Rene Boudet. After an exotic early career in Egypt, where he had the pleasure of having his small gas tankers seized by Colonel Nasser, Rene managed to get them back by seizing them in turn when they ventured out of Egyptian waters. These funny little gas tankers became the forerunner of a vast worldwide fleet of millions of deadweight tons of liquid gas carriers. The great ability that Rene brought to the business was the salesmanship of getting many of the famous names in shipping to build gas carriers (including our partner Herb Hamilton). Rene then took those ships on time charter, and traded them. The net effect at that time was that virtually every gas tanker of any size was under time charter to Boudet's company, Gazocean.

Much as John D. Rockefeller had done a century previously, Boudet discovered that control of the shipping of liquid ammonia and LPG gave the shipper a hammerlock on trading in ammonia, as the complexities of scheduling ships, cargoes and terminal space were extremely difficult. He who controlled the ships effectively had the trade by the gonads. Into this den of pirates we were pitchforked by our circumstances. Gazocean were not aware of the depth of our problems, but could smell that there were some lucrative profits lurking around us, and so we went into a huddle with them. As the USA was barred to us, we had to look elsewhere. At that time most ammonia in Europe was based on naphtha. As US ammonia was based on natural gas at 20 cents per 1,000 cu ft, giving a feedstock cost of 6/7 dollars per ton, and naphtha at 20 dollars per ton gave a feedstock cost of 20 dollars per ton, and had another couple of dollars more for other process variables, the European ammonia was basically priced at FOB US Gulf, plus freight from the USA. So where we were buying in the US at around 28 to 30 dollars, in Europe the cost was more like 40 dollars. In the size ships we had to use from Europe, where we could not load more than 10,000 tonnes, the freight was a handsome 26 to 27 dollars, helped not a little by the monopoly position of Gazocean.

The only place with ammonia to spare was Petroquimica in Lisbon, so we were forced to buy from Lisbon. The price was, of course, a disaster. The margins in Sable had been finely calculated. The Rhodesian Government would not hear of one cent increase in the price of fertiliser. It was at these times that I really felt for Harold Wilson! We had cut the price of fertiliser in half. We were now saying to the Rhodesian Government: "We were wrong. We couldn't halve the price. We could only cut it to 55% instead of 50%. If you could farm at 100% then you sure as hell can farm at 55%. We can drop to 50% as soon as the Iranian plant comes on stream." Their attitude was: "No way! Just soldier on, brothers. It's all your fault and the Government will fall if the price has to go up." Most people will never comprehend the air of unreality which pervaded Salisbury at the time. We had no option but to soldier on.

We bought two cargoes from Petroquimica, and I was getting to enjoy Lisbon. Then – BANG!! Petroquimica's plant blew up and was out of action for three months. We had to find another source, and fast.

Gazocean came up with a bright idea. How about Australia? From having virtually no ammonia, Australia had acquired two plants simultaneously, in Brisbane and Newcastle, where there was a market for one. This meant that there was an exportable surplus from Australia. In fact, as I discovered later, they in fact had one hell of a problem, and Gazocean saw our needs as a way to capitalise on theirs. The ammonia plant in Brisbane was operating, and they were scheduled to start up on their urea plant. The urea plant drew its carbon dioxide from the operating ammonia plant. As was fairly normal in those days, the guys starting up the urea plant kept on saying to the ammonia plant: "Tomorrow, guys."

The result was that the ammonia plant was kept on running, but at 600 tonnes per day, and, with only 10,000 tonnes of storage, they had a monumental problem. They had nowhere to put the ammonia, and they couldn't shut down the plant. The only white knight on the horizon was Gazocean, who happened to have a ship in Australian waters. We now know that this ammonia was bought at a price in the low teens. We, of course, were to pay what Gazocean had established the traffic would bear – $67 per ton!

We agreed to buy a 14,000-tonne lot from Gazocean in Australia. I still remember Xavier Reumaux of Gazocean telling me that he had included in his price $3 for "documentation". This would guarantee no hassles.

So the *Kristian Birkeland* duly arrived at Brisbane, picked up 10,000 tonnes, and went to Newcastle to top up with 4 or 5,000 tonnes more. I had sent Jimmie Cromie, our Terminal Operator, to Australia to load, as I found that by having him there, getting the cargo loaded cold, and impressing on the captain the necessity of trying to sub-cool on the voyage over, we could save as much as 150 tonnes from being lost through flaring. Although I had Jimmie over there, I also had a foreboding about the cargo. The Brits were by now pretty well aware of our activities, and I just had the vibes that they were looking for a big one.

The whole point about sanctions was the public posture. The Brits had got a lot of third world kudos for their spectacular efforts around the crude oil tankers *Iaonna V* and the *Manuela*. All those beautiful headlines about tankers full of contraband for Rhodesia showed that Britain was really serious about sanctions. In reality, it was an elaborate charade, as there was, in fact, a secret agreement that Britain would allow Rhodesia to get all the refined product it needed, as long as it did not flout world opinion by opening the Umtali refinery. By virtue of its position as the controlling shareholder of BP, who owned the Durban refinery, it was able to discreetly see that this was done.

To keep up the front, nice headline-grabbing actions were needed. Tankers were always good for a headline or two, and were wonderful PR tools for the Brits to show the rest of the world how serious they were. The hell of the situation for us was that, through Lloyds, the Brits would know as soon as a ship was booked for Lourenço Marques. There were no more than 20 tankers in the whole world that we could use, so it was a piece of cake to watch us.

All of this led to a phone call at 2 o'clock in the morning to me from Jimmie Cromie. "Mr Hill, I have an order here signed by Mr Hasluck, the Governor-General of Australia, which says that the ship is prohibited from sailing."

I asked Jimmie whether he had completed loading, and, in particular, whether he had passed the 14,000 tonne mark. He said: "It's funny that you should ask that. As we crossed the 14,000 tonnes level on board, a man came up to me and gave me and the captain the order." Bastards! Our letter of credit was not good unless there was a minimum of 14,000 tonnes on board. If they had done it earlier, then they would have had a can of worms on their hands. They would have had to take it back and they had nowhere to put it! Now the Australians had a million bucks of our money, and they had the box as well. We were well and truly on the ropes.

I asked Jimmie to send, by telex, all the documents he had, to find out all he could, and then get on the first plane home. I went down to the office, and awaited the telex.

The Australian Government had by proclamation, the day before, given powers to the Governor-General to stop the export of any goods suspected to be going to Rhodesia. He had then issued an order pursuant to that proclamation banning the *Kristian Birkeland* from sailing. I found the Australian Trade Commissioner Ron Strange's number in Johannesburg, and telephoned him over breakfast. I read to him the opening telex, and asked him for an interview. At 9am sharp I was in his office.

He broke the ice by offering me a cigarette. He winked at me and said: "We have a personal supply which comes in duty free from Rhodesia every month. Help yourself."

Well, that was an encouraging start. One of the unreal aspects of the protocol of sanctions busting, it was always denied, but it was equally well known what one was doing. We had a solemn discussion, in the course of which I denied that I would dream of shipping Australian goods to Rhodesia, and I asked him what I needed to do to show that they were not going to Rhodesia. Mr Strange said to me that he saw his job as selling stuff, not preventing it from being sold. We must produce customers in SA. So we duly produced orders from Triomf (the largest fertiliser company in South Africa) and Impala Platinum Mines. These were sent off to Australia, and the British advisers then got the Australians to demand that the chairman of "this Post Office Box company" (Impala Platinum – a subsidiary of Union Corporation) sign a sworn affidavit, and supply a copy of its balance sheet to them. Well, the Chairman of Union Corporation was not exactly delighted. In fact, he was mightily pissed off. He did give us an affidavit, though, and a copy of the Union Corp annual report. That stopped the Australians for the moment, but we just couldn't cover the 14,000 tonnes on the ship and they wanted every tonne firmly spoken for. Although Philip Clarke had helped with an order from Triomf, there was no way they were going any further.

As we discovered later, there were many wheels within wheels. The Australian Ambassador was sending long coded cables to his foreign ministry. The British were intercepting and decoding them before the Foreign Minister in Australia got his copy. The British High

Commissioner was reading the mail to the Foreign Minister before he had even received it. Well, this got the Aussies really pissed off. Fancy your pals reading your mail!

This was not a smart move by the Brits. The Aussies wanted to find an excuse to let the ship go, because by now another problem had arisen. The *Kristian Birkeland* was occupying the only wharf in Newcastle, and ICI had a phosphate ship waiting to dock. Captain Vik (the Norwegian captain of the ship) was told by the Aussies that they were going to bring up a destroyer from Sydney, and he would be taken out to sea, and kept there under arrest. Then Captain Vik played his trump card.

"This ship is Norwegian territory. You can stop me from sailing. But you can't make me sail. If I sail, I sail for Lourenço Marques, unless you are willing to sink Norwegian property." So we had a stalemate. ICI was screaming their heads off about their phosphate ship, and the press sentiment had turned in our favour.

A cynical article in the newspaper *The Australian* took issue with the Government. It maintained that the only goods allowed to be exported to Rhodesia were for "humanitarian purposes". Under this guise, Australia exported wheat to Rhodesia. The article asked the question, "Cui Bono?" The answer? Starving Australian wheat farmers, of course, who needed a market for their wheat. It went on to complain about starving Australian ammonia manufacturers, no less deserving of the humanitarian assistance from their Government!

We now had a climate which was clearly in our favour, but we had to put up a show. In desperation, I phoned M. A. Du Plessis, South Africa's Secretary for Commerce and Industry. He offered me an appointment three weeks hence! After much cajoling, he told me to come before 8am to his office, as his appointments started then. I got there at 5 to 8, and started to pour out our problems. The crafty old gentleman held up his hand. He was on his way to his next meeting and didn't really listen. "You need an end use certificate."

He summoned a flunky, and, in one of the masterful passing of the buck and responsibility tricks much used by the Government, he ordered the flunky to give me an end use certificate "to sort out the problem". I tried to explain to the flunky that our problem was that we only had an import permit for 3,000 tonnes and the ship had 14,000 tonnes. He gave us an end use certificate for 14,000 tonnes. After all, his boss had told him to sort out our problem, and that was what was needed. It also had the great advantage that his boss could issue a bland denial later.

I phoned Ron Strange and told him I would have an end use certificate by noon. I wanted him to familiarise his Government with our terms. We would be giving them four hours after they had the certificate in the hands of their Ambassador to allow the ship to sail. Otherwise we would cancel, sue for damages, and never again buy Australian ammonia. Ron pulled out all the stops, and the *Kristian Birkeland* sailed that evening.

Later, when the ship arrived in Maputo, we heard the full story from Captain Vik over a copious supply of his liquor. We decided that we had to go to Australia to try to get them as suppliers.

Ron Strange made all the arrangements and, to our surprise, when we arrived there were two large black Government limousines to meet us, together with a welcoming gentleman from Foreign Affairs. They booked us into hotels and made travel arrangements for us to visit Brisbane, Newcastle, and, of course, Canberra. As we had been the cause of much mayhem, this was a little surprising, to say the least.

After the rather favourable press publicity in our favour, the Australians seemed keen to help us. We had a very interesting meeting in Canberra. The leader of the Australian team was called Rex Carmody, head of Customs. A giant of a man with hands the size of legs of mutton, he led the discussions. He explained at length the Australian problem. In the course of his expose we heard about the British Government this and the British Government that. Seeing an opening, I said very innocently that I knew nothing about Australia's constitutional position. In South Africa we had kicked them out years ago and South Africans ran South Africa. Did the British Government run Australia, or did the Australian Government run Australia? I thought the table would crack as Carmody gripped it. He said, "The six guys around this table spent 5 hours with our foreign minister making the point that Australians run Australia and not the whingeing poms." The activities of the British at Cheltenham, where they tapped the telexes from Ron Strange to the foreign minister, had also pissed them off mightily. They wanted a formula. If you aren't actually sending stuff to Rhodesia, it's actually not too difficult to prove. The formula we adopted was that they would give us a cargo on trust. We would later send them evidence of the disposal of that cargo. If we got ammonia from other sources, and sold a bit to SA and Mozambique, it would work. So home we came, convinced that we would get at least one more cargo out of them.

We had the interesting divertissement of visiting the two plants which supplied us. In Brisbane the plant was owned by Dow Chemical and Armour. The boss there was interesting and gave us quite an insight into the fight for markets with ICI. He asked us how much "muscle" we had. I told him I really didn't understand the term. "Well," he said, "if ICI is buggering us around, we will dump a half a million tons of caustic soda into their prime market at half price. That's muscle!"

With all the alarms and excursions going on about ammonia, it was inevitable that this would spill over into the power struggle raging in Sable. It was clear to all that the supply of ammonia was the Achilles heel of the company. So, although the consortium had virtual *de facto* control of the company, we had the company by the balls by sitting astride its lifeblood. (As has been said, when you have them by the balls their hearts and minds are sure to follow!) The Walrus (Evan Campbell), as Chairman of Fisons (a subsidiary of Fisons UK), decided that it was time to wrest control of raw material supplies from us.

He had been a tower of strength during the *Kristian Birkeland* crisis. He was actually a lot better guy to have on your side than against you. I always think of Lyndon Johnson's comment about a difficult member of his Government. "It's better to have him on the inside of the tent pissing out than on the outside pissing in!"

He proposed, though, that I was making one huge fuss about the difficulties of getting ammonia, and that in reality it was quite easy. Fisons would show how easy it was by getting a cargo. (AECI declined because they had authored the *Crystal Gem* fiasco where the Brits demanded proof that AECI was not fronting for Rhodesia and the ship sat on demurrage for six weeks and the cargo was sold to South Africa and replaced by the SA trade.) This move provoked a crisis in our camp. It was obvious that we could not really stand in their way, as this would make it clear that we were protesting too much. At the same time we had the consortium by the shorts with control of the raw material. It did, however, provide the prospect of getting raw material supplies, whether we won or lost on this one. The essence would be elegant timing, and careful attention to detail.

The man detailed to do the job was one Renus Dieleman, the MD of Fisons. I decided that the very best thing to do was to give him a very careful briefing about what was necessary. If he were to follow my instructions to the letter, without deviation, then he would be successful. I made sure of this by having a meeting between Evan Campbell (the Walrus) and Renus at the Walrus's house in Salisbury. I made sure that Campbell Coppen also attended the meeting. I wanted a witness. At that meeting I explained to Renus what he would have to do in order to satisfy the authorities concerned.

Renus proposed to buy from Gazocean's sole competitor, Mundogas. Mundogas was based in Bermuda, and the cargo was proposed to come from the United States. In view of our US experience, it was essential that the cargo was shown as going to South Africa. Renus was in a position to do this by using Fisons's local connection in South Africa.

They had large import permits for "fertiliser raw materials". All that would be necessary was to use these permits as a front, together with a purchase order from Fedmis, and he was home free. As he had to open a letter of credit for the cargo, this should be done from SA, backed by the import permits available to Fedmis.

Renus listened to my long explanation with considerable boredom. Complicated, difficult and fussy! He was bringing in all the raw materials needed by Fisons, without any problems. I was an hysterical maniac, and he would show his boss, and the consortium, what a bullshitter Hill was. He told me not to worry, he had it all under control, and asked if I would please stop trying to teach him how to run the fertiliser business.

I was convinced that disaster loomed. I therefore had to plan to turn this impending disaster into both a means for us to keep our grip on the jugular, and to use it as a springboard for creating new supplies for the plant.

The answer lay in the structure of sanctions. The sanctions were being run by the Brits. The Americans were naively obeying sanctions, and everyone else regarded sanctions as a game at which you must not be caught cheating. Although the Brits were actively engaged in policing the sanctions, all that they could do was draw the attention of a government to an apparent breach of sanctions. There was no power to check on the action of an individual government, who would report to the sanctions committee as to their satisfaction with their investigation. If the terminal could buy from a variety of sources, and deliver to a variety of destinations, it would be possible to convince each seller that their stuff was going to a "pure" destination.

The question was how to make it work in the face of the impending catastrophe I was sure was looming. As far as I was concerned, the guts of the problem was first to ensure that the cargo bought by Dieleman would first be landed in the tank. Then we would have to get it out secretly, and give out that all the cargo was still in the tank. We made a quiet arrangement with the CFM that they would deliver our tank cars at the 9pm shunt, and take them out with the 5am shunt. As the loading took place in the heart of the plant, it would be very difficult to observe what was going on, and very difficult to measure any kind of quantities. We were therefore set up to move the stuff in as much secrecy as could be achieved.

I now insisted that I liaise with Mundogas to get all in order for the shipment. To cap it all, they were using a Swedish flag ship, the *Roland*. So we had a British-based company, buying American ammonia loaded in a Swedish ship. In a nutshell, the three countries which were relatively serious about sanctions. I told Chris Marner of Mundogas to be very circumspect in all communications. My code name was "Orange", his was "Lemon", ammonia was "tiger juice", and so on. We were aware of the Cheltenham eavesdropping set-up in Britain, and knew that the Brits were eavesdropping on all traffic. We were always conscious that there were no secure links.

The most difficult thing to impress on most people involved in sanctions busting was that most seemed to regard it as a swashbuckling game, with little or no penalties. For the reasons given earlier, ammonia was a top political hit target as it gave wonderful headlines, so most players only learned this the hard way. So the guys in Mundogas thought they were involved in a rather romantic game. Besides, it would be great to put Rene Boudet's nose out of joint by swiping one of his markets. Due to this, and in spite of the warnings, they went about the whole affair in a macho manner, without too much regard for security. Renus promised them an everlasting flow of business, and at the prices established by Gazocean – a lucrative one.

It didn't hurt us in our negotiations with Gazocean for Mundogas to appear on the scene. I was able to disclaim being the bad boy, but I pointed out that it was their pricing policy that was cutting out the ground from under our feet. This stood us in good stead later.

The *Roland* duly loaded her cargo and set sail. The voyage from the US Gulf to Maputo was 23 days. Nails were bitten to the quick during those days. Something had gone wrong with the Brits. The *Roland* had rounded the Cape before the shit hit the fan. It started with a query from Mundogas. The company had been visited by a Customs officer in Bermuda, who inquired as to the final destination of the cargo. The stock answer was that the person dealing with the matter was out of the office. This managed to hold Customs off for a few precious days, and we then advised the Customs that the vessel was due to dock one week after the actual date. This relaxed them somewhat.

It soon transpired that the US authorities were also in on the act. Renus had opened his Letter of Credit as instructed through an SA bank. This was Hill Samuel. But he had done it from Salisbury in his normal way, and had not taken the precaution of getting Fedmis to do it for him, covered by a raw material import permit. The US authorities hit Hill Samuel in New York, and demanded to know the source of the funding. This was Hill Samuel in SA. Right. They then asked for the import permit.

The import permit was not forthcoming, and the US authorities promptly froze all of Hill Samuel's accounts in the US, effectively closing down their banking activities. The Brits raided Mundogas's offices in Bermuda, and caught Chris Marner with a pile of documents which were all totally incriminating. As this was happening, the *Roland* was docking. No ship has been pumped out as quickly, before or since. We moved the cargo out of the terminal at a frantic rate, over a thousand tons a day for the first three days, but then had to wait for the return of the tank car fleet.

Back at the ranch, all hell had broken loose. The Brits wanted to toss Marner and his boss, Fred Jackson, into jail. The two were vociferously protesting their total lack of knowledge that the cargo was destined for Rhodesia. Fred Jackson became convinced that this was now actually serious. All the romance of sanctions busting was forgotten. He told the authorities that he would go to Maputo, and stop the unloading of the cargo. So Fred turned up in Johannesburg, and met with me. My strategy was to delay him to the limit, and to get all of his ammonia out of the tank, without telling him that I had done so. He wanted his ammonia back, as he saw that as his only way out. He figured that he could pick up the ammonia in about six weeks.

This gave us the opening I was looking for. I prevaricated with Fred, who now knew that the cargo had been offloaded. I had also spoken to Rex Carmody and told him that we were in the process of offloading a British/American cargo into the terminal and the whole thing was a smokescreen to block Australian ammonia. He really hit the roof. Perfidious Albion was at work. We got another *Kristian Birkeland* cargo on the trot. So I was happy to allow Fred to lift his cargo. I just wanted enough time to rail out the whole *Roland* cargo first. I told Fred that until it was resolved I would leave the ammonia alone and not rail it.

He was running around with Hill Samuel, who were shrieking blue murder from the rooftops. In the end it was shown to the US authorities that it was not a requirement of law that they had to see an import permit before they opened a letter of credit. This got their bank account unfrozen. Fred then took off for Maputo, and I promised him that I would join him a few days later.

Once in Maputo, the system was programmed to give him the run-around of his life. He first went to one place. He was listened to for a couple of hours, and then told that he really needed to see someone else. That person could not see him until tomorrow. Then that person listened to the sob story for a couple of hours, and sent him off to someone else, where the process was repeated. After four days, he arrived back at the office from where he had started. When I met him he was tearing his hair out, swearing that Mozambique was the most disorganised and bureaucratic place on the face of the earth. We didn't have the heart to tell him that the whole thing had been programmed to allow us to get the whole cargo railed out. At this point the SA Government started making waves as well. Long afterwards we found out why.

When the Government issued the end use certificate, they had screwed it up. There was a simple system for ensuring that there could be no forgeries. The certificate was typed on the letterhead of the company in question, endorsed by the Government, and given a coded number. In the case of Australia it was AUST/1, etc. As they were consecutively numbered, it was not possible to fake it, as there would then be two certificates with the same number.

The clown who did ours, coded it AUS/16, meaning it to be AUST/16. This was the code for Austria, and when it arrived in Canberra, the immediate reaction was that it was a forgery. So there was much shouting, and, of course, attention was drawn to the lack of import permits. The Government corrected it, but to have a new crisis about ammonia immediately made them start to get twitchy, especially as they had knowingly issued a fraudulent end use certificate, and it appeared as if this might now be a chicken that would come home to roost.

South Africa had been hotly denying that it was doing anything else but normal trade with Rhodesia. In the case of ammonia, the mask started to slip. Not only was it seen to be fronting for Rhodesia in the purchase, but the banking system was also shown to be fronting for Rhodesia. This created a major panic in certain circles, as there was always international pressure to enlarge the sanctions to include South Africa.

I was summoned post haste by Nic van der Westhuizen at the Reserve Bank. Nic had been instrumental in allowing us to set up a complex of financial approvals, without which the project could never have been financed. Nic told me that the heat was far too great for South Africa. We must move everything offshore, and divorce it as much as we could from any South African connection. We could continue to use the financial facility he had allowed us, but our activities must move offshore. The only condition he attached was that we could not use any SA funds for this, but must use Rhodesian funds.

Thus it was that the ammonia business migrated totally offshore at the direct instruction of the South African Reserve Bank. Due to the fact that they did not want to be seen to be having anything to do with it, we were granted considerable latitude, and this proved to be a great boon when we started to spread our wings. Nic was a man of great wisdom and foresight. Unfortunately, his early death led to his replacement by bureaucrats with neither his vision nor his understanding of the business community.

While the whole *Roland* affair was under way, the plotters in Salisbury hatched up a plan to deprive us of the operating contract for the terminal. We had had a serious fly shunting accident whereby a number of empty tankers had been shunted into two tankers coupled up to the loading racks. This badly damaged the racks, but fortunately the excess flow valves limited the ammonia escape and no-one was injured. But it was claimed this incident showed that little old NPI did not have the experience to run the terminal. So Sable commissioned AECI to do a technical report on the terminal.

Of course, there was also a more sinister motive. If AECI could get the contract to operate the terminal, they would be able to control the ammonia trade, and they could effectively block our activities in Swaziland, which by now was creating a firestorm in South Africa.

However, as plotters they were singularly inept. They sent down a competent engineer and I sent down David Leith to help him with the report. The engineer had known both David and Jimmy Cromie well from Modderfontein (AECI's major chemical complex in SA) days. Jamie was quite famous as, during a disastrous fire on their ammonia plant, he was the only person who did not flee but stayed in the plant and shut it down, avoiding massive damage and allowing the fire to dissipate without problems. For this he was quite a hero. The AECI engineer had no intention of criticising either of them. He was shown everything around the plant. His only point was the lack of a bund wall. David quickly offered a bund wall as a desirable addition. Could he get a million bucks out of AECI for it? So the report actually had high praise for our operating staff and this little ploy failed miserably.

Anyway, back to the *Roland* saga. I finally met up with Fred Jackson, and told him I had no problem loading up his ammonia. He had been to the terminal and told me he had personally read the gauges (again, tut, tut) and all his ammonia was still in the tank. He would send another ship in about six weeks. He rushed off to the Brits in Maputo and the US authorities and told them he had stopped the railing of the ammonia and was going to pick it up shortly.

I then awaited the arrival of the *Kristian Birkelend*. I flew Ron Strange down to Maputo for the discharge and showed him we were putting it into an empty tank. I told him I had contracted to act as a depot for Iran, and that shortly a ship was arriving to pick up a cargo for Iran, which it did, and we were quite genuinely able to point out to the Australians that their cargo had definitely not gone to Rhodesia, but to Iran. Fred gave the same story to the Brits and Americans. Neither Governments were *persona grata* at our terminal and our stratagem of night movements had done the trick.

Well, we thought that had ended the saga. Then I had a call from Gazocean. The *Roland* cargo had been discharged and Iran now didn't want it. Gazocean had a ship and the Iranians wanted them to take it to us. Their ammonia tank had cracked and was leaking ammonia all over the plant. The Iranians needed to get the ammonia out of it in a hurry. A few hours later I had Ardeshir Molavi on the phone. Although Shahpur Chemicals had not yet declared their plant operational, they found they were able to let us have some ammonia. It would only cost us a 20 dollar premium over our contract price. With the Gazocean information under my belt, although we desperately needed the stuff, I told them that we had a storage problem, we would have to rent expensive tank cars from South Africa and faced demurrage on the vessel, etc, etc, etc (it was only 11 days from Shahpur to Maputo). The best I could do was accept it at a 10 dollar discount on the contract price. It took less than an hour for Ardeshir to be back agreeing to this. So the *Roland* ammonia duly returned to our terminal miraculously cleansed of British/American origin. And the complicated movements had created a hell of a smokescreen and showed that our terminal was indeed a trading terminal in the export/import business.

The last country we had to deal with was the US. The vessels *Gas Lion* and *Isfonn* were still an issue. And our erstwhile American friends were trying to muscle in on terminal operations. They wanted some revenue out of the terminal. Finally, they brought a case against us. Unfortunately for them, the USA picked up a copy at the High Court and had a pretty open and shut case that they were involved in sanctions busting. And they told South Africa that the US Government was going to suspend all open general export licences for South Africa. This was very bad news, as South Africa got their hands on much quasi-military equipment through this means (such as Lockheed Hercules freighters). If I didn't go to New York and speak to the authorities, they promised murder and mayhem towards us.

So, it was off to New York. The US authorities set up a meeting with the Attorney General in New York as well as the head of export control. I was bombarded with questions. The head of export control quickly recognised Dr Batliner, the titular head of our company, Pilger Anstalt in Liechtenstein. According to him he had crossed the good doctor's path many a time. Export of IBM computers to Russia was the good man's latest scam. And, of course, the Government of Liechtenstein did not co-operate in preventing this. After all, Dr Batliner was the prime minister.

Well, the subject quickly got around to the *Gas Lion* and the *Isfonn*. After quite a bit of fencing, someone asked the direct question: "Where did the ammonia from those ships go?"

Answer: "To Rhodesia."

You could have heard a pin drop. No-one was expecting such a direct answer. They then pounced on me and said that I had personally given the assurance that the ammonia would not go to Rhodesia. I denied ever having given such an assurance, and then in triumph they produced a letter.

"Had I written the letter?"

Answer: "Yes."

Well. Case closed.

I said to them: "Read the letter."

It said: "This serves to confirm that the good ship *Gas Lion* will by no means be diverted to Rhodesia."

So they all said: "That proves it. You lied to us."

I said if they read it carefully I had not mentioned the cargo. Everyone knew that Rhodesia was a landlocked country and it was impossible to divert the *Gas Lion* or any other ship to Rhodesia. The ship went to Lourenço Marques; the cargo was offloaded and sent to Rhodesia. I had not promised them anything about the cargo!

The head of Export Control looked me in the eye. He was an enormous black man about the same size as Rex Carmody. He leaned back in his chair, pointed his finger at me and said: "My friend, you know, and I know, what we wanted in that letter. This time, you get away with it. In any future deals we want specific assurances about the cargo."

Very meekly, I said that, of course, I would provide them whatever he required. However, I pointed out that we had a lot of customers, including Rhodesia. Their ammonia was going into a tank where it was mixed with all other ammonia. American molecules would certainly be mixed up with molecules of ammonia from less fussy countries. I could not stop their molecules from going to Rhodesia!

The AG said that no American ammonia could ever go into our terminal. It was pointed out to him that if you put your money in a bank, you didn't get the same banknotes back. It was agreed then, that if we put 10,000 tons in the tank I must produce Customs clearances for 10,000 tons destined to other than Rhodesia. The head of export control and I became quite friendly thereafter. If I wanted ammonia I should phone him in Washington, send a proper letter by fax and he would release a cargo to me. After I had proven its destination as agreed, he would let me have another. So from our point of view we had another source.

Eventually, of course, Shahpur Chemical finally got their ammonia plant going. Until the great oil crisis in 1973, we had no serious difficulties with ammonia.

The next item was the Attorney General's indictment. He wanted me up before the Grand Jury. It was interesting to see at first hand the American system of justice. A Grand Jury hearing is a secret conclave at which the AG parades his witnesses and asks questions. I spent a full day with him before the Grand Jury inquiry while he asked me questions. When the answer was not to his satisfaction, he asked the question slightly differently. He carried on in this vein until he had the answer he wanted. So, before the Grand Jury, the only questions asked were those to which he knew the answer and it was the right one for him.

Cordell Hull had told me that it was nothing short of a Star Chamber proceeding and if the Grand Jury indicted you it was assumed that you had to be guilty. It was extremely lucky for Cordell that when the shit hit the fan in America he had sent a telex disclaiming any further part in the Sable project. It was this telex which was used to deny him any part of terminal operations. I allowed the Attorney General a copy of it, which saved Cordell from indictment. The big troublemaker Ed Bartlett, who brought the case against us, was not so lucky. They nailed him to the cross and he got a suspended sentence of one year.

But at last the Iranians got their act together and we started to get ammonia without a panic. The problem which now arose was that, because of the drastic cut in the price of fertiliser, our market was running at 90,000 tons of nitrogen per year. Even on our optimistic projections, we thought that would be five years down the pike. But it was on us. Rhodesia Railways told us we had second priority over Genta, who were bringing in fuel. Genta had a 10-day turnaround from Lourenço Marques to Salisbury and back. Our turnaround was more like 12 days to Que Que and back. The average on the railways was 30 days! We had 86 tank cars. At 12-days turnaround, this meant seven tank cars a day, which at the official filling rate of 26.9 tons meant 188 tons per day, which translates into 411 tons per day of ammonium nitrate. We needed the full 800 tons per day.

Because we had not been able to afford a weighbridge, we had a dipstick installed on the tank cars which was used to fill them. For safety reasons, after plotting the weights actually achieved, which were lying in the range of 25 to 27.5 tons, I asked the railways to use a lower figure for the freight charge, as by using a dipstick we had to set it at less than the payload. No way. No matter what was in the tank cars, they would charge us for 26.9 tons, and we could dispense with the 24-hour delay to weighbridge the cars at the main port.

There is a gas space because ammonia expands much more than the tank car does and thus reaches a point where the whole tank car is full of liquid. The relief valve then pops and lets out the surplus.

This is not really desirable as you get a cloud of ammonia vapour which is toxic. But the payload calculation is done on the basis that when the temperature reaches 113 degrees Fahrenheit, the tank car is full. So we investigated just how hot the ammonia got. It was, after all, loaded at 0 degrees centigrade. Even though daytime temperatures in the Limpopo Valley regularly exceeded 90 degrees F, we found that the highest temperature the ammonia reached was 75 degrees F. Calculation showed that at this temperature we could get 29.5 tons in before the safety valve popped. Allowing for the plus/minus effect of the dipsticks, we decided to go for 28.5 tons average. So on average 1.6 tons would be carried for free! This, of course, helped us to the tune of increasing our production by 25 tons per day – a drop in the bucket of our needs. And we had the Government on our backs moaning about the shortage, forgetting that we were far over their projections.

So we went into the whole logistical system. It was totally haphazard. We looked into the train schedules on both sides. Once you got on the main line, the Portuguese carried it straight to Chicualacala. There they delivered the train to Rhodesia Railways, whose train went straight to Gwelo. It waited for another train for Salisbury and made a drop-off at Que Que. The reverse schedule was similar. The actual travelling time was around 30 hours. It was all a question of getting on the right train. That meant catching the right shunt and being ready for it. It also meant ensuring that you caught the connection at Chicualacala.

After much cajoling and continuous monitoring, we managed to get our turnaround time down to seven days. That meant 12 cars a day with, now, 28.5 tons or 341 tons per day, which gave us about 750 tons per day of ammonium nitrate. But we had two full-time expediters at work – one in Mozambique and one in Rhodesia. And we had only two incidents of safety valve blow-off. It might be noted that the currently affirmatively run railway now takes at least 30 to 40 days for the same trip.

Sable was finally blowing all its critics out of the water with its performance. Of course, not one word of this success ever reached the public. Very few people even knew what Sable was or what it did. What it did do was stimulate a boom in agricultural production which went a long way towards ameliorating the effects of sanctions.

We had one amusing saga. The Salisbury plotters were forever trying to get at us. They could not believe that we were not taking a fat kickback or some such deal on ammonia, and about every six weeks I had an auditor coming down both from Sable and the Ministry. We had had the saga of the cracked tank at Shahpur and Gazocean was on the phone. We had a cargo arriving in the *Kristian Birkeland*, and Shahpur wanted about 2,500 tons of ammonia to commission their tank, which had been cracked. They needed the tank to be in commission before they could start up their plant. As the *Kristian Birkeland* was sailing to the Persian Gulf after discharge, the simplest solution was to leave the ammonia on the ship.

I had been wrestling with the ship anyway as the railways had some movement problems and it looked as though we would have about 2,500 tons too much to fit into the tank. It was time to have some fun with the Rhodesians. First, I put to the Iranians that I wanted US$68 per ton for the ammonia. After some back and forth, they proposed to borrow the ammonia and repay me with a 50% increase. I accepted this in principle.

Then I got onto Jimmy Walker at the Ministry of Industries in Rhodesia. Pointing out that, due to railway problems, we were going to be overstocked and faced a week to 10 days of demurrage, I felt it was the Government's fault and we would demand that we got it out of the hide of the farmers. Jimmy freaked. He started running around trying to get the railways to move their butts. All to no avail. I let him sweat for a couple of days and went back to him and told him I had arranged free storage with the Iranians, who would return the ammonia later. Well! I was the knight in shining armour and the great solver of problems, etc, etc, etc; and yes, I must do it immediately.

So the Iranians got their ammonia and commissioned their ammonia plant. That was the only thing we ever did to make money out of the ammonia supply, as we picked up the extra tonnage for our own account. And were heroes for doing so.

I asked Vic Hurley, one of our early farmer supporters, just how bad things were. He sighed and said: "I had to settle for a four-seater aeroplane instead of a six-seater!"

So, of course, the vultures gathered.

EXIT AMERICANS

The Americans were responsible for the ammonia supply and the technology of building phase two of Sable, as well as providing the technical support for running the plant. We had a very attractive management contract which had taken a lot of convincing to get. We had a meeting at which Jimmy Walker from the Rhodesian Ministry of Industry had invited a treasury official to attend. This individual suggested we go to tender to get a management contract. I objected and when he asked me why I said: "Because it's our money. We are very emotionally attached to it!" I thought he would die from laughing. He said no-one had ever claimed to be emotionally attached to their money. We got the contract.

Whilst Herb Hamilton was performing and sending out the likes of Lashlee, we were happy for him to draw against our management contract. (We got a fixed fee from Sable and had a *per diem* arrangement with Hamilton.) People like Lashlee are the great gems in the chemical industry. I unashamedly picked his brains and in the end, after two years of working with the master, I too became an expert in the field of nitrogen chemicals. When that dried up, they still continued to draw their half share of the profit, however.

Then someone let slip a juicy piece of information. Hamilton owned a gas tanker called the *Alexander Hamilton*. She was small (7,500 tons) and had been put on time charter to Gazocean, but the return was nothing like what Rene Boudet had told Hamilton he could expect.

Hamilton had finally found a salesman who could outsell him!! So he cut a deal with Rene. He would get a kickback of 5 dollars a ton on any ammonia shipped to Rhodesia.

Armed with this juicy titbit, I met with Rene in Paris to discuss our arrangements with Gazocean. In the course of the discussion I casually confirmed the kickback arrangement with Hamilton. I passed it to Peter Beningfield, who, of course, went ape, and refused to pay some US$90,000 to Mississippi Chemical, who had supplied the cargoes on the *Gas Lion* and the *Isfonn*. This led to much acrimony.

With all the shenanigans going on about ammonia, it was evident that some things were coming to a head. Xavier Reumaux of Gazocean, when I was visiting Paris, told me of the last cargo he had offloaded. The vessel in question was the *Cerons*, a 10,000 tonner belonging to Messageries Maritimes, a large French company and carrying the French flag. He was summoned to the foreign ministry and told that the British were complaining that the French were the major sanctions-busters with respect to ammonia. They felt compelled to report to the UN Sanctions Committee. Xavier, of course, denied knowing anything about Rhodesia, and had advised us that the French were considering banning the discharge. Armed with this information, we secretly went to the high court in Lourenço Marques. We were told that, although the French had jurisdiction over the vessel, it was in Mozambique waters and we as the cargo owners also had rights. So two jurisdictions had a say. The effective question was who had the power to enforce their jurisdiction? This was not actually a point that the British wanted highlighted, in view of the *Crystal Gem* fiasco, where they had succeeded in stopping the discharge. We got an order from the judge to the Port Captain ordering him to see that we got our cargo and authorising him to use the army to enforce it. So the French politely ducked, but the guy in Foreign Affairs in Paris sighed and opened his bottom drawer. He told Xavier that this was a bad one. He would have to use up his best piece of documentation showing British infractions of sanctions, to trade with the British. If they called off the dogs in the Sanctions Committee on the *Cerons*, he would likewise call off the dogs on this terrible infraction by the British.

Thus did it work in Europe. The Americans tended to play the game straight, however. At a meeting of the Sanctions Committee, in front of all the third world members, who were mostly unaware of what actually went on, the Americans accused the French of being the buster of sanctions on ammonia to Rhodesia. The French turned round and said that they didn't know what the Americans were being so sanctimonious about. After all, the first two cargoes they had taken to Lourenço Marques were American!

There was a howl from the third world accusing the Americans of being two-faced, paying lip service to sanctions, etc, etc. Hence the Americans had to be seen to be doing something about it. Hence the threats to South Africa and hence the Grand Jury inquiry.

Cordell Hull insisted that his company could not have anything further to do with Rhodesia. We would have to build the ammonia plant ourselves, and we would have to provide the ammonia. But they wanted their share of the ammonia profits, which were spectacular, and we had to pay off all their financing. They wanted their share of the management services contract. I believed that we had to pay off the financing, especially as our names were on the promissory notes. As far as the management services contract was concerned, Cordell had made it clear that they could not perform. So I refused to pay them anything. The same went for the profits on ammonia. They had utterly failed to perform; in fact, it had taken *force majeure* when asked to meet their guarantees and could not supply ammonia. As a result, we had had to set up the whole Lichtenstein procurement operation. We got no joy from them in the ammonia plant design. We had bought the two compressors for the plant, done the airplant, and were busy with the electrolysis plant. We did not have a synthesis loop.

Apart from a much later development, the Air Liquide project (the airplant) was the most flawless project we ever did. We had a contract with Risco which called for oxygen to be delivered on 1st January, which gave us less than 18 months to build the plant and commission it against a one thousand pounds a day penalty. We made it with 10 days to spare and it ran for over two years non-stop. Air Liquide finally got their reward, as they won the largest oxygen plant contracts in the world with Sasol II and III. Sasol had visited our plants and were much impressed with the performance of our airplant, which was, of course, a toy next to their 13 plants which they bought.

Anyway, Ed Bartlett (Hamilton's financial manager) decided to take us to court. In so doing he publicised their full involvement, on oath in the High Court. The American ambassador picked up a copy and the US Government plastered their blood and guts all over the landscape. The Americans were all charged with breaking sanctions on Rhodesia in the US courts. Their counsel in South Africa was Sydney Kentridge, who was instrumental in promoting a settlement in the case they brought against us. In the course of the settlement, it was agreed that Sable would take over the terminal and their shares in Gas Pipelines. We were granted the contract to run the terminal and the exclusive right to use it for third parties. We also got the contract to build phase two on a cost-plus basis. We kept our shares in Gas Pipelines and Sable. They were left with their shares in Sable. Eventually, when we finally sold out, they were taken out as well. Cordell, who had run with the hare and hunted with the hounds on this one, stayed friendly with us and, when he left Hamilton, was instrumental in making it possible for us to get one of the most lucrative construction projects anywhere. But that is another story.

SABLE – COMPLETION

Sable phase 1

With the departure of the Americans, we now had to face up to the problem of the ammonia plant. As long as Iran was not in production, we faced high tension with every ammonia cargo we bought. The problem was that the Brits now knew that we were importing ammonia for Sable, and were always looking for political spectaculars to show how hard they were enforcing sanctions against Rhodesia.

Air Liquide had a subsidiary company, Societe Chemique de la Grande Paroisse. Through this connection, we met an individual, Michel Bonnet, who proved to be a great helpmate. Grande Paroisse was closing down an old ammonia plant built in 1937 with a nameplate capacity of 170 tons per day. We were all convinced that, because of the gas purity from electrolysis, and the old design of this plant, with the new catalysts now used, we could easily squeeze 240 tons per day out of it. Sasol had built a similar plant. We had compressors on order, which had a nominal capacity of 325 tons per day, which could fit this old plant, so we bought it, lock, stock and barrel, for US$25,000. It was this purchase which gave me my taste for secondhand plants, which has endured to this day.

We had an outstanding team for the project. Mike McGuigan had cut his teeth on the airplant, and turned up trumps. For the project manager on electrolysis, we had taken on Julius Yodaiken. He also turned out to be a real find. Mike was one of those people who are as rare in construction as rocking horse manure. He had been a bricklayer's assistant in Ireland, and had put himself through Chemical Engineering at Dublin University. Mike had a total "hands-on" view of projects at the most basic level, and knew how to build not only cheaply, but highly effectively.

The project management was in the hands of these two really capable people. We had two others – Terry O'Sullivan and Peter Wesselbaum. Terry was a great hands-on man, who really could get work out of people. Peter had been the heavyweight boxing champion of the German Navy. He was the best construction foreman I have ever known. He was an absolute ball of fire on a site. He was everywhere, galvanising action wherever he went. The team we had that built Sable was unbeatable. They also built Swaziland and the new terminal in Mozambique later. For the moment, though, building Sable was all that mattered.

With the departure of the Americans, the Sable board became dominated by the enemy. Although Rhodox technically held control, huge pressure was always exerted on Campbell Coppen by the ring. Rhodesia was a small society with an establishment which ran the business of the country from the bar at the Salisbury Club between 5 and 7 every evening. It was difficult for any member of the establishment to resist that pressure.

The ammonia project at Sable was predicated on the concept that hydro-electric power would form the basis of Rhodesia's power needs

Sable – the world's largest water electrolysis plant

for at least 50 years. There were as yet vast untapped resources on the Zambesi, besides the great resources in Mozambique and further north. I had fallen for the supreme elegance of the Lurgi high-pressure electrolysis system, which actually, because of the pressure, had a lower specific power consumption than atmospheric pressure systems, but produced the hydrogen and oxygen at 30 bars pressure. Not only did this save on compression energy, but it simplified the gas treatment section. The only drawback was that I could not devise a really cheap heavy-water plant to go with the system. This was why heavy-water never became a feature of Sable.

We had had a number of technical problems in looking at the whole power issue. Sable was to consume 20% of the total power usage in Rhodesia. Such a vast amount of direct current would create a huge output of harmonics into the whole power system. It was all mumbo-jumbo to me, but it was explained to me that the harmonics had to be removed, or they would concentrate at points in the system, and might destroy equipment.

It appeared that harmonic suppression would involve huge capacitors. I had learned that these were also used for power factor correction. In Phase I at Sable, I had put in cheap asynchronous motors because I felt that, if we had to correct the power factor, we would do it all at once and so save on the capital costs of our big motors.

The ESC were feeling pretty chuffed with themselves. Although we had had a real Donnybrook over the cost of power, they had succeeded in sticking us with an MVA tariff, whereas they bought power on an MW tariff from CAPCO. When we started up at a power factor of 0.8, they were over the moon, as our tariff was all based on demand and initially nothing for units. When we finally had the big switch-on day of our harmonic filters, though, Sable's power factor went to unity, where it has been ever since. In fact, it was possible to even feed a leading power factor into the grid. The fat profit expected by ESC disappeared.

Meanwhile, back at the ranch, AE and CI were starting to try and seize gradual control of Sable. They appointed a new general manager, one of their men, called Frank McWilliams. Frank was a really nice guy, and was actually not up to the task of murdering us, which was why he was put there. He was a typical AECI technocrat. We easily out-manoeuvred them in their clumsy attempt to take management of the terminal. Frank also made the mistake of giving the Board bullshit at the monthly meetings. When he was asked to give reasons for the fall in efficiency of the acid plants, or whatever, he made the mistake of giving an answer which was technical bullshit. He only did it once or twice, and I had to cut him up totally, before the Board. Campbell Coppen therefore approached John, saying that it just wasn't done to cut up the General Manager before the Board. I was quite unrepentant and retorted that, as long as he bullshitted the Board, I would cut him up at Board meetings. We finally made a quiet arrangement whereby Frank would send me an advance copy of the report and I would go through it. After I had approved it, it would be submitted to the Board. This effectively gave me technical control of Sable, because Frank had bigger fish to fry than Sable. AECI wanted to build a new ammonia plant in South Africa and Frank wanted the job. (He got it.)

All my life I have looked at what people were doing overseas and bringing these ideas to South Africa. That takes the whole technical risk out of projects. (Always remember Andrew Carnegie's dictum: "Pioneering don't pay".) The whole of the nitrogen fertiliser business in Southern Africa had been controlled by the cartel (AECI, Sasol, Fisons), by virtue of the fact that they controlled ammonia. The cost of entry was prohibitive, as ammonia was the most capital intensive of all the fertiliser products. No-one realised that by building the ammonia terminal in Mozambique, we had opened the world's low-cost ammonia resources to South Africa. We could land ammonia at half the price being charged in South Africa.

During the first few months of operation at Sable, and the fight with the Americans, I had lain low. Once we had nearly got everything up and running, we started secret negotiations to build a similar plant in Swaziland. This took a long time and was done in conditions of great secrecy. We knew that it would create a mega-firestorm and we wanted the right authorities to be too far committed to back down when the inevitable might of the cartel started to complain. Swaziland was a saga all on its own. It all at once formed the basis of a great fortune, and it also finally sank us. That, though, is another story.

When Swaziland broke, the two South African AECI directors of Sable, "Wapie" Wapenaar and William van der Byl, went mad. As

Sable owned the ammonia terminal, they determined to use their power to take it off us, and thus block Swaziland. They had also, by now, come to use it for their own activities in South Africa.

We had one memorable Board meeting in Salisbury. At that meeting, Wapie, after asking about the terminal ownership, and finding out that Sable indeed owned it, but NPI had management and the sole right to use it for ammonia, not related to Sable, said to the Board: "You mean we own a terminal and we can't use it?"

For once, John wasn't writing telexes in the Board meeting. William was sitting in his usual place, at the far end, with a pile of biltong in front of him, which he steadily cut up with a wicked-looking knife, and fired off barbs into the meeting. William supported Wapie.

John said to the meeting, "If you mean by 'we own a terminal' you mean Sable, you are right. If by 'we can't use it' you mean Sable, you are wrong. Sable has first right of use. If by 'we can't use it' you mean AECI, you are dead right. You, AECI, come to NPI if you want ammonia."

At that point, it was clear we had a war on our hands. William and Wapie became hell bent on trying to stop us, but they had constraints. They couldn't do anything which would be seen to damage Sable, and they actually needed the ammonia. Sable Board meetings now became a war zone.

We had started out with one key advantage. With the departure of Ed Bartlett, a financial person was urgently needed in Salisbury. I packed Peter Beningfield off to hold the fort – a decision which later gave rise to mixed feelings (in the sense of seeing your mother-in-law driving your new car over a cliff!). Peter was the world's supreme chocolate farmer. He had been sent up from Durban to Johannesburg, to Whiteley Brothers, to be placed in the care of Jimmy Low. Jimmy had the reputation of being able to get anyone through his accountancy exams, and, as Peter battled, he was sent to get the Low treatment. Finally, Jimmy Low got him through. He succeeded in getting the twins of Campbell Coppen and Evan Campbell totally dependent on him and eating out of his hand as far as Sable was concerned. He did this very much at the expense of NPI, who he now attacked with tremendous ferocity. We had to keep our noses clean with the construction contract, but Peter went out of his way to be as obnoxious to NPI as he could be. And he was very petty. He was also a master exponent of the Michael Korda principle: "Master players attempt to channel as much of the information as they can into their own hands, then withhold it from as many people as possible."

The electrolysis plant was coming forward at the rate of two cells per month. It came in huge crates made of Baltic pine. We used a lot of it for shuttering and scaffold planking, but we brought some back to Johannesburg. John wanted one for some purpose, and I wanted to line my sauna with it. Peter had spies on site who told him the plane had taken some planks back to Johannesburg. He went berserk and ordered all timber on site to go under his personal control (and then proceeded to move it to Salisbury for himself). These types of petty frictions caused strains and made what was a very difficult situation much worse.

The big issue, of course, was the construction contract and ammonia supply. The Rhodesian Government was paranoid about the cost of ammonia. AECI also convinced everyone that I was pocketing big profits on ammonia supply. No-one had forgotten Hamilton's kick-backs on the *Gas Lion* and *Isfonn.*

To pinch money in the ammonia trade would have been an incredibly stupid thing to do. In any case, we didn't need to make money by stealing from Sable. We were perfectly capable of making money legitimately I endured seven major surprise audits from the Government, Sable and the cartel, though. It actually gave me the greatest possible pleasure to have them crawling all over the office, and to offer them free rein with all our files, records, etc, knowing that the whole thing was a total waste of time, as they would find nothing. We were clean as a whistle.

They didn't believe we were clean, though. We had to be stealing from them. The more they searched and found nothing, the more sure they were that we were not clean. They had to have something to get their teeth into, because the Board would never believe that we were totally clean. So I gave them something which they were able to make a huge fuss about and it kept them from asking some very embarrassing questions which could have cost us a bomb.

When we agreed to a cash-plus contract, it was agreed that the entire cost of running NPI would be a cost of the contract, as we were doing only that, and running the ammonia business. It was agreed that John and I could charge first-class fares for our overseas travel, plus US$100 per day, which we did not have to account for. If we wanted more, it would have to be justified. It was also agreed that our salaries and perks would be part of the cost.

Very early on in the NPI days, I discovered John had certain habits which dated back to his early days of running his own company. John was a tax evader, rather than an avoider. He once told me that "to do in the tax man", you had to steal at least £100 a week from the petty cash.

Our business was actually far beyond that level of tax problem, but John couldn't change his habits. I had also been brought up differently, but one had a choice. You could either sulk and fume, as Peter did, or have endless confrontations, or join him.

One of the things John established was that all his liquor accounts came to the company. I therefore joined him. Where John ordered (and drank) vast amounts of whisky (at least a bottle a day), my tastes were different. I ordered wine. Those were far-off days, and you could get Mouton Rothschild, Lafite, La Tache, Romanee Conti, etc, for very modest prices. I acquired a marvellous cellar. Over the two-year construction contract, my wine account came to something like R10,000.

The second item that the company paid for was the running cost of my car. Our shareholders' agreement provided for (then) a Mercedes 280SE or equivalent. That's what John bought. I bought Dominique's cousin's Lusso Ferrari. The cars cost the same. Mine was eight years old, John's was new. Over the two years of the contract, we spent some R5,000 on maintenance and repairs to the Ferrari.

Sable's auditor was a guy called Mike Hooper. He was instructed to audit us with a fine-tooth comb. There was a field day at the Board with my liquor account and the maintenance costs of the Ferrari. I pointed out to Campbell Coppen that our salaries were modest. For tax reasons, we took perks instead. At every Board meeting, though, when the construction costs were presented, these figures caused mayhem.

One of the real problems we had in these audits was in our contract with Roberts Construction. Although we had given them the continuation work on Phase II, there was nothing approaching the value for them that there had been in Phase I. Also, they had bought a big block of shares in Sable, which we were obligated to buy back at par. We had agreed to an annual engineering fee to Roberts, which was really in place of interest on their investment. This fee was clearly and obviously out of proportion to their work, but the agreement was crystal clear – it was an engineering fee. I didn't want Mike Hooper, though, to start asking questions about it, because if he had asked me, I would have had to have told him the truth, and that would have cost us a bomb. We would have had to have explained the justification for such a fee, which would have been tough.

The red herring worked like a charm. No-one even questioned the Roberts fee. The cartel had something to get hysterical about, and I got a reputation for an extravagant lifestyle. The truth is, we drank very little of the wine. The Ferrari I bought at book value from the company (as John bought his Mercedes). John's car became basically worthless, but I sold the Ferrari finally for £105,000 (at the time R525,000). Not a bad return for R8,000 and 15 years of driving bliss. I sold off most of the wine cellar for £50,000 just before the Standard Bank sequestrated me. Three bottles of Romanee Conti (alas, we drank the other nine!), which were bought for R12 per bottle, went for £800 each! Some investment! Most of the things we have bought for pure pleasure have been stunning investments. I digress, though.

We were having a great deal of difficulty with our fellow shareholders in Sable. I had structured Sable with a capital structure of R$5 million of equity and R$28 million of debt. The pricing structure agreed with the Government was designed to redeem the debt, with interest, over five years. Thereafter, the cash flow would all accrue to shareholders. It doesn't take a genius to work out that, at the end of five years, the equity earnings would be over 100%. Also, our agreement gave us a "put" right at nine times earnings, and an obligation to sell a "control" block at 11 times earnings. We were very happy with this prospect.

I was of the opinion that the *force majeure* clause in our pricing agreement with the Government gave us the right to put our prices up modestly, to put us in the position forecast in the negotiations. The Government was paranoid. Ian Smith had come to power on farmer support. They wouldn't do anything that might affect their electorate. In vain did we point out that we had halved the price of fertiliser. We now thought that it should be a 45% discount instead of a 50% discount. No bloody way.

I wanted to go to arbitration. The cartel did not have the stomach for a fight. They wanted a dividend. We said: "Stuff the dividend. We want what we were promised." Mike White, the head of AECI in Rhodesia, and I saw eye to eye on that one. He was all for my plan, but William van der Bijl thought he saw an opportunity to screw us. If he could cut the profits for three years to virtually nothing, he could take us out for practically nothing. We thus had a totally irreconcilable situation between us.

To really put the heat on us, they then cut off our funds. It was all done very sanctimoniously. "We are getting to the end of the contract, and Sable can't pay out money unless we are happy with an audit." Poor old Mike Hooper, down again to Johannesburg with clear instructions. Find the shenanigans! Any queries – hold all payments! We, of course, had all sorts of creditors beating down the doors, and, of course, AECI took care to let them know that a serious audit was under way. They hinted, of course, that some serious problems existed. This didn't help the state of mind of our creditors.

Fortunately, at this point I was able to survive by means of a stratagem, and hoist AECI with their own petard. AECI had finally succeeded in getting the South African Government to impose a tariff on ammonia entering the Customs union. The day before it was imposed, I cleared 20,000 tons of ammonia in the tank into South Africa. I never told AECI, but, one week before the duty was due to be gazetted, I wrote a very, very careful letter to Neil Steyn at AECI.

I pointed out that a duty was to be gazetted. With the cost of the ammonia under contract from Iran, the duty would amount to some $25 per ton. Accordingly, I advised him that all future invoices would carry a figure of $25 per ton as a "provision for duty". We duly invoiced them and they happily paid up for months and months. They never asked us for a bill of entry, so we were able to pay our creditors with their money. They had thought that they had us by the shorts in Rhodesia and they couldn't figure out where the hell the money was coming from to pay our creditors. We were rolling in the aisles laughing at them.

Finally, of course, Sable had to pay us. They did so with very bad grace. Mike Hooper confessed to me that they were baffled as to how

I had managed to deal with some big, tough creditors. The timing was exquisite. Then the other half of AECI started pestering our ammonia division. They had exported some urea, and wanted a drawback of the duty they had paid. Customs told them they hadn't paid any duty. They claimed they had. Customs said "Prove it"; so they wanted bills of entry. We sent them consignment notes. They phoned and complained. We sent them more consignment notes. Finally, the boss, Neil Steyn, phoned me. He explained very carefully to me, in words of one syllable, exactly what they wanted. As we had been paid the day before by Sable, I was happy with what was to come.

I sent the Bills of Entry over to be delivered at 4.30pm precisely. I wanted them to have a happy night after they read the Bills of Entry. No such luck. At 8 o'clock that evening I had a call from Neil Steyn. He said to me, "Oliver, you no doubt expected this call. My people have been telling me quite a story. You have defrauded us out of $400,000!"

I said to Neil: "I think you should read my letter very carefully, Neil, before saying that. I think you will find that all we asked for was a provision for duty. Are you telling me that, in fact, a provision is no longer required?"

Neil said: "Yes, OK, OK, I have read the letter. You win on that one. What bothers me really is that it shows a gross failure by my boys to be on top of things. They should have found this out months ago! I think it would be appropriate, in the circumstances, if there was a cheque at 8.30 tomorrow, in my office."

I said to Neil: "Of course. In fact, I have done you a huge favour. Just imagine all the paperwork I have saved you. Now you can get an instant cheque out of me, because it would have taken months to get it out of Customs!" I won't quote his reply, but at least he had a sense of humour about it, and we enjoyed many laughs over the years at the delicious irony of AECI squeezing us mercilessly with the one hand, and financing the squeeze with the other! And, at the end of the day, they got back the whole lot, and not just the drawback portion they would have got from the export. They came out way ahead.

Meanwhile, back at Sable, we were forever at an impasse on the Board. William decided that it would be quite simple to resolve it. He proposed that we would simply define Sable as being what it was, and that it could do nothing else. He claimed to have brought peace in South Africa with Louis Luyt in Triomf by this means. I countered by saying I would be happy to leave the definition of Sable to what we had proposed to the Rhodesian Government. When William saw that, he said: "But this defines the whole chemical industry!" I said we were happy with that.

At this juncture, Sid Hayes appeared on the scene. Sid was running a conglomerate called Tobacco Auctions. There were two tobacco auction houses in Salisbury, and both were cash-rich organisations, seeking to deploy their cash elsewhere. Sid had acquired 55% of Albatross Fisons Fertilisers from Albatross of Holland, and thus, through Chemical and Gas Holdings, an indirect interest in Sable. Sid was wildly and insatiably interested in conglomerate building. He saw Sable as a prize to be grabbed. In spite of the pricing fight with Government, Sable was now a cash machine, as the ammonia plant had started up and was running flawlessly. Of course, we had expected it with the electrolysis feasibility, but the ammonia plant, as the airplant had done two years previously, ran at full capacity for its first year. The reason that the cashflow was high in spite of the pricing deficiency was that, because of the drastic cut in price, the market had expanded to some 40% above projections, and we found that we were running the ammonium nitrate section, which had been designed for the estimated market 10 years hence, at full capacity. Because of the high cost of the ammonia plant, it was sized for only two-thirds of the ammonium nitrate, with the idea of adding a third compressor and second loop later in the decade, together with additional hydrogen capability. This actually meant that Sable required to import until this time around 30/40,000 tons per year of ammonia. Also, far from easing up, sanctions were now getting tougher.

We were entering the great oil crisis. The Shah of Iran had found it relatively easy to tell the UN to go to hell when Sable was the only buyer of ammonia. As the price sky-rocketed, Iran decided it didn't need Sable, and would comply with UN sanctions, so it started looking tough.

Because of the start-up of the ammonia plant, the Sable Board had believed that ammonia imports would stop. Our contractual quantity from Iran was now up, and the Board dithered about an extension to the contract. In the meanwhile, Neil Steyn at AECI knew that imports were needed to South Africa. He rushed off to Iran and tied up all the surplus needed, so, in short order, I found we had no ammonia, but we had a terminal. Neil had ammonia, but no terminal. To me the logic would be that AECI would never squeeze us in a nut cracker. There were other problems, though.

Some months earlier, Rhodesia had bought a cargo of fertiliser in a ship called the *Crystal Gem*. The vessel arrived in Lourenço Marques, and the shit hit the fan. It was a British flag! The Consul went on board and forbade the discharge. AECI Rhodesia was the buyer, and rushed off to SA to get them to front it up. The Brits were wise to what was going on, though, and were itching to prove that SA was fronting for Rhodesia. Neil said to me at the time that he wasn't paid to make false affidavits and documents for Rhodesians. AECI couldn't get anyone to do the necessary falsification, so the cargo actually had to be bought by South Africa, and used in South Africa, and substitute product was shipped from SA. This bloody nearly doubled the cost, and the affair was a fiasco. The result was that there was a great deal of wariness about another *Crystal Gem*. She had been at anchor and at demurrage for six weeks whilst the matter was resolved.

Neil refused to supply Rhodesia because he had given an affidavit to Iran, which the British Government had, to the effect that he would not ship to Rhodesia. Once again, ironically, our great enemy gave us the wherewithal to make a fortune. I claimed a share of every cargo for Mozambique/Swaziland at AECI's cost. The side benefit was that AECI demanded, and got, normal trade credit from Iran. So we rode on AECI's back, and, in any case, only paid 30 days after we drew ammonia from the tank.

We were feeling very restive over our situation in Rhodesia. On the one hand I had this tremendous emotional thing about Sable. It was the first thing I had created, and it was indeed wondrous. Every time I walked on the plant, I got a fantastic buzz. Everything there was there because I had lovingly fought for it and agonised over it, and little old me, with nothing, had brought it all about. It was almost an inseparable part of me. Intellectually, though, I knew that there was no future for us there. The power of the Anglo establishment was marginalising us at every turn. There was fierce jealousy (as Campbell Coppen told me) of the wealth I had created for myself. John was seen as old and established; I was only 30 and was seen as a brash young upstart, especially as my attitude was the exact reverse of Peter's. I treated everyone on their merits and not their position, and was pretty cocky.

Sid Hayes wanted control of Sable. That meant he had to get us out. The final act was about to begin.

TA – TOBACCO AUCTIONS

Tobacco Auctions was one of the two tobacco auction houses and was controlled by the Cooksey Trust. There were no sons and Miss Cooksey had married an amiable gentleman, who became the chairman of the company. Business was not his long suit, so they employed a tough barrow-boy from London in the form of Sid Hayes to run the company. Sid was out to use the fat profits and cashflow from tobacco auctioning to build a conglomerate. One of his first steps was to buy a controlling interest in Albatross Fisons, one of the fertiliser cartel members. He soon found out that they had a minority position in Sable, which was, in fact, clearly the big fish in the fertiliser pond. He wanted to get control of Sable and figured that, in Sable, he would flatten us where AECI and the Walrus had failed, and thus get control of Sable. He knew, of course, that Rhodox did not really see itself as a fertiliser manufacturer, so would not be an obstacle to his plans.

It was the Anglo-American style to use the mailed fist in a velvet glove. Through, I suppose, Anglo's long experience, they understood that the naked use of power was counter-productive. If Harry Oppenheimer expressed a wish, that wish would be carried out. It's like the old story of asking what table you give to the gorilla that walks into your restaurant. The correct answer, of course, is: "The table that he wants."

Our negotiating team with Sable was myself, Tim Jooste of Cliffe Dekker and Todd, our lawyers, and Peter Beningfield, the third partner in NPI, and in financial charge at Sable.

Sid was the antithesis of this Anglo attitude. He believed in a real rough house. Fortunately, he was instrumental in having Peter kicked out of Sable, which was a bad mistake. Peter had really ingratiated himself with the "Walrus and the Coppenter" and was their best weapon against us, but Sid made a deadly enemy of Peter. Peter was booted out of Salisbury and returned to Johannesburg, where I put him to work immediately. The first thing that we needed to do was to formulate a claim against Sable for the contract completion. As is usual in any contract, there will be claims and counter-claims. We had reduced overheads considerably in NPI as things had tailed off, but we were involved in our new terminal in Maputo as well as certain contract work at Sable. We also had some old equipment hire matters to settle.

We managed to draw up a pretty impressive list of claims. Topping these were my wine account and Ferrari repairs. Sid had got together some cash in Switzerland and, as we found later, this was his constraining factor. That was all he could pay in cash. He wanted to pay us 50c in the dollar for our shares and he wanted to keep the terminal. It was agreed that the settlement would be global and comprehensive. We wanted just one figure, so that we could place the money where we would pay no tax. Sid wanted to stick Sable with everything he could, so that he could get our shares in Sable for TA for as little as possible. To this day I would love to see the accounting treatment Sid gave the settlement compared to ours!

In the end it became a real Donnybrook. Sid stormed and threatened and carried on like a banshee. There was only one issue that for me was a make or break issue, and that was the ammonia terminal. It was clear to me (not to Sid) that the ammonia terminal was the queen on the board. It was a sword of Damocles hanging over the heads of the South African industry, which we were about to cut off with a new fertiliser project in Swaziland. I was going to get the terminal come hell or high water.

At the time, Sable owed the terminal $1,250,000 handling charges. The terminal was fully paid for I offered Sable a write-off of its ammonia-handling debt, specified as being guaranteed by us to be not less than $1,000,000, if they would give us the terminal. We also wanted payment of our construction account, and we wanted $30,000 for our 50 shares of Gas Pipelines. We used to get paid by Sable for running the terminal, by Sable supplying ammonia to us, which we sold to Quimica Geral, and so got cash for operations. This ammonia was then set off against Sable's debt to the terminal operation. The extraordinary thing was that no-one asked me why, if Sable owed $1,250,000, were we only going to warrant to write off $1,000,000. It all goes to show, when you are negotiating a comprehensive deal, you have to know your business inside out. Funnily enough, neither Jooste nor Beningfield ever saw, or questioned, the point either.

We had, after a month of bruising negotiations, resolved most of the issues. We even had a draft contract drawn, which was largely agreed on. The sticking point for me was the terminal. I was, however, adopting with Jooste a completely intransigent stance about how we were getting ripped off at 50c for our shares. On the cash settlement of the contract, he and Beningfield were laughing, because they figured they had really put one over Sid.

We had a typically difficult meeting in Jooste's office with Sid and his financial men, and David Schneider, who was Sid's lawyer for the deal. At last Sid sighed and said: "OK. One and a half million and we do the terminal your way." Jooste opened his mouth and said "No way", and was about to launch forth. I gave him a knee-breaker of a kick under the table and turned to Sid and said: "OK, let me just talk to Jooste a minute. We'll think about it."

We went out of the room and I motioned to Tim to just keep quiet. I phoned Ruben De Silva, who was the terminal manager. I instructed him to forthwith pump $250,000 worth of ammonia to Quimica Geral. I instructed him at the same time to telex Frank McWilliams, telling him that we were doing it, and asking him if he had any objections. (He telexed back that he didn't.) I then said to Jooste: "Don't blow it now. We've got Sid by the shorts. We will now get back the whole of the 50c he is doing us in for, plus plenty more." We went back into the room and Tim told Sid that his terms were acceptable. We signed up that afternoon and were paid later that week. Two weeks later, we finished off the final accounting. Sid hit the roof over the ammonia transfer. He leapt on a plane and stormed down to Johannesburg. Peter begged to be allowed to conduct the meeting. He allowed Sid to rant and to rave and then, perfectly slowly, dissected Sid's complaints.

"Had we lied to them?" "No."

"Had we misrepresented the financial condition?"

"No."

"Had we advised Sable we were pumping the ammonia?"

"Yes."

"Had Sable agreed?"

"Yes."

"Had we complied, to the letter of the agreement, with all of our obligations?"

"Yes."

"So Sid, what's your problem?"

"You should have explained the significance of the cut in Sable's debt and you should have explained to Frank McWilliams the significance of pumping over the ammonia in the context of the agreement."

"What you are really saying, Sid, is that your team didn't know what it was doing and you are now asking us to give you US$250,000 back after you took our shares off us at half price. Right?"

Sid nodded slowly and said: "Well, I guess that's about right."

Peter then said to him: "Well, what do you really expect the answer to be?"

It was, of course, rhetorical, but thereafter we at least had his respect and he thereafter came and consulted me frequently on affairs to do with the chemical industry. We now had our money, we were out of Rhodesia and could pursue our three new ventures – Pertamina, Swaziland and the new ammonia terminal.

Our lawyer, Tim Jooste, was a dyed-in-the-wool Stellenboschite. Through the negotiations with Sid, he was always having to defend my liquor account. He believed firmly that SA wines were just as good as this fancy French and German stuff I has been buying. I must convince him after the rough-house at Sid's hands that these fancy wines were better than anything we had in SA. Thus started one of the NPI traditions. We held a celebration party, at which I produced some of the wines we had argued over. At that party, no-one was allowed to drink anything but what was put in front of them. We started with Dom Perignon and Taittinger Blanc de Blancs. With the hors d'oeuvre, we served an eiswein. With the entrée we served Chateau Lafite Rothschild 1961 and Chateau Mouton Rothschild 1959; with the main course we served La Tache and Romanee Conti, 1961; and with the dessert, a trockenbeerebauslese. At the prices of today, those eight bottles would fetch at least £12,500! And Jooste came to agree that nothing like it had ever been produced in little old SA!

With the old terminal we had a problem, which was why, in the end, Sid let us have it. The agreement with Quimica Geral was for five years, at the end of which time we had three options. We could give them a half share gratis. We could sell the whole thing for $400,000. Or we could remove it. Sid saw no solution.

Removing it was not thought to be an option. To destroy the insulation, cut up the tank and re-erect it would have been virtually the same as building a new one. In any case, we had bought a large piece of land further up the river at Matola over 100 hectares in extent. So we agreed to build a new terminal on that site. We could, with the excess soil on our site, construct an embankment in the marine reserve and extend the rail line and pipeline to our own site. And then I made a most felicitous discovery. I read that a contractor in the States had made a pile of money because he had won a contract to dismantle a tank farm in Texas. A superhighway was being constructed. He then also won the contract to build another tank farm alongside the highway. He had taken a licence from the hovermove people – better known for hovercrafts – to move tanks. All you did was to strap a hoverskirt onto the tank, fit a large blower which lifted the whole tank and made it in effect a hovercraft. It could then be towed by a bulldozer to another site. All you needed was a reasonably flat piece of terrain, and hey presto you could move the tank.

I flew off to England and bought a licence and a hoverskirt. I then visited Al Hake, the contractor who had moved the Deer Park tank farm in Texas. According to him, all we needed to do was to build a 60-metre-wide embankment, prepare our new foundation, and move the tank. One D8 bulldozer would do the job. The English specified the fans, and we had a solution which was perfect. We did not share this news with anyone, as we knew that the enemy were hot in discussions with Campos (the manager of Quimica Geral) with the idea to boot us out and take over the terminal.

We then set about building the embankment to our new site. We had to move about a total of 700,000 cubic metres of earth.

Enter Dick Dyson. Dick was a pal of John's and was a civil engineer. He advised us to contact "Honest" Tom Stubbs – an earthmoving contractor. He told us Honest Tom did most of the Escom sitework as his prices were invariably lower than anyone else's. He made money on the Pizazz (the extras on the contract).

The one problem we had was a small river which ran right across the site to the sea. We had to put a 200-metre culvert across the site. Tom included it in his price. He put three machines on the job at a supposed 45,000 cubes per machine per month. He knew nothing about concrete work, however, and had contracted with us at a price he got in South Africa. Unbeknown to us, he then got a price in Mozambique which was three times that which he quoted.

No trouble to Tom. When I came down on my weekly site visit, he buttonholed me and said that our design was bad. We had a 1.5 by 1.5 metre culvert and he said it would work better as a 2 by 1 metre culvert. *There would be no difference in price.* I made sure of that and then forgot it. I wasn't going to fall for the old contractor's "change order" trick. Well, friend Tom duly completed his job and then I got the culvert bill. Three times his contract price. I was incensed and demanded we go to arbitration. Which we did. And we lost!! So I appealed.

This all took a hell of a time and then he went bust.

We put our old construction team from Sable of Terry O'Sullivan and Peter Wesselbaum onto the job and the new terminal went up apace. I had decided to build a larger terminal in two tanks to give us greater operational flexibility. We, of course, had to keep the old one going to keep Sable on the road. The South African gang were at the time in a recession and had lost a certain amount of market, so imports were not a high priority. Also, AECI had finally got the go-ahead for its new ammonia plant, a 1,000-ton-a-day unit based on coal gasification. Thirty months later it would be in production. What the hell did we need a new terminal for? Frank McWilliams said to me: "How can you possibly cover the cost of a new terminal in 12 to 18 months?" I didn't have the heart to tell Frank that actually it depended on what you charged for the ammonia.

Also, Wapie (the Executive Director of AECI in charge of explosives and fertilisers) had tried to persuade us when they came on board Sable to forget this crazy electrolysis scheme and to go coal gasification. Apart from the higher cost, my old reliable, David Leith, told me of the horrors of the AECI No 2 ammonia plant. He told me it took three full years to get it up to capacity and was forever shutting down, so that its early capacity was like 25% year one, 50% year two and 70% year three. Thereafter, it gradually crept up to around 85%.

Our rule of thumb for a plant is 340 days per year of full stream operation. On the basis we worked out, if AECI's new plant followed David Leith's pattern, our forecast for production was 85,000 tons in year one, 170,000 tons in year two, 230,000 tons in year three and maybe 340,000 tons per year thereafter. We also thought it would take longer to build than they thought. So we actually reckoned on three to four years at 150,000 tons per year, and a decreasing tonnage, but still large, thereafter.

And we had a contract with Sid for five years. The basis was simple. We would quote a price to him FOR. To induce us to bid, he had to pay us $250,000 per year (the estimated cost of running the terminal). If he accepted our bid, he got a rebate of $25 per ton on the first 10,000 tons shipped. So when AECI finally got in on the act, Sid quoted our price to them, so that effectively, when they got the contract to supply Sable, AECI paid the running costs of the terminal. And, of course, by then we would be in full production in Swaziland, so there we would be using 30,000 tons per year.

And as AECI started up its new ammonia plant, the full horrors of its cost came home to roost. We had fought a long campaign against the plant, but they pulled out all the stops. We warned the Government that the cost of ammonia was likely to more than double! Eventually, Harry Oppenheimer intervened. In the annual report of AECI, in his chairman's report he stated: "One of the projects for which Government approval is awaited is the number 4 ammonia plant. This plant will produce ammonia at a lower price than any ammonia manufactured anywhere else in the world and railed to Modderfontein." The final price of ammonia was trebled, but no-one took Harry on on this statement! That is what power is about.

Of course, the duty on ammonia was raised sharply. This created the most profitable bonanza for us. But to capitalise on this we did not want the trade to realise what they had given us. So we raised hell about the duty. It was a long-fought battle, but in the end Joep Steyn, our old enemy at Trade and Industry, was determined to put it through. And he did. We moaned and complained and even got a duty-free dispensation from him for the estimated needs of Swaziland. We had to play along with that.

But the duty set the price of ammonia at the so-called "dry mixer" price FOR Maputo. The duty was the dry mixer price less the CIF cost less an allowance for port charges and terminalling cost. Our ex-head-of-Customs consultant advised us that if our offshore company marked the ammonia up so that no duty was payable, that would not constitute a Customs fraud unless the profit was kicked back to South Africa. Well, no fear of that! So AECI fixed the price we could charge for ammonia at a level where our ammonia profit exceeded by a wide margin any profit made anywhere in the world on ammonia. In our peak year we pocketed over 9 million dollars! Not bad for a three-million dollar investment! We recovered the investment in the first year of operation. So much for Frank's comments about not getting a return on investment!

Eventually, of course, the trade after many fits and starts built their own terminal. It was done by Sentrachem. If anything, these Sentrachem guys were more arrogant than Sasol and AECI. They knew it all. We were asked to bid on it, but I knew that all they wanted to do was pick our brains. When AECI built their large tank at Modderfontein, I bid for it and was subjected to a two-day grilling by their technical team. Much valuable information was given by me gratis, and, in spite of having the lowest price, we did not, of course, get the contract. So when Sentrachem asked me to bid, I studied their documents carefully and realised they had made the same mistake we made with the first tank. We had been given no choice, as we had to take what Hamilton had in stock. Our first tank was designed as storage for a plant, not as a terminal. Its operating pressure was 20-inch water gauge – about 50mpa. Our new terminal was designed for 200mpa. That meant we could receive hotter ammonia, and, if delivered at contract temperature, the heat gain through the pipeline was insufficient to require flaring. We also installed a gas return line for excess gas evaporated so that the ship's compressors could help refrigerate it as they required gas in any case to displace the ammonia liquid.

So I declined to quote and advised that I considered their design "too dangerous". And passed my letter on to the South African Railways (SAR). They, of course, freaked. Sentrachem must consult me and rectify their design, as the SAR could not allow it to go ahead if the design was "inherently dangerous".

So I had a very abusive call from Johan van der Walt of Sentrachem. He was one of those Afrikaners who refused to speak English, so we had a bit of an impasse as my Afrikaans is strictly social and definitely not technical. Eventually, I told him that I was willing to consult with them and to set their design right for R100,000. He, of course, hit the roof. This cheeky upstart Oliver Hill was trying to tell the mighty fount of chemical knowledge how to build aliquid gas storage. For weeks he ranted and raved and eventually the SAR set up a meeting and asked me as a favour to come.

So I relented and explained to the SAR that the design called for 1,000 tons per hour discharge (very high) through a long pipeline and that with the heat gain, lack of a gas return line, and the low design pressure of the tanks, some serious ammonia blow-offs could result as the flare stack would probably not cope with the amount gasifying. That could cause the emergency vent to open. When a 50-ton bullet tank at Triomf had ruptured, over 50 people had died. Blowing off ammonia in the Richards Bay Harbour could cause serious loss of life. All through the meeting Sentrachem glowered at me. But with a neutral party in the form of the SAR engineers, they didn't try to contradict me.

Many months later, I paid a sneak visit to their site. Their tanks were being erected. The dead giveaway was the stainless steel straps holding the tank down onto the foundations! They had changed the design as I recommended. They still didn't give me anything for it. It is worth reflecting on the difference. Although AECI was just as arrogant, they had no shame in picking my brains on the design of large cryogenic storages. Sentrachem just thought they knew it all.

To this day I believe that the reason Philip Clarke left his job as MD of Triomf Fertilisers and joined me was that he knew an ammonia crunch was on the way. As we still had a monopoly, he knew that we stood to make a fortune. Also, he knew that bringing DAP (Di-ammonium Phosphate) into the South African market was the technical death knell of the fertiliser industry, because Philip knew not only the industry and all its players backwards, he knew all their vulnerabilities. As I mentioned earlier, our peak year for profits was an amount of $9,000,000. Philip really knew how to screw his buddies. He took a particular delight in giving it to Fedmis.

Of course, their new terminal eventually came into being. The Trade rubbed their hands with glee as they figured they now had us beat. But the terminal they built did nothing to exploit the natural advantages of Richards Bay. They had a water depth of 18 metres. If we were lucky in Maputo, we could get 10 metres of water in the channel coming in. We had more water at the wharf, up to 12 metres. That left us with a 20,000 tonner as the largest practical ship we could get in. You could get the largest gas carriers afloat fully laden into Richards Bay. We could only get the big ones in with a light load. But never fully laden. As we used to supply Mauritius and Tanzania, who had a good water depth, we sometimes got a 35,000 tonner and dropped off enough to enable the vessel to enter Maputo. A 35,000 tonner with only 20,000 tons on board actually drew less water than a 20,000 tonner fully laden. But the scheduling problems made this all too infrequent.

What Sentrachem learnt the hard way was that it was pretty difficult to secure just the ship you wanted when you wanted it. If your ship arrived too early, and your tank stock was too high, you sat with a fat demurrage bill. If you arrived too late, your customers were without ammonia. Scheduling was tough. So with the miserable 26,000 tons of storage they had built, they were reduced to ordering 15 to 18,000 ton lots: what are called "handy size" vessels. The problem with handy size vessels is that these were most in demand. The daily rate for a handy size was the same or more than that for a 35,000 tonner. Of course, your fuel consumption was a little bigger for the 35,000 tonner. But, if you could use a 35,000 tonner instead of a 20,000 tonner, your lump-sum freight was essentially the same. So your cost per tonne was spectacularly lower than that for a "handy size" vessel.

We had exploited this for years by using Mauritius and Tanzania, so, when our boytjies in Sentrachem went out to tender, we were ready.

We had a secret joint venture with Geogas Enterprises. Geogas had been formed by Rene Boudet when Gazocean was rescued by a conglomerate and he was retired. He took with him Phillipe Angostures, who had started life with with Shahpur Chemicals and Gazocean. Phillipe ran the business. The reason we kept the JV secret was that if the Ring thought we would benefit in any way in their ammonia supply, they would not have given Geogas the business. They made our old friend Piet Greyling (a former South African rugby captain) their agent. But he had absolutely no knowledge of our secret deal with Geogas.

Any tender call by Sentrachem, which gave a window of arrival dates, was, of course, studied by Phillipe. On his Master Board, he had the whole gas tanker fleet. Each one had chalked up its current voyage, and any continuation voyages marked. So it was possible to work out which vessels could meet the requirement and where she would have to load. The FOB price in every locality was known, so an hour or two of work threw up the possible tenders, the FOB price, and the charter rate. Thus, a CIF price could be worked out for all the candidates for the Sentrachem tender.

We would choose the lowest possibility, knock a dollar off it, and that was Geogas's bid. We would then check on Mauritius and Tanzania, and calculate how much we could take on board in Maputo. Mostly, it simply landed up that we took our Russian ammonia, as mostly our contact price was better than anything else you could get anywhere else, and, because of the large Russian exports from Yuzny, often to nearby destinations, there were always scads of big gas tankers in or about the Black Sea. Quite a few obviously were under time charter to Geogas. We never made less than 20 to 30 dollars a ton out of Sentrachem. And they sat back fondly thinking that they had finally screwed that cheeky bastard, Oliver Hill.

TOYS R US

Piper Cheynne

All businesses are addicted to toys. These toys range from the executive desk-top toys to Boeing 747s. Most toys have the most elaborate business justifications prepared in order to show that there is no way that these are the ultimate playthings, and the ultimate in status symbols. One observes in most hierarchical structures the way in which toys are used to display and to regulate status in companies. The number on the back of the Mercedes Benz is quickly observed by all the fellow businessmen, and this number conveys a number of messages to the observer. First, if in a large company, the number clearly places the person's position in the hierarchy. In many cases, there is a more subtle message if the number is slightly out of order for his formal position, because it indicates his position in the informal hierarchy. Consequently, a silent war is waged inside companies to get a number as high as possible to telegraph to the world one's position as perhaps being higher than it really is.

Secondly, the ability to give to the personnel high-status cars indicates that the company is prosperous. This message has to be carefully thought out if one is selling to people, because if the toy is seen to be above the station assumed for the rank of the person, it can create the impression that the customer is paying over the odds for whatever you are selling.

Thirdly, the giving of status symbols is a highly telegraphed signal to other people outside the company that high rewards are available to performers in that company.

This is just about cars. However, it is certain that the silent war which is waged about company cars is one of the most significant in the business world of South Africa. The amusing thing about this competition is that most participants are blissfully unaware that some observers of the scene understand exactly what is going on and derive a good deal of fun from watching the antics which go on.

It is necessary to make this digression because, like all businesses, we have had our fair share of toys. Sometimes these toys are unashamedly ego trips for us, sometimes vitally necessary for our business workings, and sometimes necessary for sending messages to our enemies and friends as to our state of health.

I always wanted, like all small boys, to be an engine driver. One quickly found out that there were more remunerative occupations, but most of us like to play with big toys. These toys range from aeroplanes, cars, boats and four-wheel-drive vehicles, to guns, cameras, binoculars, etc. Once, when I was visiting Nicaragua, where we were discussing a project with the Government, General Somoza, the President, lent us his yacht for the weekend. He had a little sign in the yacht which read: "The only difference between men and boys is the size of their toys."

I confess to also like the toys to which most men have an addiction. We have all derived a great deal of fun from the toys we have been fortunate to own and to play with. Most businesses will not admit to the reason as to why a particular toy was bought for the business. I say that most are bought for an ego trip and because they are a hell of a lot of fun. And some do even have a serious purpose.

The first toy we bought as a business was an aeroplane. We had to build a plant in the middle of Rhodesia, equidistant from the airports at Salisbury and Bulawayo. To spend a day at the plant site took a full three days out of one's schedule. We signed for Sable with the Government of Rhodesia in mid-December 1967. We were committed to produce ammonium nitrate within 18 months. Anyone familiar with petrochemical plants will tell you that to start with a grass-roots plant on a greenfield site, with equipment which usually runs out to 24 months on delivery such as big compressors, heavy wall stainless towers and all that paraphernalia, with a contract time of 18 months to full production, is not possible. Well, we did it, but we needed some favours.

One of the favours which I arranged immediately with the Government was the running of a weekly air service directly from Johannesburg to Que Que. By this means we were able to take off early in the morning, arrive at the site before breakfast, spend all day on the site, and return home that evening.

To do this we acquired our first aeroplane.

Hamilton had been a bomber pilot during the war, and had a pal in the aviation business – one Bill Lear. Herb had just acquired the first Lear jet off the line, and he wanted to get rid of his first effort of Lear's. This was an aircraft called a Learstar. In reality, it was a Lockheed Lodestar which was hotted up by Lear, with huge engines and various streamlining, as well as a sexy executive interior. We agreed to buy this monster from Cordell Hull, who did not know what the hell to do with it. We bought it more because our partner wanted to sell it than we to buy it. It only cost $25,000 anyway. I figured that if Cordell could fly it from Spain, where it was, to South Africa, it would be OK. Apart from the mishap of a fuel leak inside the cockpit, which flooded the airplane off Casablanca, it duly arrived with its crew in Johannesburg, and we set about crewing and setting up our airline. The chief pilot of Hamilton's was one Hap Wilson (about as masterful a bullshitter as I have ever encountered). He brought with him one Alfredo Wach-Kainsinger as his co-pilot.

As our knowledge of aeroplanes and their operations was zero, Hap was charged with setting up our aviation operations. We hired one George Parsons as our chief pilot and agreed to keep on Alfredo as the co-pilot. Unfortunately, we got an urgent fax from the civil aviation authorities grounding George with immediate effect. His big pal was one Dirk Nel, a pilot with a huge wartime reputation, who jumped into the breach.

The aeroplane was extolled by Hap as being the hottest thing around. This was in the comparatively early days of business aviation and pressurisation was virtually unknown in business aircraft, except, of course, jets. Lear had, however, put two huge 1350hp Wright Cyclone engines on this Lodestar, and it was basically faster than the Viscounts which were the regional aircraft mostly in use to Rhodesia. It had, according to Hap, when operated with the weight authorised of 22,500 pounds, easily fulfilled the IFR requirements to go to Que Que and back without refuelling – a most important consideration, as a refuelling stop at Bulawayo added considerably to our time and was not on. So Hap duly buggered off and we operated the aircraft.

My first rude awakening was on a flight to Que Que when we all felt a big bump, and the port engine started to vibrate badly. I went up to the pilot's cabin and found that the temperature had gone down to zero on the port engine. I spoke to our aircraft engineer, Ray Bleksley, who we had taken on to look after the aircraft, and he decided to shut it down. We then diverted to Bulawayo. Back in the cabin we had an airspeed indicator and altimeter, and I noticed that our speed had dropped to 180 knots and our altitude was going down. The Matopos were ahead, and they looked decidedly menacing from 6,000 feet. I went back up to the cabin to ask why we were going down. The response growled from Dirk Nel was classic: "Because we can't keep the bloody thing up." Dirk already had to try to restart the rough engine and to gain altitude, otherwise, he said, he was going to put the thing down on a small 500-metre strip he had located this side of the Matopos. He managed to restart the engine and went up to 12,000 feet faster than that aircraft had ever done in its life before.

On landing, an extensive post-mortem commenced. We repaired the engine and then I had trials conducted in Johannesburg. We found that the plane could only maintain altitude on one engine at a weight of 19,600 pounds. This meant that we could not fly to Que Que and back without refuelling unless we were willing to risk losing an engine, with all that entailed. We were forced to look elsewhere for a plane. We found a good old DC-3 owned by Protea Airways, which we bought for the magnificent sum of R30,000. She was a marvellous bird which gave us sterling service of over 2,000 hours without a single glitch.

That plane was too large an aircraft to operate for the flights to Lourenço Marques, which were typically just a few people, so we bought a Beech Baron to do this service. The advantage of this was that it was also the perfect weekend plane, as it used very little fuel – comparable to a car. After some experience of my partner taking the DC-3 off for a weekend at company expense, it was important to have a plane that at least had a sane operating cost relative to the number of people carried. Whilst the DC-3 always flew to Rhodesia with at least 12 to 20 people and at least a ton of freight, weekends did not carry the same amount of people and freight. The Baron was, however, a very important tool, as we often had to fly on late-night missions off to Rhodesia or Lourenço Marques, as we were forever having sanctions crises and, when we had the big dust-up with our American partners, it was often necessary to rush off at short notice for a meeting in Salisbury, and watch our American partners having to wait for the commercial flight. In this way, we were able to forestall most of their moves by our travel flexibility.

We soon became addicted to our aeroplanes and they were a lot of fun. When Rhodesia was finished, we had a big financial squeeze, and we finally sold the Dak. Later, we traded the Baron in on the latest and hottest thing around – a pressurised Navajo. Here we learnt a second bitter lesson. Never buy the low serial numbers! This plane became known as the "hangar lover". Even when it worked we had some bad experiences in it. Once, coming back from LM, there was the most almighty bang, and the aircraft began vibrating like crazy. Attila, the pilot, feathered the engine, and we saw the tip of one propeller blade was missing. From the bang we had heard, it had clearly hit the aircraft. As it wasn't in the cabin, it was clear it had hit low down, and I feared that it had severed the hydraulic lines to the nose wheel. Once again, we had a plane that seemed to have all the flying characteristics of a rock, on one engine, and, with a vast storm having closed Smuts, we were diverted to Wonderboom. Attila followed that superhighway all the way so as to at least have something to put down on, as we were losing height steadily all the time. Finally, we were able to hold altitude at about 6,000 feet – not a hell of a margin – but enough. After we landed and my secretary, Sue Rowe, burst into tears and embraced Attila, we found the tip of the propeller embedded only a quarter inch from the hydraulic lines.

Well, we got rid of that and bought a Cheyenne, which was little more than the same aeroplane with turboprop engines. It went like a bat out of hell and was a lot of fun, but it was never the same after Basil Brand used it for a demo at the Lanseria air show and we had a premature hot section inspection. We traded it for what remains my favourite aeroplane – a Super King Air 200. We got ourselves a really excellent pilot in the shape of Paul Newcombe. On that plane, and our subsequent one, Paul did over 3,000 hours of flying for us. I also acquired, for personal use, a Duke, which Paul flew as well. As we were not involved so much in far-off places, only Swaziland, and as the Duke was more suitable for that run, as we only usually sent at most four people down, the King Air became used less and less by us, so we put it out to charter.

Our last King Air was a real pussy wagon. I had done a demo with British Aerospace to their factory in Chester looking at jets, and saw a colour scheme which I thought had possibilities. I revamped it, and when we ordered a new King Air, I gave them the colour scheme. Graham Conlyn of NAC looked sideways at it, and thought it was horrible, but the customer gets what he wants. We got it, and Gavin Fernie and Paul Newcombe went to Wichita to collect it. When they arrived they found they were in the middle of a huge party. Our plane was actually serial number 999, and they had a huge party planned for number 1,000. However, when they looked at 999, it stunned everyone. They decided that, as there had been a serial 000 being the prototype, our plane was the 1,000th Super King Air, and the party would be around that one. So Gavin and Paul had one hell of a three days in Wichita, and that plane was universally acknowledged as the most beautiful King Air flying! At least when we landed at Plett, it flattened all the other boys!

What was to be our swan-song was a proposal from my brother-in-law. There were two pre-production Concordes which had been used as test beds and which we could buy for two million pounds each. I had the idea to buy one, and to outfit it as a bizjet. We would sell it into South Africa at the Concorde price, which was £27 million. We would get permission to set up a company with financial rands which would then have cost us about £18,000,000, so that we would have had £9,000,000 towards the cost of the plane. With that size war chest we could easily have outfitted the plane to bizjet standards and had plenty left over for fuel! The ultimate in biz one-upmanship!! But John had neither the imagination, sense of humour, nor the understanding of how the deal worked to go ahead with it. We never got our Concorde.

The other toys people are obsessed with are cars. Cars are wonderful toys at a certain stage of one's life. I have had a succession of cars, including two Mercedes sports, three Ferraris, and a Rolls. The message which we wanted to send out to everyone who was hell bent on trying to destroy us commercially was that we had plenty of money. Actually, apart from the Mercedes sports I gave Dominique, all the other cars were bought secondhand, at prices far below what the enemy were spending on their big number Mercedes, but the kudos we got was far more. We enjoyed the effect because those bozos didn't even realise how cheaply we were buying that image. Also, every single car was sold for far more than it cost. I know the rand has dropped a lot, but, for example, the Lusso Ferrari which I bought for R8,000 in 1970 was sold in 1990 for £105,000! But selling it was, in fact, a big mistake, as the last one sold went on auction for three-quarters of a million pounds! Even after inflation, that was some deal! At the time, John bought a 280SE Mercedes for something like R9,000. Not only did we get the effect we wanted at a far less cost than the *de rigeur* car, but I bought the car at its depreciated value of about R1,000 from the company, as did John. I did rather better on resale!

An interesting sidelight was the comment from Anton Rupert. We were talking about our cars over lunch in Stellenbosch, and after admitting to having a secondhand Ferrari, he admitted to a Mercedes sports, adding hastily, "secondhand, of course!" The people who make the money tend not to waste it! I noticed on a programme about Warren Buffet that he had a nice SUV – bought hail-damaged, of course!

Apart from the serious message, of course, these toys are one hell of a lot of fun and very good for the morale of the guys in the company. They feel they are on top when they see this being done, as it differentiates you from the dour bureaucratic ways of the opposition. They may be bigger and richer in reality, but we were smarter and had a hell of a lot more fun. The morale of everyone is, in the end, the one weapon which is priceless.

Neil Steyn always had a birthday party every year. At that birthday party all the big honchos of the chemical industry used to attend. Francis le Riche of Sentrachem always gave the speech. Neil always implored me to arrive first and to plonk the Ferrari or the Rolls in front of his front door, so as to be highly visible. He told me Francis always ribbed him about the size of the number on the back of his Mercedes. "Can't you guys afford a higher number?" He always rubbed Francis's nose in it, especially with the Ferrari. It made our guys feel good.

I think that toys have their place in the business world. The only time they do not is when you start to believe that those trappings make you somebody special. That, unfortunately, is what mostly they are used for, and that was a tendency we had to root out vigorously, because once you start to believe your own propaganda, you are doomed.

When we were forced to leave South Africa, it was pretty clear that getting a new passport out of the SA Government would be nearly impossible. So, as a last resort, we considered becoming international refugees and so decided to buy a boat. After much searching, we found one belonging to Ben le Bow, the owner of Ligget and Myers Tobacco and Western Union. We took out a mortgage on our London flat to buy it.

The motor yacht was a great classic, named *Candida*. We were advised that we should put the vessel on the charter market, which we duly did. We had a successful operation, as we were able to get about 60/80 days a year of charter. We had some rather famous charter guests, such as Barbra Streisand and Donna Karan, Paul McCartney, Ivana Trump and others.

Candida yacht

Renamed *Uthingo*, the yacht, completely refurbished, is now moving to Tanzania, where we will be offering cruises around the islands, both on a full-charter basis and also offering single cabins for a weekly cruise around Zanzibar, Mafia, Pemba and the Quirimbas.

In the long term, we will probably retire on it and spend a good deal of time in Europe.

PERTAMINA

During the time of extreme difficulties in getting ammonia supplies for our plant in Rhodesia, I was a frequent visitor to Iran. I spent a good deal of time with Macdonald, the manager. It was apparent that it was very difficult to get the ammonia plant at Bandar Shahpur to perform properly. The conditions in the Persian Gulf at certain times of the year are appalling. The temperature was 125 degrees F, with 100% humidity. It was impossible to be outside air-conditioning for more than half an hour at a time. According to the site manager, the productivity of a man was only 25% of what he expected in the US Gulf.

Mac told me that the ammonia plant at Shahpur cost $35,000,000, whereas an identical plant in the US Gulf cost $18,000,000. I asked him to elaborate upon this astonishing figure, and he said: "Well, for starters, we had to spend $6,000,000 on creating a site to build on." I said to Mac, half in jest, that Per Bye, our mutual Norwegian shipping friend, would sell us a ship for only $3,000,000 – half the price – so why didn't he build the plant on a ship, and then sail the ship to Shahpur and use it as the foundation. He could then have it built in a "civilised" part of the world and sail it to the Persian Gulf. Mac, somewhat to my surprise, did not reject the idea out of hand, but commented that if anyone would be receptive, it would be Baghir Mostofi, the boss of the National Petrochemical Company, who was the other half of Shahpur, and the Chairman of the company. Mac suggested that some work would have to be done, and also warned that there was not an ammonia plant on the cards for a while yet for Shahpur. Mostofi took me out one evening to one of the local night clubs, and I took the opportunity of discussing the idea with him. Mostofi was intrigued by the idea, and encouraged me to investigate the possibility.

On my return to South Africa, I mentioned to John Hahn what I had suggested to Macdonald, and said that he had not thrown me out, but had suggested that the idea had some merit. I also said that it would need an awful lot of selling. John, as is usual when an idea takes hold, became obsessed with it. He started telling me about the Persian Gulf during the war, and how all the bad boys were sent there, as it had an awful reputation for conditions. As I explained the theoretical concepts as to why it should actually be cheaper, notwithstanding the cost of a ship, he became positively lyrical.

Although at the time we were in the throes of a long and difficult negotiation to extricate ourselves from Rhodesia, John took off to Germany to go and sell the idea to Lurgi and Grande Paroisse. This was a great relief to our team of Tim Jooste, Peter Beningfield and myself, as, during negotiations, John normally busied himself with writing telexes, would suddenly hear us discussing something, and interject without understanding what the point was all about. It was a great relief to give John a new toy to play with whilst we set about the serious business of getting out of Rhodesia.

John came back with a typical layout drawing of a 1,000 ton/day ammonia plant, and an outline drawing of a 30,000 ton bulk carrier from Per Bye. I sat down with Mike McGuigan, our chief engineer, and we decided to try to fit the basic plant into the ship, to see whether, in theory, there was enough space. After some re-arrangement of equipment, and re-routing of piping, it appeared as if we could fit all the components into the ship, and our drawing office produced a schematic drawing of the idea. Thus armed, we went to Lurgi, to show them the results of our endeavours. Lurgi were reasonably cool, but our friend there, Erik

Menges, suggested that we should go and see a Mr Whitehouse-Vaux in London, as our idea might find some interest there.

We duly went to visit Mr Whitehouse in London. He had a lovely office looking out on HMS *Belfast*. We told him that we had a concept for the building of plants in remote and difficult areas in a far shorter time and at far lower cost than usually applied in these cases. Mr Whitehouse was undoubtedly one of the most enigmatic and exciting characters in the world

Whitehouse and Ibnu inspect engineering model

of oil. He had been through the mill as a navy diver and worked for British Intelligence. He had spent 10 years with the Shah of Iran, and his current assignment was as a special assistant to the President of Pertamina, the State Oil company of Indonesia. His main task was to build up and run the shipping fleet, which at the time was 3,000,000 deadweight tons.

Mr Whitehouse also had various projects under his wing to do with petrochemicals. Pertamina was an amazing growth success story. Under the dynamo, General Ibnu Sutowo, it had expanded from a production of less than 100,000 barrels a day to 1,500,000 barrels a day and had refineries, ships, petrochemical plants, an airline and a host of other interests. It was expanding at breakneck speed, and had various special assistants, reporting directly to the general, each in charge of literally hundreds of millions in projects. As it was inconceivable that anyone in Indonesia could be in a senior position without high military rank, Mr Whitehouse was always respectfully referred to as "Admiral Whitehouse".

We ran into difficulties almost immediately. Mr Whitehouse wanted to know what we were offering. We didn't want to tell him, as we thought he might just take the idea, say "thank you very much", and walk away. Mr Whitehouse told us we would have to convince his consulting engineers of the merit of our project. We didn't want to tell them either, so in the end we got Sir Frederick Warner, of Rhodesia connections, to talk to Peter Wilson of Manderstam and Partners, Mr Whitehouse's consulting engineers.

After all this fencing, we cut the talk and showed Mr Whitehouse the drawing we had put together. He loved it! Although we did not know it at the time, it fitted a political slot perfectly. First, everything that floated fell under his wing. That gave the project to him. Secondly, there was no love lost between Pertamina and the Ministry of Industry, and this project, done successfully, would really put their collective noses out of joint. This disaccord was due to the fact that there had been inordinate delays in getting projects built, due to a vast bureaucratic delay, and the sheer difficulty of doing things in remote areas. This project, therefore, fitted into a nice political and economic slot. Also, the huge price rises of the first great oil crisis were just starting, and Indonesia was a net importer of fertiliser.

Mr Whitehouse dragged John off to Paris to meet the General, while I returned home to carry on the negotiations for the sale of our Rhodesian interests. In Paris, General Ibnu looked at the drawing, said, "I'll have one of those, thank you very much", and took off. He told us that we were to sign the contract in New York on 4th November, as the stars were in their most propitious positions on that day. With some misgivings, I let John start putting together a technical package and a set of contract documents. I warned him about several pitfalls, but was politely told not to try to teach him to suck eggs. He started working on the details for the project in August.

In September, we finally reached agreement to sell out of Rhodesia. Our friend, Nic van der Westhuizen, at the Reserve Bank, allowed us to keep a substantial sum of that money abroad to pursue the Pertamina project. I came over to Frankfurt and Paris, where the negotiations were going on, just in time to avert a total disaster. John had told the general that the entire project was going to cost $50,000,000. I had specifically told John that we had agreed with Lurgi that the battery limit ammonia plant would probably cost $50,000,000. This did not include the urea plant or any of the offsite facilities. More importantly, it also didn't include a profit for us! It was an urgent necessity to get a realistic price put together. The contract drawn up was a disaster. John had promised delivery in Indonesia in 24 months. The main compressor was on 22-month delivery ex-works Europe. This meant that, even if it were ordered on day one, we would be at least 6 months late. Also, the canny Mr Whitehouse had insisted on a clause that "time was of the essence of the contract". This made the whole proceeding a farce.

To cap it all, John had breezily agreed that we would give them an option to get a 1,500 ton a day plant for only $10,000,000 more. This was what Pertamina now wanted. The only problem was that no-one had yet built a 1,500 ton a day plant, and whilst it was not seen as a great problem, the fact was that there was no experience with a monster like that. To agree to that as well, which meant that everything would have to be designed from scratch, made it totally impossible to even consider less than a 36-month contract period.

The result of John's negotiations was that we had a contract to build a plant in 24 months for 60 million which would take at least 36 months and would cost (by our estimate at the time) at least 175,000,000 dollars to build. Not a particularly promising contract!!

At this point John decided that he had loftier matters to deal with and left me, together with our partners Lurgi, Grande Paroisse and Coppee Rust (the contractor for the urea plant), to sort it out. We had endless meetings, slowly forcing the price up and modifying the specifications, so that price increases could be presented as a change of scope, rather than the mess-up it was.

At the same time we had to arrange full financing for the project. Our old buddy, Cordell Hull had left Hamilton and was now heading up project finance for American Express. This unique bank sat with loads and loads of interest-free money from all those lovely travellers' cheques, and wanted to get into international banking. Cordell, having been a contractor, knew that the ability to offer project finance to a contractor meant that much more profitable contracts could be got, and that grateful contractors could easily pay a nice fee on top of the customer's normal project finance fees, and never miss it. So, by financing contractors, and getting the usual fees, and some rather more unusual fees, project finance could be made into a very lucrative business. Cordell got Morgan Guaranty and Bank of America to join him as lead banks, to put together a syndication of 190,000,000 dollars for the project. Each lead bank put up 10 million, but then immediately were to split the total fees, all paid up front, of around 6 million. (As they said when the funds were disbursed and paid to them: "Not bad pay for a morning's work!")

Cordell had one major problem. We had a little company, with 10,000 dollars net worth. He kept telling John that he could not provide finance from all the major world banks in that magnitude, without someone of substance to take full contract responsibility. John kept pointing to Lurgi, Coppee Rust, *et al.*, but, of course, none of them was in the least bit interested in assuming financial responsibility for a contract which would, at the outset, be guaranteed to lose them at least 50 million. When we went to New York, we had still not resolved the problem.

On 2nd November 1973 we had a final price: 175 million.

We had a schedule: 36 months. We had a customer who would pay 150 million. He wanted 24 months. We had 190,000,000 million promised. We had to have a large, rich partner who would give the necessary financial guarantees. I told John we couldn't do it without something giving. In the end I got a private guarantee from Bill Whitehouse that we would change the contract to a cost-plus contract after the event. He was a man of his word.

The whole gang of us trooped off to New York. Ibnu was throwing a party at the New York Hilton for 2,000 guests, and the signing was set for just before the party. We all traipsed up to the General's suite in the Waldorf Astoria for the signing. At the door Bill Whitehouse said to me: "Just wait here for a few minutes. He thinks he is signing a contract for 50 million. I just have to tell him there a few changes and it is now 150 million!"

The General was quite composed as we trooped in. He said "Inshallah" and signed. Bill brought out the champagne, and crowds of people congratulated the General for another world first – the world's first floating fertiliser plant. There was general euphoria all round. In the taxi on the way to the party, however, Cordell tossed a bucket of cold water onto the mood. We still had no responsible contractor.

At the party I sat next to George Fabry, the financial director of Coppee Rust. George was a typically crafty European, and he applied a great deal of insight to the problem. Everyone wanted the deal. But it was clear that there was one insurmountable problem. As long as there was a fixed-price contract in place which was a money loser on paper, no-one would take it on. Whilst the customer had bowed to the inevitable, it was not in writing, and a decent interval would have to elapse before it could be renegotiated. George proposed to Cordell that the real problem was, in fact, not the money, as Pertamina was in reality the Government of Indonesia, plus oil. Better, in fact. The problem was that little old IPI was a few capable people, yes, but no track record of building a mega petrochemical plant. He suggested that if the banks could be satisfied that a responsible person would guarantee to see the project through, with Pertamina's money, the banks should be happy. He would form a company, Coppee Rust International, which would issue a completion guarantee, and Coppee Rust would guarantee the availability of people to do so.

In the end, greed won. George's formula was accepted, for which his company received a nice little fee of $750,000, and we had a project.

Now the problems started. We had to put together the syndicated loan. The problem was that Indonesia had been prevented by the IMF from borrowing for more than one year and less than 15 years. The type of syndicated credit Cordell was selling was typically a 7-year deal. Banks simply didn't lend for 15 years, which is precisely why the IMF had happily allowed Indonesia to borrow money for over 15 years. They had, however, reckoned without the crafty Cordell. He drew a loan, of which 94% fell within the normal period, leaving only 6% to be stretched out, with the final payment in year 15. This was a rather unusual loan, but it was saleable. The result was that every bank in the deal insisted on its own lawyers being in on the discussions, and on separate opinions about the status of Pertamina and the IMF rules, as well as just about everything that could go wrong. Every major law firm in London got in on the act and we had about 15 prima donnas performing and earning their money. In the end, though, in March 1974, we had our loan agreement, and we had a cheque for the $60,000,000 down payment.

There were many moments of high drama during the negotiations. There was considerable doubt among many engineers as to whether a plant could go into a ship. It all went to show how narrow people's minds were. One engineer from Creusot Loire (our compressor supplier) was shrieking that you could not put a boiler into a ship, as the insulation would fall apart due to the movement of the ship. Someone finally pointed out that most ships for the past 50 years were steamships and were driven by steam boilers! Cordell, himself an engineer from MIT, in a meeting with John and myself, was worried about compressor foundations. He said that you needed thousands of tons of concrete to hold in place a 30-megawatt compressor.

John pulled out one of the aces in the hole: "If I can show a 30-megawatt compressor without an ounce of concrete to support it, will you finance the project?"

Cordell replied: "Absolutely."

John then proudly said: "How much concrete have you seen under the engine of a Boeing 747?"

With the point that ships were propelled by, in effect, nuclear power stations, and large compressors were hung under the wings of aircraft, gradually all the doubters became convinced that it wasn't such a terrible idea after all. Fortunately, as a mechanical and chemical engineer, Cordell played a major role in convincing the bankers that they were not financing a mad boondoggle.

With 60 million in hand, John went mad. He rushed off to Norway and got Per Bye out looking for ships. We also looked for shipyards. At the time we were laughed out of court. The world was enjoying the greatest shipbuilding boom in history. Nobody even wanted to know our troubles for the next five years, which represented the length of their order books. A nasty complicated project occupying their yards for up to three years was the last thing they had in mind. We were therefore left with buying and fitting the plant into what we bought. At this point, Lurgi, who had now got some money and were starting some serious engineering work, begged John not to buy a 30,000 tonner. They thought it might just do for the urea plant, but were worried about the ammonia plant. Nothing daunted, our John insisted that he had to show Bill Whitehouse that he was on track, and insisted on immediately buying two ships. One was a steam bulk carrier, the *Resolute*, and the other was a motor bulker, the *Marudio*. The *Resolute* was renamed the *Dominique* and was registered in Liberia. Then we started looking at the *Marudio*. After a month of frantic work, Lurgi came to me and showed me a drawing of a 70,000 ton bulk carrier. They could fit the ammonia complex into that. The 30,000 ton *Marudio* was just too small. So we had the first of many crises. John exchanged bitter words with Lurgi, who told him they had begged him not to buy until at least a formal engineering layout had been done, and he was waving Mike McGuigan's drawing at them and saying they had already done it.

This was all pretty sterile, so I took off to Norway to see Per Bye, who, as our broker, now had a ship to sell chop chop, and another one to buy chop chop. He told me that the market was now softening for what we had bought, but was still firm in what we wanted to buy. I actually couldn't see why this should be, but if the market was softening I sure as hell didn't want to be stuck with the *Marudio*, which had cost us the princely sum of 5.25million! (The *Dominique* cost us 3.5 million). So we put her back on the market. After we had paid Per his commission, we were a mere half a million down the drain. I was determined not to get caught again, and as John was now in a somewhat chastened mood, I started negotiating for a 70,000 tonner. It soon became apparent that the sellers of ships were all Greeks. In the face of what was reported as an unprecedented shipping boom, and having dropped half a million on our only experience to date, it seemed to me that, if smart people were trying to get out, and we had had to drop money on our ship, we should not rush things. Now Lurgi were yelling their heads off about being unable to get on with engineering until they had a ship. John was trying to jumboise the *Marudio*, but, as she was very narrow, the jumbo section would have had to be much wider than the ship, so Lloyds were saying that we would have to go on a "battleship" design to stop her from turning turtle with the 300-foot-high towers we had in the plant.

This confused the whole scene, which was actually in a state of shambles, and we now had the Pertamina team assembled in London, asking appropriate and (for us) embarrassing questions.

Finally, we found a ship, and for three weeks we haggled. Then I flew to Port Elizabeth, where *Aristeides* was loading manganese ore for England. They were asking $12,500,000. I had to break the bad news to Bill Whitehouse that we were going 7.25 million over budget. This was the first of the many changes on the way to a cost-plus contract. It would be a hell of a problem to get him to pick up the tab on the *Marudio*, as Lurgi had placed the blame for that cock-up squarely on John's head. I therefore told Per Bye to appear to be backing down on the *Aristeides* (the ship in PE), as I felt, in spite of the urging, that the market was falling. In the end, by waiting another three weeks, Per got the Greeks to kick back, to our Liberian company which owned the *Marudio*, 800,000 dollars. This more than compensated for the cock-up on the *Marudio*, and left us with a slush fund which was bound to be needed. (It was.)

Now we had our ships, and the contract was under way. I sent our financial manager, Peter Beningfield, who was also a partner in NPI, to London on a permanent basis, as we did not want any more *Marudio*-style adventures. Peter was just what was needed to keep some sanity around, as he had a total lack of imagination, and never got carried away on the wild flights of fancy that John was fond of indulging in. As we now only had about 30 million left in the bank, it was necessary to bring some control into affairs, as John had a tendency to think that the money could just all be spent, willy-nilly.

We had to hire a whole new staff to administer the project, as we were, after all, the prime contractor for the project. Our staff left over from Rhodesia were quite inadequate for the project. We went out into the market to hire people, but, as is always the case, the bulk of people who reported for the project were the dropouts from the major contracting companies.

The result was that, under tremendous pressure from the Pertamina team, we had to bring in a team ready-made. Our old friends from Rhodesia, Roberts, were only too happy to help out. They had helped greatly with our offshore structures, and, with their great difficulty in getting money out of South Africa to spread their international wings, this contract was a godsend. They were able to get paid 100% in foreign exchange to their offshore company, whilst spending quite a lot of rands. Millions of dollars flowed into their coffers, as they moved an administrative and engineering team of over 100 people to England and Germany. The problems of putting a major petrochemical plant into a ship had never been tackled. In the end we spent 20 million of Pertamina's money solving the problems, and, I have to say, finding out that a ship was not the way to go, but that a purpose-built barge would have fitted the bill better!

All this expertise was finally put to good use when the Mossgas project in South Africa came into being. The old Pertamina team brought experience, gained at enormous expense to the project, and it is safe to say that many millions were unquestionably saved as a direct result of that experience.

The problems associated with the project were colossal. The size of the power station for the plant kept on being increased. When asked the reason why, it was first the huge cooling water requirements. We had to use seawater at a design temperature of 80 degrees F. To get to an acceptable temperature on the closed circuit for the plant, the heat exchangers became too massive and expensive, so we had to make them smaller, which put up the pressure and therefore the power requirements, which increased the need for more cooling water, and so on. Then it was necessary to air-condition the plant, and, as the power load and the confinement increased, so did the power for air-conditioning. This increased the need for more water, so we were running a vicious circle.

Then Roberts asked to be allowed to place a million-dollar order on a well-known firm of structural engineers, W. S. Atkins. When I asked how many tons of steel it was for, the design price worked out at more than we were accustomed to paying for structural steel, designed, fabricated and erected! They then explained that each piece of steel needed 80 pages of calculations because of the three-dimensional stresses and loads, and that we would have to get a computer program written to do it, as it was beyond the capacity of even a firm like W. S. Atkins to do in the time allotted.

Then Lloyds found that the ship was inherently unstable. We had to ballast it with 5,000 tons of concrete, which gave Cordell his compressor foundation, but even that wasn't enough. The carbon dioxide removal towers were 25 feet in diameter and three hundred feet high. We had to cut them in half in the end, to restore stability to the ship.

The noise was another problem. The plant had four very large centrifugal compressors, which made a tremendous noise, which in the enclosed steel hull would have generated a totally unacceptable level of noise for the operators. The noise damping cost a fortune.

Because the ship had to be insured on its voyage to Indonesia, we had to comply with the special requirements of Lloyds Register of Shipping. No single insurance of 150 million had at that time ever been placed in the London market. Lloyds Register therefore laid down design parameters which required that we could prove that the plant was inherently safe in full operation whilst heeling at an angle of 15 degrees at a speed of 16 knots in a force 6 gale. We had to design all structures for the 100-year wave on the route of the delivery voyage. (This, incidentally, was on the Agulhas bank.)

We soldiered on through all of these problems. The urea plant had nowhere near the same problems. The space was more than adequate, and, as all its utilities were coming from the ammonia plant, Coppee Rust was able to get on with the job fast. A cost problem arose with the *Dominique*, however. The shipyards in Europe were skinning us alive with charges for the slightest work. We therefore decided to load her up with cargo, and take her to South Africa, where we would put a thousand Zulus to work. She was classed by the American Bureau of Shipping, and our contract called for her to be classed 100A1 by Lloyds Register. So we loaded her up with a hundred combine harvesters and five tons of tuna fish for Pick and Pay, and set sail.

The SAR were most helpful. They were building a container wharf in Durban, and for a modest fee allowed us to occupy the quay for three months. We learnt what it takes to run a ship cheaply. With a thousand Zulus wielding chipping hammers, we discovered that there actually wasn't any steel in the bulkheads at all – only rust. After diligently chipping away, we had no bulkheads left, and they all had to be replaced. All of this activity caused a great deal of speculation in Durban, the more so as John gave strict instructions that no-one was to tell anyone anything, only that it was a secret project and could not be disclosed. This, of course, fuelled the speculation, and the more people were told to be quiet, the more tongues wagged. At last I decided to tell the simple truth, and interest faded. It was, nevertheless, very embarrassing to Pertamina, who insisted on referring to us, and to Tim Jooste in particular, as "Panamanians".

The good ship *Dominique* brought us some fine wines, as well as a lot of good equipment from Europe, which came in very handy later on. I kept two of her lifebelts for my wife, Dominique. It is quite an emotional thing to see a ship named after you!

All fixed up, the good ship *Dominique* sailed for Europe without incident – except for our beautiful cherry picker crane. Brand new, Terry O'Sullivan succeeded in overturning it and dropping it into the hold of the ship. Miraculously, the crane driver walked out, but the crane was totalled. Such was the inflation that the replacement cost was double after only six months. We only got paid out on the old price. Bang went some of the slush fund.

Meanwhile, back in London the *Aristides* was finally renamed and in her new home. She was now the *Mary Elizabeth*, not after the two Cunarders, but after John's wife. Our project manager Bricker was determined to build the ammonia plant in Liverpool. He managed to get a complete dock and warehouse for a nominal sum from the Mersey Docks and Harbour Authority, and proceeded to create a construction site for the project. We had to buy a massive 200-ton crawler crane, besides a number of smaller ones. Bricker started hiring a workforce which, in the end, was well in excess of a thousand, besides the hundreds employed by our various subcontractors.

We soon had a foretaste of things to come. The last thing which had to be done before final acceptance of the ship was to dry-dock her, and pull the tail shafts. So, in she went. On Sunday, Bricker thought he would just drop in on the ship, only to find that some of the enterprising inmates of the docks had decided that the 16 tons of propeller would fetch a tidy sum for them on the black market, and were in the process of removing the propeller onto a large flatbed truck. We instructed Bricker to press charges, but were told that if that were done the ship would be blacked, and we would be stuck there for keeps. Also, we would have to pay dry-dock charges all the time. We decided to drop the issue, but it was really a taste of what lay in store.

Britain in 1974 was in a chaotic state. A stockbroker friend of mine said that the stock market was discounting the end of the capitalist system. Burmah Oil was forced to liquidate its holding of 25% of BP for a lousy 150 million pounds, by the Bank of England. Truly Britain was in a mess. Into this mess walked a bunch of South Africans. We were told by all concerned to stay well back from the labour unions. We were, after all, representatives of one of the most odious governments on earth, and we would be as a red rag to the Labourite bull. The English would handle them.

Building a plant on a ship was a unique thing for the English labour unions. All shipbuilding work in Liverpool fell under the boilermakers' union, and they claimed that all the work was theirs. We didn't see it quite that way, as we had 12 other craft unions whose skills we needed. The boilermakers were adamant, however: all our business was going to go to the boilermakers' union, and union rules would apply. Until you know these rather quaint rules, this doesn't sound too bad. Apparently, the work is held to be so arduous that for every job you must hire two people. While one works, the other will rest. When the working one is tired, he will rest, and then the other one will work. Lest you think that, at the least, this will remove the need for tea-breaks, loo stops and lunch,

I must hasten to tell you that resting is too tiring for that, and those breaks are totally necessary as well.

In short, we had a problem with the boilermakers' union. In fact, the situation got totally out of hand. The boilermakers' union staged a sit-in, in which they welded up the gates, and denied us access to the dock. We were all for breaking down the gates, but were told we would have to get a court order, as the police would not lift a finger to help us. As soon as the order was presented, the union retreated to the ship, and pulled up the gang planks. They refused to receive any papers served on them as we couldn't reach them. The English counselled patience, whilst the ship was occupied for months.

Finally, to top it all came a great storm. None of the workers were seamen. The ship broke loose from her moorings, was blown across the dock, and crashed up on a mole. The terrified sit-inners took off like lamplighters, and we managed to recover the ship, much damaged. Lest we think that only Iraqis indulge in wanton and senseless destruction, the mess on board was disgusting. Everything was destroyed and vandalised. So much for civilisation.

LONDON

Number One Belgrave Placel

With the Pertamina project under way, I was spending two weeks of every month mostly in London. We had set up a company in Germany as the bulk of the engineering work was done there, but administration was in London, and construction of the ammonia plant was to be done in England. Pertamina's consulting engineers were in London, as were ours. And Cordell was based there. Travelling back and forth from South Africa every two weeks was a pain in the neck. To ease the whole thing I decided that I had to have a residence in London. So my wife Dominique located a beautiful flat in Belgrave Square. We discovered later that it was owned, in fact, by Goldfields and was the former residence of their Managing Director, Sir George Harvie-Watt. The flat was immaculate. We fell in love with it. But it was way outside our budget of one hundred thousand pounds. Little did we know that we were in a big slump and Goldfields just wanted shot of it. So we tentatively offered one hundred and ten thousand pounds and found ourselves the happy owners of Number One Belgrave Place, on the corner of Belgrave Square.

We bought the flat through our Cayman trust and set about furnishing it. We had just two weeks to furnish the whole place and put all the things in motion one needed to do to live there. Dominique did it. How, I don't know, but I got accustomed to hearing her on the phone saying: "I want it this afternoon. Not next month. Now!"

The apartment made a huge difference to my travels, as I simply needed to take just a briefcase; no suitcase. The Underground to Heathrow stopped on Hyde Park Corner, 100 metres away, so I never had any hassles with traffic, etc. When you are in a hotel you are always saddled with luggage which you have to drag around with you. When you can operate with hand luggage only, it is no big deal to be on an overnight flight.

One of the things I had a bug for was collecting antiques. In South Africa I was forever buying Africana and in London we got bitten by the collecting bug. We discovered very early on that the 18th century artists of England were out of fashion. So we acquired some 18th century portraits: Gainsborough, Reynolds, Romney, Lawrence and Hoppner. We paid an average price of around three thousand pounds per item. It was never as an investment. We liked them. And we had a hell of a lot of wall space. Then we bought Dutch art of the 17th century. Not madly fashionable, but a hell of a lot more expensive than the portraits.

John, of course, did not get as big a distribution, as he had already had a huge bite of the cherry. And he had a farm. We had a PR consultant who quoted an aphorism. There are three ways to go broke. The fastest is horses, the nicest is women and the surest is farming. It's still that way today.

It wasn't long before John was using our flat and ensconsing his wife there when we were away. He also let his children use the flat. They ate and drank everything we had, ran up huge telephone accounts and were nearly arrested for disturbing the peace by having rowdy parties there. Bloody annoying to arrive and find the flat a total mess and all food and liquor gone. Eventually, John got himself a flat in Eaton Square and our lives became easier.

His wife became insanely jealous of our paintings, especially our Breughel – a beautiful ice-skating scene. Later, when we had one of our periodic financial crises, John, at the behest of his wife, forced me to sell the Breughel. I had paid £38,000 for it and Thomas Brod, who sold it to me, gave me £75,000. Not bad after three years. Four years later it was sold for $1.5 million. We also built a beautiful collection of porcelain, the wonderful soft paste porcelain of Sevres and Minton pate-sur-pate ware. Our lawyer, Morris Fluxman, who used to rent the flat from us in the summer, told me his wife said it was like living in the Wallace Collection. If John had not carried on and forced me to sell, we could easily have paid off the Standard Bank in Swaziland with a few paintings. He also pinched a Joshua Reynolds from me when we finally closed up shop.

The apartment was also important from a business point of view, as it created the right atmosphere when we had to deal with all the folks in Europe and the States. And although we were forced to sell a lot to keep the show on the road, the few items we have left are still worth almost as much as we paid for the entire collection.

Many years later, when we sold our English art, we got stunning prices. The picture of Earl Grey by Sir Thomas Lawrence, for which I had paid £3,000, sold for £90,000. We also had a wonderful picture of Lady Hamilton by Romney (she was Romney's mistress before she became Nelson's) and he painted many portraits of her. The Romney expert at Christies told us it was not by Romney, but Dominique did a fantastic job ay the Witt Library and proved beyond any doubt that it was indeed a "lost" Romney. So what cost me £3,500 sold for £85,000.

In furnishing the flat, Dominique bought a commode said to have come from Northumberland House. Much, much later we found some yellowed papers hidden in it signed by the Heber-Percy's (the family name of the Dukes of Northumberland) and an article in the *Connoisseur* magazine describing the item.

They have, of course, some of the finest Adam decor in the world, especially at Syon House, which is like a jewel box. Anyway, the commode indeed turned out to be an original Adam commode, painted by Pergolesi with metal work by Matthew Boulton, and indeed done by Adam for Northumberland House. We bought it for £10,000 and sold it to Aspreys for £150,000. Later, our tame antique dealer was shocked. He said that a piece like that with its provenance was worth at least one and a half million!

We made the best investments of our lives buying things we loved.

We had to set up an office in England, and Sir Frederick Warner, the senior partner of Cremer and Warner, our consulting engineers, told us the office building three along from them was for sale. We bought it lock, stock and barrel, and had lovely offices on Buckingham Palace Road. We so enjoyed the Guards band which marched down the road every day at noon. Added some pleasure. It was also highly convenient.

Manderstam and Partners (Pertamina's consulting engineers) were just up the road.

In furnishing the offices, John used a friend who had lived next door to him in Johannesburg. Bernard was an architect. I insisted on putting four Charles Eames chairs in our foyer to create the right atmosphere. They cost £2,500 each. John hit the roof. He complained to Bernard about what his mad partner was doing. Bernard told John that they were the ultimate and thereafter John stopped grumbling.

When the offices were closed down after the project, I asked Gallagher, our local accountant, what was happening to the furniture. "Oh," he said, "we are selling it at book value." So I bought the four Eames chairs and their footstools for fifty quid apiece. But my Reynolds portrait, bought by me, was stolen by John. Some you win. Some you lose.

PERTAMINA PART II

The problems of building an ammonia plant into a ship were enormous. I have mentioned some of this briefly. John's 24 months for delivery was a pipe dream. The engineering problems were enormous. Due to the fact that half of the plant was built in the bowels of the ship, and space was at a total premium, the maintenance problems for the plant would be greatly multiplied. Terrestrial engineers suddenly found that the simple task of pulling a tube bundle was now a major problem. You couldn't just drive up a crane and pull it out. You had to have created crane rails, space to pull the bundle, and be able to get it out of the space. All this compounded the engineering problems and added immeasurably to the time taken planning the operation. The heat build-up in the confined spaces was gigantic, as the plant was operating at sea level, being on the equator. The hull acted as a fabulous transmitter of noise from the huge centrifugal compressors and turbines, and bringing the noise level to within health and safety parameters required a huge engineering effort.

It was a great tribute to Lurgi that they, in fact, solved all those problems. I have to say, though, when I first set eyes on the engineering model Lurgi built, my heart sank. We had actually created the Frankenstein monster of chemical engineering. Building into an existing ship was a fatal mistake. We thereafter redesigned future plants to go on purpose-built barges, with wide, flat decks, and thus avoided the major problems of building into hulls. It was also much easier to deal with the acceleration forces on the equipment during the delivery voyage.

I mentioned the problem of the design out of the structural steel with W. S. Atkins. Today, of course, everything is designed by computers anyway. To do it by computer more than 40 years ago was quite something. The ammonia converter for this monster was a 650 ton vessel, which was cut into the bows. The acceleration forces acting on this, under Lloyds' requirement of a speed of 16 knots, heeled at 15 degrees and meeting the 100-year wave, were enormous. The steel structures and hull reinforcement needed were huge. The stiffness of the piping, as it was heavy wall piping, was a problem, with the hogging and sagging of the ship under design conditions.

Another problem factor was the fact that no-one had ever built a plant of that size. As Lurgi designed the front end, and Grande Paroisse the synthesis loop, we had the guaranteed performance syndrome. Typically, to meet their performance guarantees, Grande Paroisse would build in a 5% contingency in their interfaces with Lurgi. Lurgi, to meet its guarantees, would build in a 5% contingency on its interface with Grande Paroisse. Each set of engineers had built in their own fudge factor anyway of around 5%. This led to the plant being very oversized. In addition, John was asked by Lurgi for the piping design criteria. Such a question was actually meaningless to John. He said, "100 years." This led to massive overdesign of pipe sizes to drop velocities to ridiculous levels.

Over a dinner with Erik Menges of Lurgi, I asked Erik, taking all the factors into account (bearing in mind Lurgi was under no financial penalty or constraints, only a capacity and feedstock and purity guarantee) what, on paper, the design capacity of the plant was. He came up with a figure of design 1,800 tons a day, without taking engineering contingencies into account. If you then took the factors built in and the equipment contractor guarantees, Erik and I, in fact, concluded that the real nameplate design was 2,000 tons per day. Pertamina was therefore getting one third more plant than it had contracted for.

One of the other problems we encountered was the massive size of the equipment. For ordering 1,000 ton per day plants, there were around a dozen vendors in Europe for the huge vessels. However, the unique size of our synthesis loop left us with about three. Rheinstahl and Thyssen were fully booked and the only other vendor was Cockerill in Belgium. We couldn't really get very keen prices as a result.

Just to erect the reactor was going to cost a million dollars, as we had to contract for a giant 1,000-ton offshore floating crane, and specialist barge, and bring it to Liverpool.

Europe was not really equipped for this kind of work, but it would still be cheaper than trying to do all this in East Kalimantan. We looked longingly at the Hitachi supertanker dry-dock – 3.5 kilometres in length, 100 metres in width with a 700 tons overhead crane with 100 metres under the hook. You could put the whole thing together for half the cost in such a dock.

In the meantime, John was running around the world trying to sell more floaters, and becoming more grandiose by the day. We had a wonderful deal in Ecuador. The president had three years to go and wanted to go out in a blaze of glory. He wanted a 600 ton ammonia plant and a matching 1,000 ton urea plant. "Nonsense," was John's reaction. That heavy, virtually unrefinable Ecuadorean crude needed a Synthol plant. (That is the South African SASOL process used for oil from coal.) "You don't need a boring little hundred million dollar project. You need a billion dollar project." A great opportunity to build a sane project as a floater was thrown away. Gallagher, Beningfield's side-kick, was almost in tears. He had worked for months, and saw the project literally thrown away because of complete megalomania.

When you have a construction contract of such magnitude, your ability to make profit is enhanced by the way you use it. The first thing we learnt about at Sable was to establish a payment regime which always keeps you in cash, well in advance of your expenditure. A vigilant client, of course, always tried to achieve the reverse. In this case, because we claimed to have such high front end costs, we got an unprecedented down-payment of 40% of the fixed-price contract value. Even after initial disbursements, we had 30 or 40 million left, and I had drafted the progress payments clause in such a way that we never had less than this amount in the bank for years. At a time of high interest rates (14% on US dollars), we made almost more money on interest on our payments than we ever made on the contract.

When you are this liquid, you have the ability to do a lot of manipulating to improve your profits. Sub-contractors will kill for cash contracts. My main concern was to get the contract changed as agreed, to a cost-plus contract, and the idea was to manipulate everything so that, when cost-plus came, we would do well.

The first thing I did was call for an estimated breakdown of our expenditure by currencies. Because the interest rates on dollars were at an all-time high – the hard, and even soft currencies were comparatively low. Of course, the forwards were even more so. A sensible person would have hedged anyway, so I told Beningfield to take out forwards covering our estimated expenditures in certain selected currencies at the estimated payment dates. If the contract became cost-plus, these forwards would become a one-way bet. It was absolutely clear to me that it would become a one-way bet.

Most contracts with Indonesia for large industrial projects had one very simple characteristic. As the project progressed, the money given to the contractor tended to equate the plant and equipment delivered to Indonesia, and erected. Although there is always a contractor's lien, enforcing it in Indonesia was impossible. Effectively, the asset is in their country and the cost of construction can never be reclaimed. Also, the chances of getting an export permit for equipment – well, don't bother to try. Effectively, you the contractor are held by the shorts by Indonesia.

The problem of 1974/75 was the adjustment mechanism of inflation caused by the oil crisis, which I have referred to before. Inflation was running at around 50% per annum and every contractor was in deep trouble. Almost all contracts had to be re-negotiated, so most contractors never even had a liquidated claim against which to exercise a lien. We were unique. We had, as time went on, more and more of Pertamina's money, as well as more and more of their assets – taking shape as working plants. The closer to completion, the more we had of the money and the box, and that in a jurisdiction where we could fight like hell. This clearly gave us an unspoken bargaining position when it came to contract re-negotiation. It was not necessary to point this out. This was one area where Peter really came up trumps. He would put on a long face and explain the consequences of contractor bankruptcy, without making any threats at all. The message went home, though. Actually, it was hardly necessary. Whitehouse was, in fact, one of the most honourable men around. He had every intention of making the contract cost-plus. The problem was the money to pay for it.

Pertamina was in a classic situation. Because of IMF restrictions, it borrowed very largely on the short-term market, ie less than one year. These borrowings were all rolled, mostly on 90- and 180-day bills. The problem of borrowing short to invest long is a classic in all business disaster scenarios. Pertamina had borrowed billions in short-term investments. In addition, Pertamina acted as an effective tax gatherer for the government. Pertamina collected the oil taxes (say 70% of the oil price), and after 90 days paid it to the government. That gave Pertamina a permanent float on steady oil production at say $2 per barrel x 1,500,000 barrels/day x 90 days. That's around $270 million.

As the oil price rocketed to $15 per barrel and more, Pertamina's float rocketed by well over a billion dollars. This money was quickly spent on fixed assets. As the oil price peaked, two things happened. First, the float stabilised, and then it started down. It accelerated down as Pertamina's market collapsed as Indonesian crude was priced out of the market. First, the Government took it on the nose. As they started to panic and pressurise Pertamina to pay, the inevitable happened. Pertamina bounced a 50 million dollar note to a bank in Texas and the shit hit the fan. Most of Pertamina's notes became due and payable immediately. Pertamina went bust.

The politics around Pertamina were complex. Suharto maintained his hold on power by balancing the Communists, army and religious factions. The army held onto all the key positions. They were kept happy (at least the top guys were) by the large slush fund at the disposal of Pertamina. We had contributed $6 million to this fund when we got our down payment. This was the only thing in our contract that really bothered me. There was no way to conceal this cost from an auditor. It was what it was – a payment to a Liechtenstein Anstalt on the orders of Mr Whitehouse.

Because Ibnu Sutowa controlled Pertamina and its huge slush fund, he had considerable power, but the Pertamina crisis stopped the inflows into the fund. The so-called technocrats or "Berkeley mafia" in the Government structure (because they all went to Berkeley University), saw an opportunity to kick out Sutowa and get their hands on the Pertamina slush funds and the political power that represented.

Our project became a political football. On the one hand, the South African connection enabled them to plaster Ibnu for dealing with South Africans. On the other hand, they had a real problem with the project. If it went ahead and was successful, that success would be to Ibnu's credit. They didn't, therefore, want the project to go ahead. We still held the money and the box, though, and we threatened to sue for extra money on the basis that the massive oil crisis-induced inflation had put up our costs beyond belief.

Fortunately for us, we took the prevention of advising the lead banks, who by now had paid out all but the retention on the project, of our syndicated loan. Morgan Guaranty hit the roof. It was busy putting together a billion-dollar syndication for the Bank of Indonesia, which required that all outstanding contractual matters had to be settled. Pertamina management was therefore told in no uncertain terms to settle our contract.

If there was one thing I wanted above all else, it was to stop the project, as currently designed. The ammonia plant would have been an example of how not to build a floating plant. Ernie Four of Coppee-Rust was, however, desperate to complete the urea plant as a floater, because Coppee-Rust would then have the only floater in the world, and the urea plant in the *Dominique* was actually not a problem. Ernie really wanted to displace us in the floating plant business. I never told Coppee-Rust of my misgivings about the ammonia plant, but it seemed to me that we were in a unique position to get a phenomenal settlement out of Pertamina and make a quite unconscionable profit without actually building anything.

Putting on an air of great reluctance, when we were advised that Pertamina wanted to discuss the future of the project in Singapore, we proposed to go. I had a big scene of doom and gloom from Jooste and Beningfield. We were down to our last 20 million in the bank and we had bills to pay coming up from creditors of around 40 million. With the gloom of pending bankruptcy and how we would have to beg on our knees to Pertamina for salvation and similar sentiments, I got hold of John. I told him I was going to Singapore and I was going as a hawk – I wanted no doves – and that our bargaining position was, as I saw it, virtually impregnable. I wanted him to read the riot act to them. He was usually quite good at that because he charged everything like a bull at a gate, and would never listen to anything that he didn't currently believe in. This time he came up trumps. He put some balls on Jooste and Beningfield, and this pep talk sent them to Singapore in a good fighting mood.

Singapore in those days was really magic. Orchard Road was a series of two-storey buildings with one five-storey emporium where we all bought our *de rigeur* batik shirts and had dozens of pairs of trousers made. The Shangri-La was a magic hotel. It even had a 9-hole chip and putt course there beside the pool.

The negotiation took a relaxed week. On the Indonesian side were Whitehouse and Tabrani, on ours Jooste, Beningfield and myself. Basically, we would meet for an hour in the morning and an hour in the afternoon. Bill Whitehouse then laid Singapore at our feet in the evening. He had connections and organisation there which made for one of the most memorable weeks of my life. In those days, when you went walking down Orchard Road in the evening it was magic. The air made you almost literally float in a perfume of frangipani.

The first formal meeting took place in the morning, at which Peter presented our case. We wanted all our costs plus a 10½ million settlement fee. I have to say, it was a flawless performance by Peter. In the afternoon, after reluctantly conceding costs, Tabrani presented a termination fee of 2½ million. We then retired for the day. I took Bill Whitehouse on one side and suggested that we split the difference, give us 6½ million and let's have a bloody good holiday for a week. Bill winked at me and said: "Let them fight it out for the week."

I knew we had a deal at 6½, but Peter and Tim really went at it. We had our ritual morning meeting where we chopped our asking figure and our ritual afternoon meeting where Tabrani upped Pertamina's. The rest of the time we played golf, swam, ate satay round the pool, shopped and did all the things tourists do. In the evening Bill laid on Singapore night life and introduced us to the Singapore young citizens association (lovely young ladies). Quite a hedonistic week.

At the end of the week, Tabrani finally came up with the magic number of 6½ million. By this stage, Peter was really quite a hawk. He debated about the total inadequacy of the offer, etc, etc. I asked for a short break. I took them next door and said to them: "If you guys blow this now, I am going to kill you." Jooste and Beningfield's faces were a picture. Here was the great fighter wanting to settle! They could not believe their ears. I told them to come down to earth. With the side issues on costs all settled, we had an amazing deal. It shows how vital it is to know your numbers inside out. I knew we had about 5 million in nuts squirreled away, that Pertamina had in effect agreed to. Both of them were totally ignorant of the nuts I had carefully squirreled away. Unfortunately, one of the nuts we lost through total incompetence. Anyway, there it was. 6½ million. A lot of money in 1975. Plus the rest.

We went back to London, where Tim and Whitehouse drew up a termination document. Because Coppee-Rust were to continue with the urea plant on land, they held a separate negotiation, but as a guarantee of the main contract they were given copies of our settlement. The only things left out were the figures. I did not want them or anyone else to know that. We had to close down and hand the plant to Combustion Engineering, who were going to build it on land. The close down would take 18 months and I had to do a deal with Roberts to do it. We had provided in our costs for a monthly fee to Roberts of $50,000, plus the personnel costs. They were a greedy lot, and if they knew our profit they would have gone ape. So I had quite a Donnybrook with Bill Bramwell on the close-down contract. He actually was as happy as a pig in shit with $25,000 a month fee! We never told Roberts!

Back in London, the big signing day was approaching. Radius Prawiro, the Industry Minister, had come to London to sign. We had to undergo an audit to get our money to date, plus part of our fee and our costs. I was sweating over the audit. What about the 6 million? Were they going to disallow it? Were they going to nail Whitehouse? We actually had no experience of dealing with this kind of thing. In the end, Bill Whitehouse told me that Prawiro wasn't going to make waves over that. He had just taken a 5% kickback on a 400 million dollar urea order. The only thing we had to show the auditors was that it wasn't a secret profit of ours.

Whitehouse and Ibnu inspect engineering model

We had the usual last-minute hiccups. Prawiro wanted to show that he was no pushover. We got a list of his requirements at 10 o'clock in the evening. Signing was 9am in the morning. We had actually just told Bill to tell him to piss off, but we assembled in the Indonesian Embassy in Grosvenor Square for the signing on the basis that the contract was final. Ernie Four was there and had just been given a copy of the final document to see, with the prices. He came rushing over to me and I braced myself, expecting him to be shouting for a bigger cut for Coppee-Rust. He started out saying: "This settlement figure ...". I cut him off and said with an absolutely straight face to him: "Yes, I agree that it is a total swindle by Pertamina. We, in order to get a settlement, have accepted this miserable pittance." Ernie was stunned. He said: "I was about to congratulate you on the most stunning enormous deal I have ever seen a contractor get, and you are complaining!!" I gave him a grin and conceded the point. We signed up and I set about collecting the "pizazz" built in.

The first item on the agenda was the forward exchange contracts. We were sitting on a 2.5 million dollar profit on the forward exchange contracts. I wanted to cash them in immediately. Beningfield and Gallagher were totally against it. They kept saying: "But we will then have to buy the marks at a higher price." I was saying to them: "Dummy, Pertamina will have to buy the marks at a higher price, not us. We will have pocketed the profit, and our agreement is worked very carefully in such a way that this profit belongs to us." I was actually tearing my hair out in the end, because I could not get Peter to understand the point. I went to John with the bank instructions and just said to him: "Trust me. Sign here. I can't get Peter and Kevin to understand this, but we either pocket 2.5 million or give it to Pertamina!" John signed.

One of the other little goodies that I had put in place was to do with spares. I had told Peter that, in getting spares prices, the vendors were to quote with a 30% discount in favour of Consolidated Enterprises – our Cayman Islands treasure chest. When we went to collect, I found that the vendors, like Borsig and Creusot Loire, had happily marked up the spares as ordered, but Peter and Co had not got the discount commitment in writing at the same time. Both companies bluntly denied that such an arrangement had ever existed, so Peter cost us a good 3 million by pure administrative failure.

It was a salutary lesson. I started by saying that, in contracting contracts, the real profit is made on side issues. We used to have a saying: If the customer says "Paint the shithouse door yellow", then paint the shithouse door yellow. What is unsaid and is vital is that you must have a little change order book which is signed there and then, preferably with a price having at least a 500% mark-up, or better still "TBA" (to be advised). That advice was in a sheaf of documents and hopefully is at 1,000%. It could almost be said to be the art of contracting. Whenever a big company orders a plant, there is the order price. There is also a contingency amount set aside in the budget, under the control of the customer's project manager. He is the customer. If he wants a yellow shithouse door, by God he is going to get it, and the cost doesn't matter to him. He is going to spend his discretionary budget.

Conrad Wysocki told me that in building the porous prill ammonium nitrate plant at AE & CI in Modderfontein, the profit on the extras exceeded by a wide margin the profit on the whole contract. And the extras added only 10% to the price! So you win some and you lose some. But you should never lose due to your own incompetence.

We probably made about 25 million dollars on that contract. If we had had people with more of what I call a contractor killer instinct, we could probably have easily made another 10 million.

After Pertamina, we had to close down the project. This took the best part of two years. John, of course, spent that time swanning around the world, with an entourage in tow, trying to sell projects. The problem was that he never really understood why we had got our two huge projects. We got Sable because it was a political and economic necessity for Rhodesia and Anglo was sulking, which left an open field. We got Pertamina because we had a gimmick which fitted a political profile at the time. That is not to say that such opportunities never arise. They do, but you need to recognise them and deliver the customer's requirement, which, for our kind of project, usually has a large "political" content. Ecuador was just such a case in point. It was a complete shoe-in, but it got stuffed up by complete megalomania.

But one project did come up, which was the forerunner of others to come. The Pertamina problem was essentially one of so-called "stranded gas". And the biggest source of stranded gas was the north slope of Alaska. The usual solution was then LNG (Liquid Natural Gas), a development which had been pioneered by our old friend Rene Boudet. But with the sea frozen for half the year, this was not to hand. To get the oil out from Alaska, a pipeline had been built at enormous cost from the north slope to Valdez in Alaska. There were huge problems as the viscous oil needed to be hot and there were big issues with the permafrost. No-one wanted to even think of a pipeline for gas, as in any event there was no market in Valdez. We had been doing a lot of work on methanol and we proposed that we could make methanol there and pipe it by mixing with the Alaska crude. We got Sasol to do some work on this idea and their report was that it really wouldn't work. So we proposed to Sasol that we could make synthetic crude and put it in the pipeline. They became quite enthusiastic about this, as their crude via their synthol process was an API 57 crude which would drop the viscosity of the Alaska crude and could readily be pumped to Valdez. Their advice was to make synthetic crude from the gas. And they gave us all the engineering we needed to put together a project.

So we took a licence from Sasol and, together with Foster-Wheeler, who were our sub-contractor on the Pertamina reformer, we costed out a floating synthol plant to be delivered to the north slope in the summer and to convert all the surplus gas into synthetic crude. The oxygenates would have to be stored and taken out in summer. Economically, the project showed great economics. So, Foster Wheeler and ourselves made a presentation to BP.

BP's attitude was that temperatures reached -40 degrees and were absolutely impossible to work in. So the project was canned.

Later, Sasol was ordered by the SA Government to do such a plant at Mossel Bay, for strategic reasons. The wheel came full circle as Sasol asked for and we gave them all the engineering studies. The result was a 30,000 barrel a day GTL (Gas to Liquids) plant, now PETROSA. More such plants are now being built. In fact, the plant we proposed might now well be done. After all, the Athabasca Oil Sands are now producing over a million barrels a day of crude in similar temperatures to those on the north slope and BP's fears about petrochemical operations at -40 degrees are now groundless. With additional gas now available in the Mackensie delta, and with the developing surplus of shale gas in the US, it is the only practical way to exploit this gas. So maybe something will come of this 40-year-old project. In the meantime, Sasol is steaming ahead with other GTL plants.

FINANCE

The chemical industry is by its very nature extremely capital intensive, and does not at first blush appear to be the industry for an entrepreneur. This is particularly true in South Africa, where the incestuous control of all the financial institutions by the business oligarchies of the country means that anything which is seen as being against the interests of the establishment will find the acquiring of finance pretty tough. And, even if granted, it will in all probability be a poisoned chalice which will be recalled at the critical moment.

That means that, for our chosen area of activities, our financing had to be imaginative in the extreme.

As a general principle, we had a very simple philosophy which for 20 years stood us in good stead. Where projects were concerned, where we were on our own in the world, we only spent our own money on fixed assets. Chemical plants do not make very saleable items, except as scrap. Assets like cars, aeroplanes, construction equipment, etc, can, if necessary, be financed, if, and only if, there is a guaranteed employment for them which will pay off the financing. Other assets like stocks and debtors can be financed because they are essentially self-liquidating. It was by breaking this rule that we finally came unstuck.

In the case of Sable, we had to fund $13,000,000, starting from essentially zero. We had nothing. To put it in perspective, the replacement cost of Sable today would be in the region of $400,000,000. Quite cheeky!

Because Sable was to be granted a monopoly in Rhodesia, with the market guaranteed, and the price guaranteed, Sable was a perfect project to be highly leveraged. We therefore had a capital structure of $5 million, with the rest of the capital to come from debt, of which the greater portion was to be guaranteed by the Government. The plan was that we would build the project in two stages, and use the cash flow from the first phase to help the financing of the second stage. The main reason for this was that we were able to structure a large profit on stage one, which was in-house technology, and which had the peculiar advantage of Hamilton's unique nitric acid plant business. Hamilton built standard plants. They were for 180 and 350 tons per day. Whatever you ordered, that was what you got, with a de-rated compressor, as they were designed around Brown Boveri's compressor frame sizes. So when the Rhodesian Government wanted two 250 ton per day plants, all we had were two 350 ton per day plants. So we sold them the plants at 250 tons per day at a price which looked (and was) a reasonably fair price. I then said that we wanted to increase the capacity and we got an increase in price to cover the increased capacity, without putting up our costs by one penny. This gave us a massive profit on the acid plants on phase one, and good profits on the ammonium nitrate plant and off-sites, which were all in-house. The construction profit on phase two was far more modest. In fact, with the guarantee from the Government of R$7.6 million, we were virtually able to complete phase one of the plant, including the ammonia terminal in Lourenço Marques, on the back of their money. We had a problem at commissioning as we owed Roberts Construction about R2,000,000, but they weren't going to be bankrupted by this and it gave us time to get in other investors – the Consortium. So, at the end of the construction of Sable, we had paid for a 25% interest in Sable and we owned the ammonia terminal in Lourenço Marques, on which we owed about R500,000, and our shares in Gas Pipelines.

The financing of Gas Pipelines was probably the most esoteric financing we ever did. With Afrox on board, the pipeline was financed to the tune of £600,000, whilst we put up $100 for one third of the shares. The company got a contract for £120,000 per year to transport the gas to Risco and put a branch line into the Que Que industrial area. When we sold out to TA, Sable paid us $60,000 for our one-sixth. Not bad on a $50 investment!

This was one of the all-time classic financings. If economic sanity prevailed in Zimbabwe, that little pipeline company should now be earning $1.5 million a year pre-tax. I suspect the real figure is less than 1% of that!

Mostly when you do big complex projects, the cash flows do not come up to expectations. This has given me a taste for projects which are simple technically and where Murphy's law has the minimum of opportunities to flourish. When you are capital constrained, as we always were, you have to do things which cost a lot less than it costs other people, and which work well from day 1. In the latter days at Sable the financing flowed smoothly because the airplant, the pipeline, the electrolysis plant and the ammonia plant hit capacity on commissioning and ran at rated capacity or above for years. The same held true for the ammonia terminal.

This latter financing was with the Standard Bank locally. They loaned us R300,000, which covered the local erection costs in Mozambique. Many years later, the manager told me that he got orders from SA to pull the plug on us. He had refused because he maintained he had made the loan on certain conditions which were being met to the letter, and, it was good business for the bank. He was sent out to grass in Parktown North! The long arm of our enemies reached deep into the banking establishment. One had to be very careful about borrowing as a result.

As we withdrew from Rhodesia, and started on with Pertamina, we had a flood of profits from our ammonia trade and eventually from Pertamina itself. Our financing of Swaziland and the new terminal was therefore as conservative as it could be. It was done for cash.

We put a tiny construction on the Swaziland site, with instructions to construct the plant. There were only four artisans. The work before them was massive. Usually, the psychology of construction workers is to pace themselves so as to be sure that they are going to get a full 70-hour week. Once they saw three years' work in front of them, their productivity was astonishing. The major part of that plant was built by that team in three years – 15 months' work for a conventional 60 workforce! And as most of the equipment was either secondhand from Aruba, or leftovers from Sable, our cash outlay for the plant we built was probably no more than 15% of what it would have cost one of our competitors. Its efficiency was below the latest technology, but our access to cheap feedstocks and low capital more than compensated for that. The margins in any case were grotesque in South Africa.

But it was in the building of Swaziland, largely with money from ammonia and Pertamina profits, all of which were earned in offshore companies, that we pioneered a financing technique which later became refined and perfected as "round-tripping". We had all that lovely money sitting in the Cayman Islands and I saw little reason why we should take it back to South Africa through the commercial rand route. Hence, as discussed elsewhere, I went to the Reserve Bank and we brought our money in through "blocked rands". The next step was to pay back the money we had borrowed from Switzerland (our Swiss company) for the financing of fertiliser imports. This was, of course, a perfectly legitimate transaction, as there is no Exchange Control on bona fide current account transactions. But the more interesting side arose when we had to pay for the import of the Swazi fertiliser plant.

Our erstwhile partner, Hamilton, had built a plant on the island of Aruba in partnership with Esso. Based upon refinery gas, it soon became uncompetitive and Esso, who had inherited the whole caboodle, put it up for sale. We bought the whole nitric acid plant and the ammonium nitrate plant, as well as tanks, spares, etc, for $125,000. The current replacement cost of those plants was about $15 million, and it was a question of how much we should capitalise the plants in the books of Swaziland. In the end, taking the dismantling cost, shipping and re-erection cost into account, as well as the new instrumentation, etc, we came to the conclusion that a reasonable price would be around $8 million. This resulted in a profit of a few million, which, clearly, to avoid tax, was taken offshore. The net effect of this transaction was effectively that our offshore companies got back most of the money they had invested in the project in the first place, and what was there was financed by the "blocked rand discount".

It was Sable that had given us a taste for secondhand plants, as the ammonia loop had cost us US$25,000 – replacement cost at the time: US$2.5 million. The absurdity of buying new instead of secondhand is illustrated by the fact that the nitric acid storage tank we bought was 70 tons of 304L stainless steel. The raw steel alone cost US$3,000 per ton, so that what we paid for the whole lot was a lot less than just the storage tank would have cost us!

A lot of agonising went on about how to deal with this issue – something which was well illustrated by a later project where what, for us, was a problem in financing can rapidly be turned around into something more sinister. So a great deal of care was taken to get a proper valuation of the plant done by top consulting chemical engineers, who valued the plant based upon its age, condition, etc, on completion, so that the value was fair, not only mechanically, but in respect of the local market.

Once one applied one's mind to what actually had transpired, it was readily apparent that finance for plant-building could readily be to hand by using blocked rands. However, with the passing of Nic van der Westhuizen at the Reserve Bank, the new incumbent, one Jan Senekal, became known to us as "Mr No".

At that time we always had an enormous surplus of foreign exchange, not only from the interest we were earning on our Pertamina funds (we normally had 30 to 40 million dollars in the bank at all times), but from the ammonia business, where all the profits from whatever source were all accrued in Liechtenstein. We had a great aversion to sending money in via the commercial route when you could do so much better through the legalised black market. The problem was that anyone who wanted to use this was viewed as a "traitor" and part of the total onslaught on South Africa. Chemical plants cost a wicked amount of money and one had to use every means to stretch our little capital so as to get maximum value for our buck.

And because of our vulnerability to the establishment, we could not afford to borrow money, except for liquid assets, which could readily be turned into cash. So while the one half of the business was to build plants at low cost, the other half was to find ways of creating capital.

Any economy which is as regimented by rules and bureaucracy has a multitude of opportunities to exploit by using the rules in a way never imagined by the writers thereof.

So one of our main themes was always to find a way, within the rules, of using the "funny money" created by Exchange Control legislation. Before the De Kock Commission recommended the use of financial rands for direct investment, the Reserve Bank flatly prohibited any more approvals for direct investment. Thus, we worked out the concept of using a cash shell on the JSE. The art was to find one or to find a company that could be made into a cash shell.

We found a company called OVCON, which was controlled by the Ovenstones, in which they owned something over 98% of the capital, and were looking to delist the company. It had a hotch-potch of rather crummy assets, and we made a simple deal. We would bid for all the shares. Because they owned 98% plus, the JSE would allow a standby offer to other shareholders, thus making the takeover of the company quick and costless. Jooste, Andrew Ovenstone and Justin Millar sat down with me and we did a simple two-page agreement, which was lodged in his lawyer's safe and which spelled out bluntly what the deal was. We would buy the company with financial rands from our offshore sources. The total cost of acquisition would be deducted from the receipt in the Ovenstones' hands, and the profit thus derived would be split with the Ovenstones using the proceeds to purchase the assets of the company at a price which would leave them with half the profit and all the assets (which they had started with originally). We would cycle the funds back overseas by paying the trade finance provided by our offshore companies and by paying out the accumulated profits in the company as dividends to the new offshore shareholder.

The question then arose as to what the share price should be. Obviously, we wanted to maximise this to make the deal as big as possible. So the Ovenstones worked out the absolute maximum value they could place on the assets (which were all property) and we came out at something around R2.70 per share. The market value was languishing at around 50 cents! The amusing point about this was the reaction of the financial press. *The Financial Mail* ran an article called "Manna from heaven", and advised minorities to grab the money and run. But no-one even questioned the astonishing price being paid. Fortunately, there were only 2% minorities and this was a cost to us of the deal. Max Borkum quickly got approval for the deal from the Committee and off it went. Two weeks later, the Ovenstones and ourselves each picked up a million dollars from the deal. Thus was developed the concept of using cash shells on the JSE to take advantage of the finrand discount.

We kept our eyes open thereafter for cash shell possibilities, as we had the continual problem of having a huge cash flow in dollars with our investment requirements being in South Africa, and we wanted those dollars to stretch as far as possible. Because the approvals we had got from Van der Westhuizen at the Reserve Bank were given without making any requirements about the overseas companies having to remit profits, we were happily able to keep the bulk of our resources in hard currencies.

Lockheed Learstar

Ammonia tanker off Lourenco Marques (Maputo)

Discharging ammonia through stainless steel hoses

Ammonia pumped through stainless steel pipes

Air separation plant

"Cerons" arrives Lourenco Marques

The Hill farm near Plettenberg Bay

Ammonium Nitrate Prilling Plant

New Ammonia terminal takes shape

Ammonia terminal in Quimica Geral

Ammonia terminal

Cordell Hull on Somoza's boat

Head to Head in the in youthful days

At last a Marlin

The next cash shell deal we did was the Capital-Cartoria deal. This company was being sold to the McCarthy Group for 80 cents per share. I phoned up Martin Glatt, the financial director of the company, and offered him 90 cents per share for the company if he would sell the assets to McCarthy Group for 80 cents per share. He needed no persuading for his shareholders, and we undertook to buy out all the shares at 90 cents and to delist the company. All was set for another elegant cash shell deal.

However, Standard Merchant Bank insisted that we get Reserve Bank approval and we trekked off to Pretoria. Jan Senekal hit the roof and expressed his extreme displeasure that we were using the Stock Exchange to get around the Reserve Bank's bar on using finrands for direct investment. But he admitted that he had no power to stop it, but used his "moral persuasion" powers to try and talk SMB out of it. Well, the shareholders who were getting an extra 10 cents weren't going to give that up. So the deal was set to go and signing was set for noon in the offices of Werksmans. At quarter to twelve, Max Borkum spoke to Senekal, who told him: "I can't put Oliver Hill in jail for what he is doing, but I would like to. But if you are party to this deal, then I am going to take away your arbitrage privileges with London." Well! That was a spanner in the works! Consternation! Then Harold Shapiro of Pollak and Freemantle came to me with an idea. Why delist? Put some of our assets into the company and leave its listing on the Exchange. He would put out a standby offer which he said no-one would take up. I thought that that was preposterous. We were offering 90 cents for 80 cents in cash. Everyone should grab the 90 cents. Harold's theory was that if Oliver Hill was paying 90 cents for 80 cents, the market would figure that I had some big plans for the company, and no-one would pick up the standby offer. He got Max Borkum to phone Senekal back and tell him this, to which Senekal had very little option but to agree.

To my utter amazement, Harold Shapiro was absolutely right. No minority shareholders accepted the standby offer. On the contrary, the shares went up to 105 cents!

Thus, we came to get a Stock Exchange-quoted vehicle. The problem with that is you have a sea change in the way you do things because you now have minority shareholders whose money is entrusted to you and you simply cannot do in such a company the things we had been accustomed to do. It was very difficult to convince John about this, because he considered the Exchange to be a den of thieves operating a loaded casino, to whom he owed nothing and a company to be his personal piggy bank.

When Philip Clarke joined us, it was at the beginning of the most sustained upswing we had ever experienced in the ammonia/fertiliser business. Our ammonia profits reached quite extraordinary levels. As we could show sustained profits reaching 9 million dollars a year, we decided that we should inject Swaziland Chemicals, together with the ammonia terminal, into Hanhill Industries (the new name for Capital-Cartoria Motors). But, we would create the biggest finrand deal of all if we set it up right. Swaziland Chemical Industries was now owned by an offshore company and its shares were all endorsed "non-resident" in terms of the Reserve Bank's permission. Thus, if we swopped them for Hanhill shares, those Hanhill shares would likewise have to be endorsed "non-resident". So, in a general submission to the Reserve Bank, permission was sought for the offshore company to set up a local holding company, whose shares would now be endorsed "non-resident", whilst the Swaziland Chemcal Industries shares, being now held locally, would have the endorsement cancelled. Thus, when Swaziland was injected into Hanhill, the new Hanhill shares would be resident shares, and could be sold for commercial rands, but purchased from abroad for financial rands. The Reserve Bank gave its approval and the takeover of SCI by Hanhill was duly announced. The shares rocketed and we made a contract to sell the whole lot at R2.70 per share to the offshore holding company. As there was no change of control involved, there was no need to offer any minorities anything or even mention the deal. The price was the market price on the day of the transaction, and Harold Shapiro got permission from the Stock Exchange to post the deal when the payments were completed.

This deal involved some R91 million. It took us the best part of six months to put through, and was actually never completed, and so was never actually posted, because of intervening events. The finrand discount was around 30 per cent when we started, but the size of the deal drove the finrand discount down to eight per cent, at which point it was abolished. We had planned for a margin of more like 25 per cent, but only turned out with a profit of around R10 million on the deal. And we had stirred up a hornet's nest on the Exchange because we had found a neat loophole in the Exchange Rules. The Reserve Bank required all finrand transactions to be evidenced by a broker's note. This was a simple means to ensure that all transactions took place at market price and thus removed the possibility of manipulating the finrand to profit. But there was a special rule which allowed for transactions at other than the market price: the "Special Bargain" rule. If there was a transaction involving more than half a million rand, it could be done at a special price. As we had virtually completed selling the Hanhill shares at R2.70, we could do the whole thing all over again if we sold them back to the resident owners at a nominal price and then again for finrands at market price. So we tried it with five million shares at 4pm on 31st December at 10 cents a share, trusting that it would go down as a misprint, and anyway no-one would be around to note it. No-one was, but Max Borkum. Max was highly pissed off because Pollak and Freemantle had got the Hanhill business for the R91 million, which brought a commission of over a million (a lot of money in those days). He went ranting to Paul Ferguson (who had done the transaction), saying that the Special Bargain rule had been in existence for 50 years and had never been used in this way. Much fuss, and we decided that the profile was too high, and anyway the discount was too small at that stage to make it worthwhile enduring the screaming match, and the finrand was abolished shortly thereafter anyway.

One of the problems of breaking down the explosives monopoly was that you actually had to build a full-blown plant to try to break into the market before you could get the credibility, and there was absolutely no guarantee that you would break the monopoly. You also had to operate this plant which was designed to be economic at high levels of output, which meant accepting a very capital-intensive design, with relatively high fixed costs. That's great at high outputs, but crucifies you when you are excluded from 95% of the market. So the operating company had to find the capital and had to fund long continuing operating losses.

Both of these factors led one straight into tax planning. The investment created huge tax benefits as a shield against profits. Operating losses were another source of tax benefits. The question was how to turn these tax benefits which we couldn't use into cash. Enter Rand Merchant Bank, an aggressive bank with unlimited resources backing it and a need to prove something. They had done odd financing for us (all very safe stuff), but didn't really have the ability to finance high-risk big projects (nor the ability to judge them). But they were hungry for merchant banking fees, and were totally unsqueamish about exploiting the tax system to the hilt. So, together with them we developed a highly sophisticated leverage lease system which enabled us to finance the explosives plants in South Africa, and other plants, with a zero capital input!

The leverage leases in vogue were quite popular because RMB had convinced the Receiver of Revenue to allow the interest portion on the lease to be capitalised up front as part of the capital investment. This meant that, on a long lease, the interest could add significantly to the cost of the investment. On this investment, in the first year alone, one got a 30% investment allowance, a 25% initial allowance and 25% declining balance depreciation – a total of 73.75% in year one. And one got a tax allowance of 130% in total! For someone in a 50% bracket, these allowances were worth a total of 65%. So, high tax bracket taxpayers were a sitting duck for being brought into leverage lease syndicates, and were offered, say, 50% of the tax saving, thus halving their effective tax rate. And there was a fat fee for arranging the deal, especially for the extra wrinkle we introduced.

We injected our operating losses in the explosives company as development costs which were capitalised as design and development costs on the machinery – the so-called "soft" costs of a plant. In any plant, the hardware usually amounts to, at most, 50% of the plant investment. In a specialist plant it can be a lot more. So, if we wanted to finance a packaging machine which cost, say, $100,000 in its box, by the time it had been shipped, foundations poured, structures built and erected, we could quite easily cost it at $4/500,000. Then Rand Merchant Bank would structure the lease and place it, take a fat fee, and give us the down payment on the lease. This always exceeded the direct cash cost of the piece of equipment, so we were able by this means to build really superior plants way beyond our normal means. And we had a happy syndicate who were only paying half the tax they expected (actually no tax at all, but half of what they would have paid to RMB). RMB: an ecstatic banker taking a fat fee for no risk, and happy to supply us with a beautiful plant. Presumably a not so happy Receiver of Revenue, who finally stopped these little games when Sentrachem pulled a billion rand leverage lease on him. In the meantime, everyone had their snouts in the trough for all it was worth.

It was fine to do this the way we structured it. But, of course, it was open to abuse (as with Sentrachem and another one closer to home).

We as a company and John Hahn personally had provided the finance to put together the Interboard deal. In exchange, we were allotted 26% of the shares. After the plant was complete, Dutton came to me and asked for help in financing a melamine plant, which cost him R1,500,000. I packed him off to RMB, telling him to charge a R3,000,000 engineering fee from Interboard to RMB, making the total cost to be financed R4,500,000. From experience I knew that RMB would throw out a down payment of around R1,500,000 and hey presto! Finance for one melamine plant. This went through like a dose of salts and Dutton had his finance. Later, however, when he floated the company, he claimed the engineering as a profit "due to the high demand for the great engineering skill of Interboard". Apart from the fact that this should have disappeared upon consolidation of the accounts, it was clearly a gross misrepresentation to would-be investors, if not downright fraudulent. Fortunately, I was long out of the company, as I had decided I wanted no part of Dutton. Against my advice, the Hahns kept their stake in the company. But it shows how what was merely a technique of turning tax losses into cash could be misused.

In the end we knew that someone would always bugger up a good thing by taking it to extremes. So we were able to use this system by keeping our heads down and mouths shut and not being blatant. But there will always be someone who will push the system to the point where someone else will wake up and spoil the fun.

Another game which was played which mercilessly exploited the Reserve Bank was interest arbitrage. A strange fact which no financial commentators have raised hell about is the fact that the Reserve Bank, under the leadership of its guiding genius Dr Stals, lost R14 **billion** in the forward exchange markets. That is a mind-boggling sum, which Dr Lombard passed by saying that it wouldn't cost the taxpayer anything because bonds would be issued to cover it. And no-one even commented on that bullshit!

What the Reserve Bank did in order to boost the reserves was to give attractive forward cover to people who raised foreign borrowings. In the normal forward exchange market, the forwards price against any currency is reflected in the interest differentials between those currencies. When you have a rigid controlled economy, where there is no free forward exchange market, in the case of South Africa, its largest multinationals could borrow US dollars at, say, 6%, invest them in SA at, say, 15% and get forward cover for nothing! Thus, risk free, an interest differential of, say, 9% was picked up. I know of a subsidiary of SA's greatest company which derived nearly half its profits from playing just this game. Whenever controls are introduced, it introduces an artificial opportunity for profit. And, bluntly, even the most sanctimonious are quite unashamed of exploiting it.

I close by quoting the late Dr De Kock, when we, the Harvard Business Club of South Africa, gave him the Business Statesman of the Year award for his report. He had cocktails with the Committee before the award, and, to my horror, Stan Goldstein, the President, introduced me as "Oliver Hill – the great expert on financial rands". I wanted to shrink under the nearest table, but De Kock smiled and said: "The financial rand system creates a great opportunity for businessmen to make profits. I do not blame businessmen who seek to profit from the financial rand system. Businessmen are trained to seek profits wherever they arise. It is my fault for creating the system and I intend to abolish it as soon as possible. In the meantime, I cannot blame you."

There spoke a mature and balanced man. A Harvard man, of course!

THE RESERVE BANK

No autobiography of mine would be complete without a chapter on the South African Reserve Bank. When the subject comes to mind, I am always reminded of the great English diarist Samuel Johnson, who defined patriotism as "the last refuge of a scoundrel".

Central banks generally fulfil a pivotal role in a nation's economic affairs. One only has to look at the record of the Bundesbank in Germany which, by following sound financial policies, created the conditions necessary for Germany's *wirtschaftwunder*. In the early years of my life, the South African Reserve Bank was an almost invisible hand, keeping a low profile as it steered economic policy.

Our early dealings with the bank generally involved a Mr van der Westhuizen and were concluded in a gentlemanly fashion. However, as global pressure tightened on the Nationalist Government, things changed. Mr van der Westhuizen passed on and the hardliners emerged. Up until the early eighties, the Bank's primary role had been to determine the money supply and protect the rand. But an old threat to all economies – inflation – began to manifest itself.

The oil crisis of 1974 is an appropriate point at which to start. Before then, inflation in SA had remained in low single-digit figures. However, the crisis caused by the soaring price of crude oil could only be solved in economic terms by allowing inflation to balance out the cost of industrial exports from the developed countries to oil imports by allowing the price of industrial exports to compensate by rising. This process took a number of years. When it was achieved, in crude terms (no pun intended), industrial countries came out on top, oil-rich countries found their place in the sun – and Third World countries such as South Africa were saddled with a crippling debt of recycled oil money.

No central bank during this turbulence could do anything but accommodate the violent adjustment process; thus, money creation was the order of the day. The resulting inflationary fires had largely died down by the time of the second shock of 1979. Most countries were better equipped to cope. Nevertheless, this triggered another inflationary round.

How, specifically, did South Africa fare? Initially, due to price controls on many commodities, and State control of many of the factors of production, inflation did not take off quite so violently as it did with many of SA's trading partners. All these conditions achieved was to flatten the peak rate of inflation, but spread it over time.

The performance of the Reserve Bank in coping with these inflationary pressures is reflected in the exchange rate. Until 1982/83 the rand held its own, but the continual creation of new money, vastly in excess of economic growth and the rising rate of inflation – coupled with deficit financing by the government – led to a collapse of the currency in 1984/85.

Sadly, the respected Governor of the Bank, Dr Gerald de Kock, was in ill health during much of this critical period. Nevertheless, monetary policy was responsible for the greatest collapse of our currency in modern times.

However, the immediate effect was masked by the boom in gold-mining profits this brought about, as well as the shot in the arm gold mining delivered to local industry – thus inflating the balance of payments. This "quick fix" bluffed everyone (more or less) into believing that all was well. The Bank continued to print money – in spite of being coupled with the highest interest rates in South Africa's history.

To this day South Africa suffers from ultra-high inflation – in spite of the fact that some years ago the Reserve Bank adopted a new policy of "inflation targeting", announcing a target which ranges from 3% to 6%. Towards the middle of 2014, as the country's General Election approached, this upper limit was breached. The country still has uncontrolled expansion in the rate of money supply and punitive interest rates – as a result of a Bank Rate of 6% (compared to the Bank of England's 0.5% Bank Rate).

Infrastructure such as the railways is collapsing or has collapsed, manufacturing output continues to slide, and GDP growth is less than 2% pa. Official unemployment is more than 25%. One is reminded of the old quip about Robert Mugabe's failed Zimbabwe state, which goes: "What did Zim use for lighting when candles ran out?" The reply, "Electricity".

South Africa too has an embattled State electricity supplier which has failed to invest in power stations, resulting in power outages and the loss of foreign direct investment such as a proposed multi-billion dollar aluminium smelter.

Much of the current economic state is the result of Reserve Bank mismanagement on a grand scale. In the mid-80s the Bank, under its then Governor Dr Chris Stals, managed to lose some R14 million on foreign exchange markets, presumably trying to prop up the rand. The Bank's Dr Lombard calmly announced that this loss would not affect taxpayers … the Bank would, when the time was right, simply issue bonds to cover the deficit. Yet in the country's next Budget the Minister of Finance had to provide a massive contribution to help cover the Bank's losses.

Since then, South Africans have watched their currency devalue to the level of that of a failed state.

On a more personal level, I have had a long relationship with the Reserve Bank. Our very existence was brought about by one of the most enlightened executives to work there – Nic van der Westhuizen. We were very fortunate in being introduced to Nic by a French banker, Maurice Bonnet, who regularly advised Nic on forex transactions. Nic was a bureaucrat to his fingertips and ran the exchange control department. Moreover, he was a patriot. If you sought the right to externalise funds, you first had to persuade Nic that your proposal would benefit South Africa. Tight and supervised guidelines would be set.

We found it easy to satisfy the rules since we did not have any money. We wanted South Africa to allow the export of capital through the exportation of capital goods. We wanted the right to invest abroad in ventures using the profits from these ventures to create our investment.

Nic accepted our rationale. He took the view that if we were successful South Africa would acquire substantial assets abroad, which would eventually bring in financial rewards. An example was the extent of our Rhodesian activities, which brought about exports and services in engineering. So it was that we didn't want to send money out of the country – only goods and services. These exports would be paid for partly in cash, long-term loans in SA and shareholders' funds arising from our profits.

Over time we developed a kind of ritual with Nic. We would sit down and unfold a long story about new companies we had acquired abroad and what we planned to do with them. We always acquired these companies with funds which accrued to the first batch of companies we bought, so that the following acquisitions did not involve getting permission to send money out of the country with which to acquire them. This, Maurice Bonnet advised, was the key to having a liberal, unsupervised regime overseas. This was as long as you didn't require financial resources from South Africa.

At that time the conditions of overseas investment were strictly supervised. Nic accepted the view that we were not using South African capital – other than hardware. We therefore enjoyed unparalleled freedom with our overseas activities.

Once a year, however, we went to confession, as I called it. We would list all our activities and the assets we had acquired. I think that Nic was fascinated by all the scheming and wheeling and dealing that went on behind the scenes. It brought some light relief into the grey world of a central banker.

Nic also recognised the dangers to South Africa through the increasing heat of sanctions against Rhodesia. This was brought home by the first oil crisis in 1974. At that time we drew our ammonia supplies from Iran. Up until then the Shah had more or less ignored the UN sanctions and our Rhodesian operation continued to obtain its ammonia, through South Africa, from Iran. However, the oil crisis created a global shortage of ammonia and the price became a free-for-all. Rhodesia became an also-ran as a customer.

Nic advised us to help lower South Africa's profile by routing finances through other countries such as Switzerland. To achieve this we set up companies which were controlled by discretionary trusts. These had been introduced overseas to avoid heavy taxation. However, they also provided a perfect vehicle for holding overseas investments. While the trustees of a trust in practice carry out the wishes of nominees, these types of trusts are not under the control of anyone but the trustees, whose sole concern is the interest of the beneficiaries. With the full knowledge of Nic, we set up a forest of such trusts – all devoid of South African control. This enabled the South African Government to deny any involvement in the large-scale smuggling which took place. It also gave us a fabulous tax structure. All our activities took place in tax havens. This was to assume great importance in later years, when most of our profits were made from ammonia trading.

As we extricated ourselves from Sable, the Rhodesian fertiliser plant we had built, we needed the profit made there for Pertamina, our venture with the Indonesian oil giant. But Nic dug in his heels, wanting the proceeds in South Africa – although Sable had not been constructed with South African capital. He eventually relented and let us keep a third, which we secured in Swiss francs. As part of the Rhodesian settlement, we had acquired the ammonia terminal in Lourenço Marques (Maputo), the port capital of Mozambique. However, we had an obligation to build a new terminal. We had to fund this offshore, although Nic allowed us funds for goods and services from SA.

However, we had a problem with the Board of Sable. We had a "take or pay" contract with Iran for 60,000 tons a year of ammonia at US$48 a ton. At that time (July 1973) I was worried about the effects of the looming oil crisis. I told the Board that the price of ammonia would go through the roof. The Board took fright and told me to renege on the contract.

I managed to persuade my friends at Shahpur Chemicals to give our company credit, so we bought 17,000 tons of ammonia for which we had no customer. We now owed Shahpur US$816,000!

Frank Macwilliams of AECI was now running Sable and we agreed that we would supply Sable with ammonia if and when required – at replacement cost! In October, the Yom Kippur war broke out and the rest is history. ... The final delivery of ammonia to Sable took place the following March (1974), at the then ruling price of US$450 a ton. Our net profit on that alone was more than two and a half million dollars. Thus we met Nic van der Westhuizen's stipulation that the new ammonia terminal would be financed offshore! We threw the rest of the money at the Pertamina deal – money that in the long run was returned twentyfold.

As the Pertamina project progressed – we set up our prime contracting company in Switzerland for the sake of respectability – we were faced with another challenge: financing our Swazi chemical plant. I came up with a scheme which interested the governor of the Swazi central bank. It involved a complicated bond issue – basically, financing the enterprise using discounted funds – and at this Nic put his foot down in terms of SA Reserve Bank approval. "Equity yes, debt no," was his final decision. We came up with a revised plan, but while we were waiting to hear from the Bank, Nic died. His place was taken by Jan Senekal – a dyed-in-the-wool typical SA Reserve Bank apparatchnik. I managed to get to see him and he told me, to my horror, that the late Nic had left no written instructions or details of our scheme. I explained the agreement and, to his credit, Senekal accepted this and we got approval shortly afterwards.

Later, when we wanted to bring in another tranche for Swaziland, the Reserve Bank turned it down. The same Mr Senekal told me that the previous permission was a mistake – a "rogue" decision. We found another way – by buying control of a JSE-listed company and turning it into a cash shell and then delisting.

All this ducking and diving, scheming and plotting, was the result of South Africa's Exchange Control regime – which still exists to this day.

A point I used to make was to compare exchange control with the Berlin Wall. It wasn't built to keep enthusiastic Germans out of Russian-controlled East Germany, but to stop those already behind the wall from getting out! The apartheid government's motive was to stop South African businessmen from investing outside of the country. In the face of this, why would foreign businessmen want to invest in South Africa? I put this to the then Governor of the Reserve Bank, Dr de Kock, and he acknowledged my point.

DIVERTISSEMENTS

Whilst we were involved with the struggles of our operating investments and the major projects, we were not idle in seeking other outlets for our ideas and our energies. For much of the staff these divertissements, which had the effect of John being away for long periods from the office, meant that they could get on with their jobs without continual interference. John had no idea of a chain of command at all and his organisation chart would have been an alphabetical list of all the employees of the company reporting to him. And he would issue illogical and irrational instructions to people, who would come to me and ask what the hell they were supposed to do with the latest lunatic proposal. So everyone was pleased when the Hahn roadshow was on the road with its entourage, making royal progresses around the world.

As Kevin Gallagher said to me cynically: "If you are prepared to take someone out to the best restaurant in town, he is usually prepared to listen to your horseshit a few times in exchange." This roadshow cost us around a million dollars a year, but it was in a way cheap at the price because having John at home would probably have cost more and would have steadily lost us our best people.

It was, of course, a lot more fun getting involved in projects. In a sense, the sheer chutzpah of the projects we had undertaken had certainly led John into delusions of grandeur about what we could do. Everything we had done had very special circumstances as to why they had happened. We could never get a project on our terms unless we brought something special to a project. Much effort was wasted on projects which were never in the end going to be feasible.

One project was brought to us by our old friend, Cordell Hull. Cordell had a mate who had been head of the biggest bank in Cuba at the ripe old age of 24, and had just made it out ahead of Castro's hit squad when he turned down Raoul Castro's offer of the Ministry of Finance. Eddie had fled to Nicaragua, where he became the bagman of Somoza, the President of Nicaragua. Eddie had a project. They wanted a fertiliser project to be based on hydropower, the same as at Sable. All the old formulas would apply. So I undertook to put together the project and went off to Nicaragua with Cordell.

A different world. We arrived at the Presidential palace at 8am as bidden for our appointment. This was just a temporary palace, as the actual palace had fallen into one of the volcanic craters in the great Managua earthquake, so dear old Somoza had to hijack whatever was left standing for use. At noon, Somoza finally came out and said he was sorry, but we had better go out to lunch. So we piled into the presidential limousine, which was one of those vast black Cadillacs, followed by his bodyguard, which was a bunch of ruffians hanging out of the windows with submachine guns waving in all directions. We must have looked like something out of a thirties gangster movie! Anyway, over lunch we discussed the project. Somoza was no fool. He told me that on the advice of the US he had been concentrating on getting his agriculture modernised, and with the oil price at $40 a barrel, he faced agricultural catastrophe. He needed a local production of fertiliser, and the only feedstock would be hydropower. He needed to build a dam to supply the power and would give to the project at whatever price we needed for viability. He was a very direct man and a lot of fun. As we departed, he said to me: "You will be sitting next to my wife at dinner tonight. If she wants to know what you have been doing this afternoon, you have been meeting with me about the fertiliser project." We then dropped him off at his mistress's house and the goon squad parked outside while the driver took us back to the hotel.

I have to say the palace was a shock. Being temporary, it was very much a seat-of-the-pants affair, and the general's whole art collection was on a vast wall facing you as you entered. Just as if it was wallpaper. But it was an absolutely stunning collection of all the best impressionists: Monet, Degas, Renoir, etc. That collection alone would have paid for the whole project. I always wonder what happened to it, especially after his assassination in Paraguay.

Mrs Somoza attacked me when we sat down. She told me she wasn't interested in the fertiliser project, but in the scandals of apartheid. But being essentially on the far right, one could separate the racial aspects from the political, so that in the end they came to political support, but were vehement about the racial discrimination. So we were able to agree. It was a good dinner. It being the weekend coming, Somoza wanted to borrow Eddie's yacht, which was on the Pacific side, and lent us his, which was in the Caribbean. The General had the largest part of little Corn Island and he gave us a military aircraft to fly us down there. I thought Cordell was going to do his nut as we came in to land. The island wasn't big and the airstrip was at most 30 yards wide, with massive jungle trees all down the length of the strip. Three wrecked aircraft lay in the jungle on the edge of the strip as a stark warning to get your landing right. Fortunately, there was no crosswind, so we set down safely. It was a great measure of the physical courage of Somoza that, when the Sandinistas seized 160 hostages in Managua, Somoza took off from that strip at midnight with no moon or lights of any description and flew back to Managua.

We had an idyllic if weird weekend in the General's holiday house, a massive establishment built of palm and wood amongst the coconut palms. His boat was a 58-foot Hatteras and we fished, bought crawfish for a couple of dollars, scuba-dived and relaxed. The airforce arrived finally at 6pm on Sunday to take us back. I was having ants because we were bidden to the palace for 8pm for dinner. Eddie was totally unconcerned and told me to stop flapping. We arrived at the palace at 10pm to find our host was not back yet from Eddie's boat.

The amazing thing about these Latinos was the wholly open way in which they conducted their affairs. Eddie had spent most of the weekend ensconced with his girlfriend in the presidential bedroom, as had, it seems, Somoza in the stateroom on Eddie's yacht. It certainly was a different society!

We only got into dinner at 11pm that night. Although Somoza was pretty dynamic, he had absolutely no idea of time at all. He was never less than three hours late for any appointment. Anyway, we got a contract for $150,000 to do the study. Consulting engineers (our old friends Cremer and Warner) were appointed to report on my study.

Our consortium agreed to fund half the study, which means that we were paid $75,000 to do the whole study. We made a handsome profit even on that. The only things necessary to check in Nicaragua were the local cost of civils (only 10% of the cost), find an appropriate site, and study the logistical problems of moving the big items of equipment to the site.

This project was a prime example of a political project in which the Government would issue guarantees for the loan capital, and the equity would be wholly financed by profits on the project. Nice if you can get it. So Eddie and his cronies (including Somoza) were going to get half the project for free and we the other half. But I would have to make it work.

I didn't need $75,000 to tell me if the project would work or not. If you specified the parameters correctly, and gave the terms of reference to the consulting engineers correctly, you had to get the answer you wanted. Thus, the basic parameter given to the consulting engineers was to assume that power was available to the project at a certain price. Given this as an input, they correctly confirmed the study I had made was correct.

So the great day came when the project studies were completed and presented to the General for his approval. I was very uneasy about the project because it was really predicated upon the premise that $40 a barrel for oil was a floor price and it would continue to rise. I never believed that, and had been selling off our own stocks of ammonia so that when the market topped out I had only two thousand tons left – bought for $48 and sold for $450. When the collapse came, we had no stock. I didn't believe in $40 oil and I was concerned that if the ammonia price collapsed the guarantees of the Government would be called upon. Since the total guarantees were something like twice Nicaragua's annual exports, it would effectively bankrupt the Government. And Eddie and his pals would not be the people who had to cope. It would be over to me.

In the meeting that followed, Somoza said: "Well, all the reports say the project is a go." He then turned to me and looked me straight in the eye: "Would you do this project?"

Much to the chagrin of Cordell and Eddie, I said to Somoza: "With the utmost respect, Mr President, you would be totally out of your skull to do the project."

"Why?"

"Because the whole project is predicated on two things. For the first nine years you are going to burn oil in your power stations to make power, which we are then going to use to electrolyse water to effectively turn it back into an oil-derived product. That does not make sense. Even after the hydro project starts up, the economics are predicated on an oil price of $40 per barrel. If the oil price drops to $20 per barrel, then the project will collapse and the Government will have to pony up. This will break your Government financially.

I would love to do the project, but in all honesty I have to tell you straight what I think."

Somoza exclaimed: "I knew that there was something the bastards were hiding from me. I never knew what it was, but something felt bad about this deal and now I know what it is!"

Afterwards he had a private tête-à-tête with me and the usual factor emerged. Everyone around him always told him what they thought he wanted to hear, or what suited them. This was what finally led to his downfall, because he was out of touch. In my travels in Nicaragua, I found considerable disaffection with him, but not anything so serious as would lead to revolution. But if he was in touch, the fertile ground the Sandinistas found would not have been there, and, who knows, he might still be pulling strings there instead of pushing up palm trees in Paraguay! So, no project, but some pleasant living the life of a President, banana republic style!

Whilst I was busy there and elsewhere, John was busy with his big project in Colombia. This was to exploit a newly discovered gas field in the Guajira, a wild area near the Venezuelan border. We proposed a 1,000 ton a day ammonia plant and a urea plant to match. Through American Express, John had met a certain Jaime Serrano, who was in the "pharmaceutical business" in Colombia. How naive can you get in those days? John told me that "these Colombians are really a wild bunch. Jaime has a farm in the Guajira and an airstrip out of which he flies his DC3. There are business rivals who try to shoot his plane down. It's like the Wild West!"

Well, Jaime got John a real Colombian passport, which John used to great advantage to dodge taxes in Britain because he habitually spent more than three months a year there, and was thus taxable as a resident. With two passports he was able to pull the wool over the Inland Revenue's eyes. The result was that he paid his taxes nowhere!

In all this South American gallivanting, we got our hands finally on a good project. The President of Ecuador had three years to go, and wanted a fertiliser project before the end of his term. He wanted a 600 ton ammonia plant and a 1,000 ton urea plant – a perfect small project of around 150 million dollars. Well, John found that he also had a problem of very heavy crude, almost untreatable in a normal refinery. So John conceived that he needed a Sasol plant to convert this heavy crude and the fertiliser project could just be tacked on the back of it. So John tried to sell him this vast project. Eventually, someone else gave him what he wanted – a little old fertiliser plant – and we lost out. But not without tossing a few hundred thousand out of the window on the Sasol boondoggle.

I discovered that Paraguay was engaged in the co-building of a vast hydroelectric project with Brazil on the Parana river and would have the right to 50% of the power from the project. So I went off to Paraguay to see if they were interested in a project there. Well, they most certainly were, although their agriculture was about the most backward I have ever seen. But there was a huge market in that area of Brazil and the project was well placed to compete.

The Itaipu hydroelectric complex was the greatest hydro project in the world. When I visited the site, they were building the diversion channel for the river. This was, at the time, the largest open-pit mining operation in the world, using 100 tons a day of dynamite, digging a channel two miles long, half a mile wide and 600 feet deep. The site has an installed capacity of 12,500 MW – ten times the size of Kariba! The opportunities there were fantastic. Paraguay had the right to supply half of everything used in the project. This would have made possible the building of a cement factory there, which would have had a captive market for ten years and which would have paid off the whole plant. It would have paid off an explosives plant, as well as a whole host of other ventures. In the end, Paraguay got nothing from all this because of the greed of the political structure. They killed off every project with their demands for kickbacks which were so high as to make the projects uneconomic. You can usually tolerate five to ten per cent in a project for commissions or fees or whatever, but in mundane commodities like fertiliser and cement you can't pay 30% and still be viable.

But that is running ahead a little. We thought that it would be quite a good idea to start with a small explosives plant there. Then we discovered that General Knopfelmacher, head of the army, had the contract to supply explosives, which he procured from Brazil and took a fancy mark-up on, and that was that. Paraguay was full of ex-SS types who took no prisoners and so that rather nice little project died stillborn.

In the course of all the visits I met a very interesting character from the Inter-American Development Bank, who taught me most of the ropes there. One of the startling features of Paraguay is the extraordinary beauty of the women. He explained to me the whole reason. In 1860, Paraguay had fought the war of the Triple Alliance against Brazil, Uruguay and Argentina, in the course of which the male population had been reduced from 180,000 to 11,000. The net effect was that only good-looking women got to be mothers, as the remaining male population was virtually worn out. Then in the 1930s there were the Chaco wars with Bolivia and these crazy Latinos went out and did the same thing and had to revive the ancient sport once again. The result is a collection of the most stunning beauties in the world. It was weird to go into the countryside to small towns and see young women, absolutely beautiful, dressed in the kind of rags you thought only Hollywood could dream up.

South Africa had, however, found a bosom buddy there. I found out that it had loaned a large sum of money to Paraguay on very soft terms. I also found out, in inquiring about farms, that certain South Africans had been given farms by the Government. The young man from the Ministry was very enthusiastic, saying that: "Your Prime Minister and Minister of Defence have both got farms in the Chaco which our President gave them." Alert to the newsworthiness of this item, I asked in all innocence to find out more so that I could get a farm next door in good neighbourliness. Well, once he started asking for details, the information stream quickly dried up. It was easy to see why such attractive loans had been made to Paraguay!

And if you think South Africa was right wing, you don't even start. The Ambassador there told me that he was summoned to the President at the time of the Soweto riots. He went in trepidation, expecting to get chewed out, as every other ambassador in the world was receiving. He did get chewed out: "What's going on? You're not shooting enough people!"

Truly the right wing in South America really knew what right wings were about. I spent some time in Argentina, courtesy of our London insurance brokers, and was squired around by their local office. Alfredo Triulsi was well connected. In no time we had a meeting set up with one of the junta members in the Casa Rosada. This is in the main square and its balcony is where Juan Peron used to harangue the crowds. It looks rather like a pink wedding cake. The interior was quite different – divided up by shopfitting panelling. We had our meeting next to Videla's office and heard all the goings-on there. The junta was keen on a project and we discussed it at some length. The junta man wanted a million bucks up front before we even started. I told Alfredo that bribes only got paid when we had the project. According to him, it didn't work like that in Argentina, so I said I would leave that question up to him.

A cocktail party was arranged, at which an assorted array of hangers-on and some of the junta were present. I was talking to one and said I thought there was considerable scope for more contacts with Argentina. After all, South Africa had a powerful steel and ferro-alloy industry.

"Ah, yes. Steel. Strategically needed by Argentina for the war."

I said: "What war? There isn't a war on, is there?"

'Why, the war with Brazil."

"But there isn't a war with Brazil."

"No, but there has to be one to establish once and for all who is top dog in South America."

Another character buttonholed me. He told me he was Chilean and his services were needed in South Africa. I asked him what he did and he explained he used to shoot communists. He had done it for Chile and Argentina and to date had accounted for over 150 communists. We clearly had a serious communist problem in South Africa and his services were available to come to South Africa and shoot communists.

Many years later, when the Argentines invaded the Falklands, my pilot phoned me up and said that some newsmen wanted to charter our plane for the Falklands islands, as there were rumours of an invasion, but that was clearly not going to happen. After my meetings in BA, I was of the opinion that the junta was mad enough to do anything. So I turned the charter down. And got to keep our aeroplane.

Another really good project reared its head. Through our contacts with the Ovenstone Group, who had had a major fishing venture in Chile, we were introduced to their lawyer in Santiago, one Carlos Montt. Very well connected, as one of Chile's cities is named after his family – Puerto Montt.

Carlos told John that there was a very nice hydro project in the far south of Chile where a large lake, Lake O'Higgins, drained into the Pacific through a short river, the Pascua. At once it was apparent that this was similar to the Kitimat development in British Columbia, where Alcan had its main smelter. The Japanese had done a study on the project and, as is usual with the bureaucratic approach, had proposed a project which would take seven years to build. What I liked about the project was that most of the flow was brought about by melt from the Lake O'Higgins glacier. That meant that the flow volume was regulated by sunlight rather than rain and was therefore much more reliable. A 2,000 megawatt project was possible. It still is one of the best hydro sites in the world for our total redesign of the Japanese proposal. Unfortunately, we finally got our hands rather full in South Africa and therefore dropped the project, which would have been a very full-time project.

Another small venture which turned out quite well for us was travel. We did a lot of travel. On the ground floor of our offices was a small travel agency owned by Nicholas Yale, the arms dealer. His wife ran the business and Nicholas wanted out. We didn't really see ourselves as being able to run a travel business, but John had a dinner with Lindsay Laing and casually mentioned that we had been offered Yale Travel. Lindsay immediately begged John to buy it and said that she and Gladys Stiefel would run the business and would bring from their existing customer base millions in business. So we agreed to a 50/50 deal with them. The only snag was that the fathers of the two girls who put up their share of the money insisted that they get in a man to run the business – one Philip Cadman.

Well, they were as good as their word and we had a very nice little business running. However, we never saw eye to eye with Philip Cadman on his idea of what the company should finance.

As we had taken away a lot of business from Rennies, they had been watching us carefully. Buddy Hawton was engaged in a big conglomerate building exercise and he wanted Yale Travel. He offered us Rennies' shares, which I insisted he immediately sold off. We made a nice little profit of R150,000 on that deal.

SWAZILAND – THE PAPER TIGER

Virtually nothing I have done created as much of a firestorm as the Swazi project. This project, and the ramifications which flowed from it, was the great issue which made me public enemy number 1 in the business community in South Africa.

It started off innocently enough. Being involved in the fertiliser business in Rhodesia, and all the back-biting and fighting that went on there, and desperate to develop a market in South Africa for ammonia, I started to investigate the SA market.

Neil Steyn told me years later about how people in AECI had poo-poo-ed the idea of bringing in ammonia by sea. They never really realised that new technology had appeared which made the whole basis of control of the fertiliser and explosives markets obsolete. For peanuts in chemical industry terms one could access ammonia at half the cartel's price in South Africa. In fact, the ammonia terminal was a sword of Damocles over the heads of the industry.

South Africa was then, and still is today, riddled with cartels and back-scratching arrangements between the major players. The result is that no-one steps out of line. I can go on and on with the stories, but the simple statistic that something over 80% of the value of the Johannesburg Stock Exchange was directly or indirectly controlled by five big players says it all. There exists in South Africa a very peculiar attitude to power. It is as if the abuse of power is frowned on, not the use. I have never really understood the subtle distinction between the "use" and the "abuse" of power.

Power exists to be used. I think the tendency is to view the public and open use of a club as "abuse". The Anglo-American Corporation has never, except in the very early days of Sir Ernest Oppenheimer, stooped to the vulgar use of a club. My earlier story of the gorilla in the restaurant is appropriate. What Anglo wants, Anglo gets. They ask for what they want in a very civilised fashion. Everyone recognises that the Anglo power is there, so everyone comes quietly.

Anglo early on recognised that Afrikaner nationalism was a profound threat to the well-being of the English economic establishment. The answer was either to take on the Government and fight a bitter battle with it, or to recognise countervailing power. After all, two gorillas tend not to fight to the death. The winner can be so badly damaged that the victory is Pyrrhic. In the case of Afrikaner nationalism, the Oppenheimers recognised a fellow gorilla and decided that it would be appropriate to give them a mining house and thus a cut of the action. The question was, which one?

I am indebted to Arthur Aiken, our next door neighbour when we lived in The Valley Road. Apart from being an auditor, Arthur was Chairman of Barclays Bank. In this capacity, he arranged for a £10,000,000 loan to Jack Scott. Jack Scott had bought his Strathmore Group into Sir George Albu's General Mining. They had developed Buffelsfontein and Stilfontein mines. In the course of this, Sir Ernest had loaned £10,000,000 to them with the proviso that if the loan was not paid back on due date, he would have the right to assume technical and managerial control of the mines (the usual Oppenheimer ploy).

Well, as is usual with entrepreneurs, things go wrong. The due date was approaching and Sir George Albu didn't have the money and Sir

Ernest knew it. Like the spider in the middle of his web, he sat back and waited for his victim to fly in, which he did. With a cheque for £10,000,000 – courtesy of Barclays Bank and Arthur Aiken.

As Arthur Aiken told the story, he and George Albu were summoned to Sir Ernest's office. Like two naughty schoolboys, he made them stand in front of his desk and gave them the dressing-down of their lives. I cannot repeat the choicier bits.

Anyway, guess who got elected to be given to the Afrikaners!

It is, of course, interesting to see that Anglo is repeating history by giving a mining house to the new gorilla (minus, this time, the choicest bits!).

Anyway, the point of this whole dissertation is that massive power exists, and its mere existence is enough to see that compliance with the wishes of the big five is carried out. In many cases it is not even that. It is more often compliance with what people think their wishes would be. After all, not too many can call up Harry Oppenheimer and ask his opinion or his wishes. The result is that they do what they think he would like them do, or, more likely, they make very sure that they don't do something that, in their minds, would make him cross. That is what I call real power. It's virtual thought control and you don't have to lift a finger. That is why Harry Oppenheimer is able to be one of the most affable and unassuming people you could ever, ever hope to meet. He had *real* power.

The result of all of this is that, when you are up against this establishment in South Africa, its power and its tentacles are everywhere. You are really up against it. No-one will do anything which might offend the perceived interests of the Big Five. Due to their total interdependence on each other, none of them will do it either, unless the prize is irresistibly large. (Like Impala Platinum was for Union Corporation.)

Into this jungle I now entered to find a way to sell ammonia to South Africa. I had found out earlier about the high cost of ammonia in South Africa, as I bought some from the South African trade to start up Sable. South Africa had a surplus and was willing to dump it, but even this dumping price was hardly competitive – R40 per ton FOR, which, with the additional railage, made it more expensive by some US$20 per ton than that from Iran. This would have left us with no margin at all, and Andy Jurgens of Fedmis was utterly determined to tie us up totally. There was no question of buying 1,000 or 5,000 tons. He wanted a contract for 25,000 tons per year from Cape Town and Durban combined. This was utterly out of the question, but he took a "take it or leave it and there is the contract" stance. Just sign off! I noticed that there was nothing in the contract covering the provision of rolling stock. I knew that Jimmy Walker in the Ministry in Salisbury would never agree to let the tank cars, now owned by Genta, the Rhodesian Government front company, go to South Africa for more expensive ammonia. Andy didn't know and didn't particularly care about this, it seemed to me, as he actually had had very little logistically to do with moving lots of ammonia. If you wanted it moved – you asked the SAR. So he was quite happy when I insisted on a tank car clause which effectively made the whole thing subject to his providing the transport. Once our terminal was operative, we never sent a tank car to Cape Town, and even before that, because the Durban railage was lower, we drew every ton we could get from AECI in Durban.

Andy was mighty bitter about that. AECI had never believed in the contract anyway and were just happy to dump whatever surplus we could take (which we did do whenever they could produce SAR tank cars). There was, therefore, a surplus in South Africa and no-one wanted it. I had had the odd flurry, as described, with SASOL wanting ammonia for Triomf, but once the Triomf affair was resolved by AECI merging its fertiliser business with Triomf, that was the end of that.

Apart from Neil Steyn, who was supply controller for AECI and thereby effectively was the ammonia supply controller for the whole trade, no-one wanted to know our troubles. I often wonder how different history might have been if AECI had leapt in and helped us with our problems, instead of seeing us as a beetle to be crushed.

The purchase of the ammonia plant for Sable for scrap opened my eyes to the possibility of secondhand plants. I had working for me a man who I still regard as the finest project engineer I have ever known, Mike McGuigan. Our association with C & I Girdler, Lurgi, Air Liquide and Grande Paroisse had given us real engineering capability in the field of nitrogen chemicals. Whilst we couldn't design a nitric acid plant, we could and did design everything else. That was from some pretty hard and bitter experience in Rhodesia.

When it came to buying a secondhand plant, taking it down, re-furbishing it, re-instrumenting it, in fact doing everything necessary to build it again as good as new, we had peerless experience, however. I did a crackerjack project taken from total design to total construction and commissioning. All was ready and waiting.

I found out all too quickly that it would be impossible to set up in South Africa. You would have to buy from the ring at their set prices, so your supplies would be unreliable, and the tank car fleet was controlled by AECI. All imports into South Africa were controlled by the Fertiliser Society. They had a raw material sub-committee, which decided what the annual inputs would be, and who would get how much. This was then taken by the Department of Industries, who issued import permits to the parties specified by the Fertiliser Society. As we were not producers, we could not join. This was a very formal little official cartel which effectively allocated market share by controlling all imported inputs. Where materials were wholly locally manufactured, of course, this did not apply. Effectively, however, the Fertiliser Society was a cartel organisation which allocated the market. Prices were controlled by a price controller who set a maximum price. This in effect became THE price. There were standard early delivery rebates, etc, but effectively the fertiliser industry was a price-fixed cartel.

I was about as welcome as a pork chop in Arabia. The idea that anyone could import cheaper ammonia was received with horror. If there were to be ammonia imports, went the view, the Fertiliser Society would handle them, and would divvy-up a share of the profits to all participants *pro rata* to their market share. Anyone who tried to steal a march by buying the cheaper ammonia because of shortage would be jumped on.

So how could this little cartel be cracked? In the end, of course, the answer was simple. There was Swaziland, right next door to Lourenço Marques. It had a small, thriving agriculture, but what was more important about it was that it was mainly based on sugar. Sugar uses basically nitrogen and potash (which is all imported) and virtually no phosphate, so it was ideal from our point of view, particularly as the price in Swaziland was based on FOR Durban or Modderfontein. The ring had to rail potash from the coast to Modderfontein, and then back to Swaziland. The market, of course, was far too small to support a factory on its own, so we would have had to invade South Africa for a large enough market. We would also have to, in the end, be a full-range supplier, ie nitrogen, phosphate and potash in mixtures. Nitrogen was, however, the priority. I went to Swaziland and interviewed the government. Rhodesia, of course, was technically a total swear word. Actually, of course, no-one in Swaziland gave a toss for the whole sanctions bit, but officially they "toe-ed the line". And while the Swazis hated apartheid, they had a strange fascination for South Africa because, of course, it was the only place in Africa that actually worked.

There was a colonial remnant in Swaziland in the form of one Reg Oldham, Secretary for Commerce and Industry. He was a colonial employee of long-standing, who knew the whole system like the back of his hand. Also, he was big pals with the guys in Pretoria. I sounded him out. He liked the 800 jobs, and wanted to know what the repercussions would be. I explained to him the unbelievably violent reaction that would flow from South Africa. He was basically unperturbed and explained to me how the whole Customs Union thing functioned.

The three High Commission Territories in South Africa – Lesotho, Swaziland and Botswana – had been part of a customs and currency union from way back. It made life a lot easier. In addition, the bulk of Government Revenues for the territories derived from the Customs duties paid, which was all collected by South Africa, and then, after an inflating factor, was paid out *pro rata* to their imports. Each territory could issue its own import permits in an unlimited fashion, and, in fact, would all pay duty at the common external tariff. In theory, none of the countries would allow itself to be used as a railway station, and exports would be deducted from their share of pool reserves. It was, however, in reality only "rail-road" exports which would be deducted. Real actual exports to South Africa mostly slipped through the net.

Consequently, imports for manufacturing purposes into Swaziland would automatically boost Swaziland's share of Customs Collections. I forget the figure now, but it was something like 30 cents in the rand. Real money. Reg Oldham said that dealing with the South Africans was really a piece of cake. Every time there was a conflict about an industry, he just agreed a quota with the South Africans and that was that. He promised to talk to Paul Kruger, the South African Deputy Secretary for Commerce and Industry, at the next meeting, and let him know that Swaziland was going to start a fertiliser factory which would also export into the South African market. This he duly did, and reported back to me that Paul Kruger had said to him that there would be a fuss, but what the hell, they would deal with it in the normal way. I now started to look seriously at the whole idea.

I took John down to Swaziland with me for a big bean feast. We had become quite close to Ahmad Tehrani, the Iranian Ambassador, for obvious reasons. He was also made Ambassador to Swaziland and had to go down to present his credentials, and there was a whole bunch of receptions, etc, laid on. We put our DC-3 at his disposal, and Ahmed, his wife Paravani, and his staff, as well as ourselves, went down.

Well, it was quite a bean feast. The whole thing about Swaziland was that any function was always seen by most Swazis as a place to get as much free food and free booze as you could stuff into yourself. Anyway, it was a great success and we made an appointment to go and see another guy who dealt with the nuts and bolts of getting industries started.

Quite different from Reg Oldham. "Industrialists," he sighed, "I suppose you want Road! Rail! Power! Water! Fuel! Housing!" Problems! Problems! Work!

Well, quite a reception! It was pretty clear we were on our own. I grabbed the Baron and went to find a site. We did want Road, Rail, Power, Water and lots more besides. When you are building an industry and you don't have any money, you have to substitute brains. I have always got sites which cost very little to buy and very little to develop because of the strict criteria I apply. You can't afford to waste money on infrastructure. You must choose a site where your earth-moving can be negligible. Your road and rail access should be such that it is easy and cheap. Your rail, ideally, should come in at one side and have the possibility of going out the other. The perfect site is absolutely level along the line of rail and slopes at 1 in 100 away from it. Power and water must be readily available. Your housing should not be more than 20km from the site. And so on.

I flew the area till I found the site I wanted. I asked the local who was with me to find out who owned a particular piece of land we had flown over. A week later I find out it was him! Typical! He had an option on it. Unfortunately, he had the farm next door to the one I wanted, so I got the lawyers to deal with it and we bought the farm for R25,000. The point is that 300 hectares of industrial land would have cost 3 million. You cannot, in our kind of industry, buy industrial land. Three million would have to build the whole plant.

The site was perfect. The Swaziland Electricity Board canal and main power line was at the bottom of the site. We had a water right of 1 cusee from the Blue Nile Canal, which we transferred to the Electricity Board canal and had to pump uphill 300 metres to our reservoir. We had a 300-metre power connection. The main railway line crossed the river at the bottom of the site and we had a flat straight length of track at the site for 2km. We got a lovely exchange yard at low cost. The site had a perfect slope down and we could bring in rail at all levels from the exchange siding, at different points. We had road access two kilometres from the main drag between Matsapa and M'babane. For 25 grand, you couldn't beat it.

We now had a site, bought and quietly tucked away, while we quietly planned the project. We had had the assurance from Reg Oldham that he would deal with the South Africans. We took over the farmhouse as an office, and erected four small houses near it for our construction staff. What I wanted to do was build cheaply, above all else, so I was determined to have a tiny crackerjack crew to build the whole thing. We could build it all with our own money, and as long as we did that, we were bullet-proof.

Once, we had a rather enlightening meeting at Sable. William van der Byl of AECI was on top form. He always sat at the one end of the Board table, cutting up biltong and firing *bons* mots into the meeting. He chose to attack me that day by saying he didn't understand NPI. What did we want in Sable? Were we buyers or sellers of our shares? I responded to him with the comment that I supposed that it would depend upon the price. Forever after, William claimed that everything I had was for sale (including my morals).Coming around to Swaziland, he commented that he thought that we were a paper tiger. All you had to do with a paper tiger was cut it up with a pair of scissors.

Then I started looking for a plant. In this kind of thing your first stop is actually the USA. There are dealers there who liquidate everything, so I went shopping there and surprise, surprise! One of Hamilton's ventures was being closed down. He had done a venture on the island of Aruba with ESSO, when ESSO decided that fertiliser was a GOOD THING. They built an ammonia plant tied to the refinery, and a nitric acid/complex fertiliser plant next to it. We bought the acid plant and some stainless steel tanks and bits of the complex plant for all of $125,000. We got a contractor for another $50,000 to dismantle and load, and chartered a ship for $60,000. So, for $235,000 we had the stuff delivered to Lourenço Marques, where we parked it in Rennies' yard. We now had the guts of a Swaziland factory, and it was a C & I Girdler design, which we knew backwards. We could re-engineer it up easily.

Mike McGuigan and I laid out an ideal plant. I would not permit any earth moving. I actually think it is cheaper to raise a pipe rack than to move thousands of cubic metres of earth to get a nice straight pipe rack when, in any event, you have to build in so many bends for expansion joints it actually costs you less to have to raise or lower pipe racks. When I visited Glom fjord on the Arctic Circle 20 years later, and saw how Norsk Hydro's plant flowed down the hill, it was clear that the South African obsession with earthmoving was nonsense.

Anyway, we laid out the plant and sent down Ralph Lee, Terry O'Sullivan's side-kick, to start construction. The whole idea with a tiny crew was to give them an almost unlimited quantity of work. Your construction workers who are really good have one criteria: how many hours a week? Mostly, if you can't guarantee 60, you don't get the best. Mostly, they like 70, with a knock-off at 12 noon Friday on week 4, back on Monday. Some blew all their money in 2½ days and came back pretty useless on Monday, but the Portuguese tend to do it so as to save enough for a house. They will live in a hovel if it is cheap enough, and save an amazing amount of money.

The problem with these guys is when they see the work tailing off, the time required to do any job extends. If they can see months of work ahead of them, your productivity is amazing. And you can really stay on top of a small crew, so I had Ralph Lee and a few best artisans working on the job. We got a small local civil contractor to do all the foundation work which Mike had designed in Joburg. I still remember the sphere.

One of the early discussions centred around ammonia storage. Did we go the medium pressure route of a sphere? In the end, John gave the answer. "If we don't give the Swazis a sphere, they won't think they've arrived!" That settled it. But I still put a small 100 ton high-pressure bullet there. To me, the crazy thing was that we started with -33C ammonia in Lourenço Marques. We then warmed it via our cooling water, which at least did help our refrigeration system, as our water was dropped to 2C. And the bonus of that was that we condensed our make-up of water out of the atmosphere and didn't have to buy it. It was hellishly expensive doing that!

Anyway, the ammonia gets hot en route and is at ambient when it arrives at the plant. If you have a sphere, you then have to refrigerate it down to 0C for storage. You then pump it to the ammonia burning tank, where you steam heat it to give you a feed pressure of around 180 pounds for the acid and nitrate plants. So first you spend money on refrigeration (power and cooling water) and then on steam (coal). Bloody waste of money, so I put in a tank to receive the ammonia at ambient, and pumped it to the burning tank at 120 pounds pressure. That saved a bundle in costs.

I may sound a bit crazy about the small things, but I always think of reading about John D. Rockefeller and the bungs on his oil barrels. John Paul Getty was the same. The people in the end who make money for you are the people who have a deep hatred of WASTE. So many people see waste and it doesn't affect them. I can remember talking to the acting manager at Swaziland while walking around the plant. He was offloading a tank car of mono-methylamine. The hose coupling was defective and it was leaking. I said to him, pointing at it: "What's that?" "Oh", he said, "mono-methylamine." I said to him: "No, that's *money*, man!" They never get the point. This same character, when we passed the cooling tower, never even noticed that the fans and *two* pumps were running while the acid plant was down. That was a mere 500Kw being wasted at 3c a unit – R15 an hour – R360 per day – more than his pay! WASTE is the greatest criminal offence of them all. Paying tax is a close second!

Anyway, my point is to design in savings wherever you can. It is amazing how few of your engineers think money. I have heard an engineer say: "Oh, I'm under budget on this one, so I've got cash in hand to spend!" It's a mentality you have to break. John Paul Getty put it quite succinctly. He said you had to create a "millionaire mentality" in your staff. You had to have a staff which treated your money as if it were theirs.

We had never built a sphere. This is quite a specialist job, and, with the sphere ahead, Ralph had plenty to do. For a long time it was the biggest cooking pot in Swaziland. John was quite right. Everyone had to see it on the road from the airport, and came looking, as we were just to the left of finals at the airport. They did think they had arrived!

I had by now also shipped down our surpluses from Sable. Typically, when you order stuff like pipework (and remember that 40% of a chemical plant is pipework), you order 10% more than your isometrics will call for. In addition, Sable, being Roberts' first petrochemical job, had been chaos. When the stuff arrived, all tagged with their codes as instructed on the purchase order, it was all piled in a corner in our warehouse. When the item was needed, there was a frantic scream from site that such and such a valve has never been delivered, so another one was bought. The result, of course, was a massive pile of duplicate valves and fittings, etc, left over. At least £100,000 worth. A lot of money in those days. I shipped the lot to Swaziland. I also bought mountains of stuff from the Satmar refinery. This was a tiny (3,000bpd) refinery at Boksburg, which had been set up to refine torbanite shale oil and was closing. All the valves had been in oil service and were perfect! I bought hundreds of valves for 1c in the Rand. I also bought the control room, which was virtually new, for next to nothing. There was plenty of new piping and stuff as well. The one thing which was a bad buy was a carbon steel tank we bought and cut up. By the time it was cleaned up and rebuilt, a new one would have been cheaper. Basically, though, we bought huge quantities of desirable equipment for next to nothing.

We were now able to keep Ralph's crew going flat out on construction. It is amazing to think that four men built most of the Swaziland plant in three years. (Not, obviously, including the labour – this was the artisan force.) To finish off, of course, we had to bring in a lot of other trades, but we put together the basic plant for a cost which would have made AECI's hair stand on end. We left Ralph in Swaziland quietly building the plant, whilst we forged on with much more pressing matters. Terry O'Sullivan was building the new terminal with Peter Wesselbaum, and then was shifted in a hurry to Durban to fix up the *Dominique* and get her into Lloyds class. The pressure to build Swaziland as a front for Rhodesia had slipped, as we were now going flat out to South Africa with ammonia, which gave us all the front we needed. And then the first great oil crisis hit.

As the price of ammonia sky-rocketed, there was no incentive to push forward with Swaziland. I did not trust the rising prices of the Iranians, saying that we had better contract for ammonia at $600 per ton for the forthcoming year. At those prices, no-one was viable. However, such was the hysteria, that the South African Government, using its strategic oil fund, paid for the ammonia at those astronomical prices, and averaged it out. The high price did not, therefore, choke off demand – it exacerbated it. Neil told me that demand for polyethylene was sky-rocketing. Everyone was being rationed. The automatic consequence of being rationed is to increase your orders. As the demand sky-rocketed (apparently), the panic became greater, which in turn increased the orders, the rationing and the apparent demand. With a pliant Government hysterically bank-rolling the high prices,

AECI ordered polyethylene like crazy. When the market collapsed, as it had to do eventually, it took many years to work off the stockpile AECI had bought.

Neil told me he was at a cocktail party at this time, when he heard someone say: "I've got 800 tons ...". Someone turned to him and said: "I'll take it." He didn't even know what it was! As I mentioned elsewhere, I went into the crisis with 17,000 tons of ammonia. At first, I sold it at replacement cost, which I replaced out of the next shipment. That was fine at $75 and even at $110. As the price went higher and higher, however, I became more and more nervous. World resources of natural gas were enormous – a lot of it outside OPEC. Once the price crossed $200 per ton, the unlimited coal resources of the world could all be turned highly profitably into ammonia. Even oil. At $40 a barrel, even SASOL was viable. It couldn't go on.

The only person who calls the top of a market is a liar. No-one knows, especially in a panic, where the top is going to be. I know one thing which is an inimitable law, though. When everyone knows a market is going to the moon, that market contains within itself the seeds of its own destruction. I confess I started to liquidate our stocks, and quite slowly at first. I would sell 5,000 tons and buy 3,000 tons. This I slowly sold on the way up. I liquidated my last 2,000 tons at $450. That actually was the market peak. Of course, in retrospect, you have to sell into volume, and you only get volume on the way up – not on the way down.

The oil crisis, of course, took the political heat off Swaziland. With world prices in orbit, the trade in South Africa was quiet. You could hardly complain about unfair competition when world prices were six times the price in South Africa, so they laid off us for the moment. It, of course, gave a huge momentum to AECI's new ammonia plant as well. Suddenly, two hundred dollar ammonia looked like a bargain. This was the hysterical era of "Coal is best". Everything must be made from coal. AECI built a calcium carbide-based PVC plant. Sentrachem built a coal-based synthetic rubber plant. I was rubbished for my "heretical" views. The climax actually came after the second oil crisis in 1979. There was a symposium on the Chemical Industry in the decade from 1980 to 1990. I was asked to do a paper and presentation on ammonia.

For the first three days I listened to speaker after speaker calling an end to the world petrochemical industry as I knew it. It was doomed. Only in South Africa did it have a future, and that was based on coal. South Africa led the world. I hastily reviewed my paper. Could I have got it that wrong? When I finally stood up, I apologised to the audience and said I was afraid I was totally out of step with the rest of the symposium speakers. Although I was only talking about ammonia, I felt my remarks covered any of the basic petrochemical building blocks. My view was that, in the forthcoming decade, ammonia in the world would come from natural gas almost entirely, exactly as it had in the last decade. A few crazies might build coal plants in paranoiac circumstances, but basically, although there might be an inflation in price of market levels, there would be no world shortage of ammonia. This was because there was a fundamental over-supply of gas, and as the 20c contracts ran out in America, American gas consumption would respond and there would be a surplus. This view went down like a lead balloon. The whole tone of the symposium was that South Africa had the world by the balls and anyone who disagreed with this euphoric belief was a traitor. Anyway, the rusting monuments of coal-based petrochemicals lying around South Africa showed up in the end who was right.

After the first oil price shock was over, and the world settled down to a higher oil price and higher petrochemical prices, South African prices rapidly rose to their traditional premium to world prices. No slouches, our boytjies in the cartel! We quickly carried on building Swaziland.

At this point, we were also terminating with Pertamina, with all that that entailed. We were putting our own money into Swaziland

and the Maputo terminal. It seemed to me to be grossly unfair that others could use blocked rands to buy SA Government bonds and be paid out in five years in real rands. Why should we not be able to bring our foreign earnings into Swaziland via this route? After all, ICI, owner of our most violent competitor, was doing just that. Thus was born one of the most lucrative and profitable concepts we ever had – round-tripping. It began innocuously enough with discussions with the Central Bank in Swaziland. They enthusiastically supported the whole idea, and, as the pattern unfolded for them, it got better and better. The whole principle they loved, because if you could issue bonds effectively at a 30% discount to the buyer, but you received the full 100%, the bulk of the interest was paid by the discount, so you could borrow for nothing almost. Even if you just put the money in the bank, at the end of five years you pocketed all the interest. What a deal! No wonder they encouraged us.

The next problem was how you covered the "soft" costs of the plants imported. Only around 50% of any chemical plant is hardware. The rest is soft cost. In Rhodesia, the Customs just told us to double the hardware and be done. There was no duty on the hardware, so there was no penalty associated with this option. We discussed it with the Swazi authorities. How should it be done? They loved the idea of marking up the hardware. Every rand of hardware coming in was 30c in the Swazi Government's pocket in terms of the Customs Union Agreement. Customs went further, however. What was the "Customs" value? It was a secondhand plant. But what was it worth? Not what did we pay for it. We had to evaluate the plant, modernised and refurbished, and bring it in at a realistic "Customs value".

The net effect of this was that we brought in R7 million in the form of capital. At the blocked rand rate, this cost us $7 million. But the nitric acid plant and complex plant were worth $8 million, which was the invoice value. We had R7 million in the bank, which was $10 million. So we paid the $8 million as instructed, which gave us back our $7 million and another million on top of it, and we still had $2 million left in Swaziland!

Once I had arranged the whole deal, I rushed off to London to tell John and Peter what the upshot of the Reserve Bank/Customs meetings had been. I wanted to use $7 million of our funds immediately, for four days, into Swaziland, for shares and to pay for the plant. Peter wouldn't do it. I insisted: "It's Pertamina's money." He said: "No it's not. It's our money." "It's paid to us under contract. This is a pure financial transaction which will be due in four days." "The bank might stop the payment." "It's all already been agreed to."

My big problem was that the blocked rand market was a highly esoteric thing. Blocked rands were created by stockbrokers through some gilt mechanism. I didn't know how and I didn't care. All I knew was that I was offered 7 million blocked rands for 5 million dollars. I could close the deal and that would be that if the money would be back in four days, this time with 3 million profit in London and 2 million in Swaziland.

In the end, Peter let us take $1 million. This money went round and round (hence "round-tripping"), but we had buggered up the blocked rand market, and the end result was that we only made 3 million instead of 5. We used "Pertamina's money", anyway, for four weeks instead of four days! No difference in principle. What it proves is what Brutus said to Cassius:

"There is a tide in the affairs of men

Which, taken at the flood, leads on to fortune …

And we must take the current when it serves

Or lose our ventures."

Procrastination costs!

So it was that round-tripping was invented. I can't say we invented it. It was a combination of factors and not least the insistence of Ray Strydom, the Swazi head of Customs, that we bring everything into Swaziland at a proper Customs valuation. People have got very squeamish about this now. When the Interboard deal was financed, Paul Egerton-Vernon made the point that London was crawling with antique dealers who were trying to buy things for £100 and sell them for £1,000. The question to be asked is not the Marxist question of "What did it cost?", but the free market question of "What is it worth?" The South African authorities took the view that any mark-up imposed overseas is a fraud on South African Exchange Control. This was one of the reasons why we employed an ex-head of Customs to advise us on ammonia to keep us clear of any Customs frauds. Our enemies would dearly have loved us to have a Customs fraud!

Thus, with fits and starts, we pushed Swaziland along. One thing was absolutely clear to me, however. We needed some serious professional people if we were going to run a fertiliser and ammonia business.

Through my contacts with AECI, in spite of Wapie's efforts to bugger us around, I became very friendly with Neil Steyn. Neil didn't really give a damn about what was bugging Wapie. He had a job to do, which was to see that AECI always had the raw materials for its business. As he once said to me: "People can carp and bitch that you have paid 25c a ton too much for your sulphur. They may or may not be right. But if the sulphuric acid plant goes down because there isn't any sulphur there, that is a big visible sign that you have failed. Your first duty is to keep these plants running!"

Neil, being totally dependent on us for ammonia, kept a good and proper relationship with us. He was an exceptionally bright and perspicacious individual who had many *bons mots* for each occasion. He also had an unparalleled feel for commodities markets and where they were going. What I learnt from him was worth millions in taking market positions. I also felt, however, that it was grossly unfair that

AECI should have the money and market power and also at their disposal the talents of Neil. I was determined to have him out of there, no matter what. We both used to go to Plettenberg Bay on holiday at Christmas. We had a house on what was known as "Millionaires' Row" and Neil had a house on what he called "Astronomers' Row." (the only view you had was of the stars!) Neil was one of those crazy fitness buggers who used to walk to the end of Robberg Beach and back every morning, starting out at 6 o'clock. That wasn't actually my idea of fun, but I was determined to find out what made him tick and so I drag-arsed out every morning at 6am and walked to the end of the beach with Neil. Of course, a side benefit was that we got first choice of all the timber washed up during the night, as well as any other jetsam.

By the end of the holiday I worked out a package for Neil which met his needs. He would join as soon as he hit the magic 55 mark, when his fancy AECI VIP pension came about. I had to compensate him for the value he would have earned anyway, but could not afford to pull him out before then. Neil was one of the most compatible people I have ever worked with. I still remember his opening remark to me, which was that in Joburg everyone said that I was used as the hatchet man by John Hahn – who was the "*éminence grise*" behind NPI! I left it up to Neil to make his own judgement. After a couple of years, he said to me: "I can well understand why you let John Hahn waste a million dollars a year chasing rainbows around the world if it keeps him away from the business!" Neil didn't dislike John. He just didn't want John's input into the business in any shape or form.

Fortunately, Peter agreed with me 100% about Neil and starting to hire proper professionals and not total "seat of the pants" operators like John. John never got rid of the small business mentality and never began to understand the difference between tax avoidance and tax evasion. He once told me that Jimmy Low (his auditor) had told him to steal £100 a week from the petty cash to "diddle the tax man". He never understood that at the scale we operated on, we employed expensive lawyers and accountants to avoid tax and nasties like exchange control. Peter used to go crazy at John's refusal to change his ways of stealing petty cash and fiddling expense accounts. It was a terrible example to people in the company, as it created entirely the wrong atmosphere. It also enabled people to steal from us, because they thought we were tax evaders, and John always used to boast of how I was "diddling the tax man" when we worked out a clever avoidance scheme. The whole thing is to keep quiet because, as James Maasdorp said to me: "You can be 99% sure you are right in your scheme, but you don't ever want to go to the tax court, because you just might lose. So shut up!"

Anyway, with the discovery of the blocked rand route for investment, we were able to finish off building the new terminal in Lourenço Marques and to build the plant in Swaziland. It was easy to do part of it, the whole ammonia handling, nitric acid, ammonium nitrate liquor, cooling towers, power supply, etc. The big problem was how to put out solid ammonium nitrate. This would depend on how we solved the problem of how to market the product. Then on the scene appeared one Tom Moodie. Tom had been given the task of selling ISCOR's and AMCOR's available fertiliser. Quite imaginatively, he did it by going into the spreading business because he had real garbage: Langebaan Phosphate, Calmaphos and ammonium sulphate. He blended this lot and spread it. What he needed, which we could provide, was a decent source of nitrogen, so we decided to go with him. We had a secret agreement to sell him bulk ammonium nitrate in a granular form. We opted for a super-cheap system: stainless steel belts cooled by water with breakers at the end! Cheap as hell. No prill towers or granulation. Absolute magic.

Then, two months before we got going, Tom disappeared. AMCOR pulled the plug on his activities, so we were on our own. Neil and I sat down and confabulated. We decided we had to, chop-chop, hire our own sales staff and go into the business. Without phosphate and potash, though, we would be dead. We had to sell the whole range. We hired a man who, as far as we were concerned, suited us. He brought an intellectual context into an industry which was known for its total lack of any such thing. The products on offer had not been changed for 30 years. Farmers were then, and still are today, being swindled by being sold citric-soluble phosphates when the crying need in many areas is for water-soluble phosphates. Much was based on single superphosphate and ammonium sulphate. The standard big selling mixture was 2:3:2 (22), the 22 being the total plant food content.

Even worse, George McKusic of Fedmis promoted the sale of supers and raw – half single superphosphate and half raw phosphate rock. It really was a fraud on the farming community. As we had now to change our horses nine-tenths of the way through the stream, we decided that we had better do something better. This was not very difficult!

When the world is your oyster, and the competition is insular, you can actually plaster them. One of the clear first problems we encountered was that, to sell in South Africa, we had to overcome a big transport disadvantage. This also sheltered us to some extent from competition from South Africa. To sell outside Swaziland, though, we had to find a way to cut our transport costs.

As is usual, with every problem there is an associated opportunity. Once again, we looked at the rest of the world and what they were doing. We also took the step of employing Dr Abel Botha. Abel worked for Fedmis. His big advantage, although he was pedantic and drove a lot of people nuts, was that he brought in some brains, which we proceeded to pick. We packed him off to the USA and told him to find out what the hell went on there. It was clear to us that US producers tended to be one- or two-product companies. How the hell did they survive in that market? We needed Abel to do some digging.

Well, it soon became obvious. Under the intense competition in the USA, the fertiliser industry had evolved along totally different lines from that in Europe. Whilst there was still big business in straight nitrogen, chiefly for top dressing, farmers wanted all three plant foods in one packet. In Europe, this was done by granulation, where all three ingredients were granulated together so that every granule had all three ingredients, in the right ratio. In America, they "bulk-blended" the product by physically mixing the granules of the different ingredients. The Americans had, chiefly by TVA, carried out intensive studies of physical mixing. The simple answer to this was that, if all the granules were of the same size analysis, then there was no segregation of granules in the blend, and the blend would be representative throughout. This gave a huge advantage, because the European system requiring a blend change meant a plant shut-down, a change-over to another mixture, and a huge inventory of finished products all of different blends. The Americans, on the other hand, mostly carried a maximum of four ingredients, and just blended to market requirements as and when needed, in simple bulk-blending operations – really just a concrete mixer.

We had to be in business fast. Even if we had had the money, a granulation plant would have taken years to build, and in any case we did not have phosphate-manufacturing capacity. We therefore decided we would have to go the American route. Chop-chop. I still remember having a lunch with Steve Anderson of AECI at the time. Steve was actually highly complimentary to me of our abilities, and then he said: "You know, I really have to congratulate you on the total secrecy you have maintained on your fertiliser marketing. We have been keeping an eye on your plant, and we know you are nearly ready to go, but no-one knows your marketing plans!" I kept a straight face. How could I tell Steve we were six weeks from production and we had done no marketing at all? That our deal with Tom Moodie had fallen flat on its nose and we were running around like turkeys with our heads cut off, trying to put together a totally radically revamped situation in six weeks!

Anyway, my project genius, Mike McGuigan, sorted out the one problem. He found a huge concrete batching plant at the Hendrik

Verwoerd Dam which we could buy lock, stock and barrel for R50,000. We would convert our workshop into a bulk store for 25,000 tons of product, and put in the concrete plant, and, hey presto, we would have a 1,000 ton a day blending plant! Good as his word, Mike did it in six weeks. When you have people like that on your team, no-one can beat you. Most people would have estimated at least six to nine months to do what we had to do, to be in business. Having put Abel to work, Neil and I determined we were going to turn our problem of no phosphate and high transport costs into a positive marketing advantage. We went for DAP.

DAP was magic. In South African parlance, 18-20-0 (38). Thirty-eight per cent plant food. When blended to the popular 2.3.2 mixture, we got 2.3.2 (38): 38 per cent plant food, against our competitors' 22 per cent. We would have to transport half the stuff. Our bagging cost would be half. The advantages went on and on. DAP had other characteristics, too: 100% water-soluble phosphate, an immediate alkaline reaction in the soil when there was moisture, which gave a huge uptake. Compared to the garbage the South African industry was selling, the stuff was a magic bullet.

By just importing DAP and granular potash, we were able to make a full range of blends, all with analyses far in excess of the competition. We turned this into an active marketing advantage. Although our transport cost was higher, we could deliver the same plant food to the farmer for less money. The farmer had only to handle half of his accustomed number of bags. His planter could run for twice the amount of time. The advantages went on and on.

We had a campaign of vilification waged against us by the trade in South Africa that was staggering. They sowed poison in farmers' minds about the high concentration burning their crops. The co-ops were poisoned about it. We were called a lot of black communist bastards who were part of the total onslaught on South Africa. The biggest co-op where we wanted to sell – the OTK – was a leader in the violent campaign against us. The Government was warned of massive crop damage with DAP.

It was useless to show the graphs of fertiliser consumption in the USA. One saw the absolute decline of single superphosphate from millions upon millions of tons, to a few hundred thousand and the growth of DAP, from nothing, to millions of tons. It was quite amazing what had happened in the USA. If DAP did not burn USA crops, why should it burn South African crops? After all, you were putting the same amount of salts into the soil. The campaign was relentless, though. How supposed scientists, working for the other side, could in conscience spew forth the garbage that they did, at the behest of their masters, I will never know.

All the fuss had one hugely beneficial effect, luckily: the ozone of publicity. We were clearly being taken seriously. You find that when you innovate in a market place, the bulk of people are too conservative to change. Some, however, want to get the latest and the best, and some of those can think for themselves. You can, after all, fool all of the people some of the time, and some of the people all of the time, but not all of the people all of the time.

Louis Luyt broke into the market with a sledgehammer approach. He was an out-and-out discounter, but he was offering an identical product. If there is no perceived product differentiation, then discounting is the appropriate way to break in. With our freight disadvantage, and the fact we were promoting a different, superior product, this would have been a bad strategy. The problem was to survive the low volumes in the market establishment years.

I had established for us a very simple set of financial ground rules. What went into fixed assets was all our own money. We borrowed nothing to build our fixed assets in any risk venture. Sable had been built with borrowed money on a huge scale, but we had an effective take-or-pay contract from a country behind it. Going into the lions' den as we were, we could not have any borrowed money. However, this was to make a virtue of necessity, because no-one in the banking community believed we would succeed against the forces we were up against, and wouldn't lend us anything, and they were, in any event, basically controlled by those forces. When we broke that rule, we went bust.

All in all, we could see that we were faced with a long haul. The basic problem was to persuade a farmer to even try our product. Our idea then became to get a farmer to try out our product for, say, 10% of his crop. Let him see the result. You can spew forth all the scientific data in the world, but farmers are pretty basic. And the smart ones came to a simple conclusion. If this stuff was really so terrible, why was the fertiliser industry in an uproar? If it was bad, it would not sell anyway. The size of the uproar convinced some that just maybe the reason for the hoo-ha was that we represented a serious threat to this business. This experience stood us in good stead later on in explosives. When you are small and poor, you can't afford publicity. Everyone ignores you. If you can get the big boys to notice you and kick up a fuss, they are creating the ozone of publicity for you. When you are getting going, you only want 5 or 10 per cent on them. That is your foothold.

One of our prime customers in those early years was Sidney Press. Sidney was the retail mogul who had created Edgars – a chain store. Sydney had a huge farm near Lydenburg which was "the model farm". He had read about DAP and he wanted it. Regardless. So the next thing was a phone call to come to Edgardale for a meeting. Dominique and I were invited to Coromandel Estates for a weekend to discuss matters. It led to a long friendship with Sydney. But as the most prominent farmer in the area, whatever Sydney did was aped by the rest.

We started establishing a toe-hold. Our strategy was to tackle the farmers most recognised by their fellow farmers as leaders in farming thought. They tended also to be the guys who had the most open minds, because they were looking for a better way. For me, this has been the guiding principle of my life. No matter how good you are, there has to be a better way.

We got some farmers who said: "All right, we'll give it a bash for 50 or 100 hectares." It then took one long year waiting for their results. The overwhelming response was in the next year to go over 100% to us. It was inevitable. After the low soluble phosphates most of them had been using, DAP was a magic bullet. Being leading farmers, the guys we had used, talked. The next year, we had their neighbours – maybe not for all their business, but a portion. The year after, they were hooked 100%. It was a long drawn out process. The early years with Abel, Neil and myself were effectively a foundation basis where we proved the inherent total superiority of the product. It showed up in accelerating demand.

We were treated derisively by the trade in these years. "30,000 tons in a market of 4½ million. Huh!" Even 60,000 tons the next year was being laughed at. By 120,000 tons in the third year, they started to take notice. Bear in mind that every ton of diammonium phosphate we sold displaced two tons of the competitors' product. That was when I got a message to meet Philip Clarke. Although not so at the time, this, of course, became one of the more pivotal events of my life.

Neil and I went to meet Philip. Neil, of course, knew him from Triomf days, but I had never met him. All I knew was that Lombard had got him to sign an order for ammonia when we were in trouble, and he was regarded in much awe by the other members of the industry. Philip was known to be smart and utterly ruthless. He had risen out of the wrong side of the railway tracks in Birmingham and was very, very street smart. He stood head and shoulders above the other players in the industry. What the hell was this meeting about? We were used, by now, to the endless stream of threats which came from Fedmis and AECI. I had never, however, personally met any of the Triomf players. With hindsight, of course, the entire history of the fertiliser and explosives industries would have been different.

As it was, we sat down with Philip. Philip has the most smooth and gentle approach. Butter would not melt in his mouth. He was all sweetness and light. What did we want? If we were determined to disrupt the industry (which is what our loose cannon John Hahn was forever screaming his head off about) by chasing prices ever lower, then the industry would have to respond. If we were, however, as he put it, prepared to restrain our ambitions, he was quite happy to give us a quota in the market, and let prices be restored. Clarke thought that the wars were bad for the industry and its image.

Well, this was pretty startling stuff. No threats. Join the club. Let the terminal become recognised by the industry. Even let them buy shares in it. Where was the catch? Well, of course, the problem was that Philip's figures were out of date. He wanted us to settle for 80,000 tons of product. He had been working on our previous year's figures. We already knew we were selling 100,000 tons, and for proper viability we needed to sell 200,000 tons. (This was before we decided we had to sell explosives.) We would probably have settled for 120,000 tons, because obviously we could cheat for 30,000 tons, but Philip didn't want, at that stage, to go higher. At the end we could probably have made a deal because Philip wasn't counting plant food – only physical tons. At the end of the day, though, Neil and I just could not believe that the trade would undergo such a volte-face. There just had to be a catch, but we couldn't figure it out. Years later, Philip told me that he had been quite genuine. He wanted us in the fold and neutralised. There was no catch, except that we would be forever small. That was, in fact, the only catch.

Although our meeting with Philip Clarke came to naught, it did at least carry a message to the industry. Contrary to the continuous barrage of propaganda being put out by John, we were not Crusaders on the path of cheap fertiliser for the masses. We were capitalists trying to carve out a piece of the action for ourselves. Of course, we wanted to be seen as the consumer's friend. The Raymond Ackerman stuff! That's pretty basic, but we weren't altruistic. At least we got that straight.

The fact was that, after three years, we had actually started to penetrate the market. At the end of the day, people realised that DAP was magic stuff, and our sales were starting to become really significant. The trade kept yelling at Pretoria that monoammonium phosphate was fine, and DAP should be banned. To me, brought up in America in the whole competitive market thing, this was crazy. Let the market decide. The barons of South African industry, however, didn't believe in a market system for one minute. South Africa believed in a private enterprise society – but not, under any circumstances, a competitive market economy. Everything was "strategic" against the day of sanctions. I suppose fascist politics always brings about fascist economics. The thing was that we just wanted to be free to sell and deal with our product in the market place, and let the best man win. The establishment, on the other hand, believed in fighting their competition by any means except a better product at a better price with a better service.

We supported Swaziland in these years with our Pertamina profits. As we got going, though, the nature of our ammonia business asserted itself. AECI was finally getting its Number 4 plant debugged and operating. That meant the market for ammonia collapsed. All we sold was our own consumption and a few tons to Quimica Geral. The problem with the Pertamina money was John. John was obsessed with ever bigger projects, and he travelled the world first class with an entourage. He couldn't travel without it, as a sort of security blanket. He wasted about a million dollars a year and the biggest cheek of all was when Mary Hahn came to see me – by appointment – to explain that, as John was doing all the work for the company by travelling around the world, he needed her to look after him, because he was the most valuable asset of the company!

Our agreement was that we could charge a first class ticket and $100 a day. Anything over had to be claimed. I always cashed a first class ticket for two economies and took Dominique, when I wanted to. I was damned if I was going to pay for Mary Hahn to gallivant around the world, at my expense, to waste yet more money, unless she and John went economy. In the 10 years of operations since we signed up Pertamina, John brought nothing into the business at all. To do nothing, he spent a million dollars a year.

The thing that irritated Peter Beningfield more than anything was the way John ran up expenses and charged them to the company. Once he bought a bracelet for his wife, for her birthday, in Tel Aviv. When Peter came to me and asked why it was necessary to spend a huge sum on a gift for Mrs MacDonald (wife of the boss of Shahpur Chemicals), and I saw the credit card reference, I told Peter it wasn't for Mrs MacDonald at all, but Mary Hahn. Peter exploded. This was just the kind of thing that drove him insane. The old mentality of stealing from the company to diddle the taxman was also stealing from your fellow shareholders. This never occurred to John.

The result of all this "diddling" was that, by 1977, Peter had had enough. He quit, and wanted to be paid out. The problem was, he had some wild ideas about what his shares were worth. He wrote up the books and claimed something like two million dollars from us! Well, this was quite a fight. We had a lot of potential, but it was going to take one hell of an effort to realise it. In the end, we paid him out in 1979. What I really look at cynically is that, because he exercised his rights in terms of the shareholders' agreement, he technically had the power to deal with his $300,000 pay-out, which was paid on his instructions, to his Cayman Trust. He did very well, and I hear that he has a couple of million there now. Because of his position today, he is bullet-proof from being prosecuted and hounded by the Reserve Bank. One rule for the establishment and another for the rest. Is there any wonder that the whole system is discredited and stinks?

The other more serious departure was Neil. Unfortunately, Neil went off to the ISMA

Conference in Rio, sans me, and the next thing he was offered a prize job with Sentrachem. We were probably at the lowest ebb of our fortunes at that point, and life was very tough. The ammonia business was diabolical because of the new AECI plant, and the ammonia contract I had with Sable was up, so we had to carry the full cost of the terminal ourselves. Sable bought from AECI and just needed us for check pricing. Life was tough. Also, John was back in town, and had brought Max Hahn into the company. Neil just couldn't take John, and when Max was added to the equation, well, enough was enough. John used to have meetings and talk utter bullshit, criticising Neil and me with no idea of the problems. The offer from Sentrachem, therefore, fell on fertile ground. This was a big problem, because I had real financial juggling to do to survive, and I really needed someone to handle the Swazi company.

Out of the blue, I got a call from Philip Clarke. "Are you still in the market for a replacement for Neil Steyn?"

"Well, yes."

"What's wrong with me?"

"What!"

Well, it turned out that Philip had split with Louis Luyt and was looking around – not that he needed a job. He did have something to prove, however, and he knew something I didn't. The ammonia boom was about to start. There just wasn't any question about it. Of course, we took on Philip. His one great strength was that he took utterly no shit from John at all, and Max even less. Neil had always felt he couldn't tell the people who paid him to piss off, but Philip had no such inhibitions, although he never really had to. The only person Philip had to flatten (only once mind – that was enough), was Max.

The three years Philip spent with us were the three last great boom years of the fertiliser industry. One more year would probably have seen the total replacement of most phosphates with DAP because Triomf finally decided it had to build a DAP plant. Imitation is the sincerest form of flattery!

Swaziland plant

Aristeides

SWAZILAND – THE REAL FIGHT BEGINS

The whole purpose of going to Swaziland was to get within the Customs Union, so that the industrial control exercised by the South African Government, in terms of its import permit policy, could be circumvented. That was the only advantage. There was a kind of cargo cult in Swaziland which seemed to believe that development was something which was given to you on a plate. Consequently, when Oldham departed for the island of Anquilla, due to affirmative action in Swaziland, we had people who were not only inexperienced in dealing with the gangsters they were up against in Pretoria, but who never really understood what it took to deal with them.

The South African trade mounted a virulent campaign against us. We were part of the Black Communist total onslaught on South Africa which was going to destroy the critical and strategic industries which had been built up. The epithet applied to me was "Kaffir-loving communist!" Most of them, of course, were fat-cat industries run by affluent incompetents who were political masters of the art of climbing the rungs of company ladders. The idea of Swaziland, which was bringing a breath of world competition into the industry, was total anathema. We were the worst news they could think of. Although there was some restricted competition from the likes of an Omnia, they could be controlled within the industry, as could Triomf, by control of ammonia.

The whole basis of control of the industry, and the prevention of any destructive competition, was based in the first instance on ammonia. This was a highly capital-intensive business. The more so in South Africa, where the only feedstock was really coal. Although refinery gas was used, the amount available was really restricted and inadequate for the needs. Consequently, the barriers to entry were huge.

Once we built a terminal – for a miserable $1.4 million – the full force of cheap world ammonia based on natural gas could hit the South African market. The South African trade was screaming that we were buying dumped material. In truth, there never was any such thing as "dumped" ammonia. It is like talking about "dumped" copper. Ammonia is a world commodity with a world price. There is no such thing as dumped ammonia. The officials in Pretoria, however, believed it all, and the lack of sophistication of the Swazis meant that our case was never properly presented and the South Africans ran rings around them. We had to try to present our own case to Pretoria.

We were about as welcome as a pork chop in Jerusalem. Joep Steyn, the Secretary for Commerce and Industry, regarded us as a bunch of renegade traitors to South Africa, who were assisting the "Communist" onslaught. When I mildly pointed out to him that the Customs Union Agreement made specific reference to assisting the less developed markets of the Customs Union towards industrial development, his response was utterly typical. The Swazis had no business meddling in white men's industries. They must restrict themselves to things like baskets and blankets, which were what Kaffirs were fit to make. South Africa would deal with the real industry.

We obviously were going to have a real uphill struggle. The first thing that they did was in respect to the consumer subsidy. In the earlier days, the Government had given a subsidy of 75% of the rail transport on fertiliser, to encourage its use. Because of the distribution distortions and manufacturing distortions this brought about, they decided to replace it with a consumer subsidy. The Swazis asked for the subsidy on fertiliser sold by the ring in Swaziland. They were told that it was not a subsidy for manufacturers, but a direct subsidy to consumers, and the South African Government had no mandate to subsidise Swazi consumers.

We applied for the subsidy. One of the factors that was clear was that all potash was imported, as there were no local reserves. We could not see how we could be denied the consumer subsidy on potash. We could also see extending the argument, because the trade was also by now importing ammonia. We felt that, if subsidy was paid to the South African trade on imported ammonia, we could not be discriminated against. However, when we came to it, all of a sudden it was changed. The consumer subsidy was still a consumer subsidy, but it could only be applied for by a recognised South African manufacturer. The more we protested, the more they dug in their heels. Gradually, over the years, as the oil crisis took over, and prices sky-rocketed, the amount of the subsidy, as a percentage, declined. All our arguments about potash were unanswerable. They finally removed subsidy from potash and put it only on nitrogen and phosphate.

The SA Government thus, quite illegally, protected the SA trade. If Reg Oldham had still been there, they never would have got away with it. The South Africans bullied the Swazis mercilessly. It is amazing how the South Africans were able to effectively impose apartheid on their independent neighbours by just pushing them around.

During the oil crisis, the cries became muted as the ammonia price sky-rocketed, and, if we had been operational, we would have had to have closed down. However, as the boom inevitably brought about its own destruction, and as oil prices collapsed, we once again became a threat. Prices levelled off at two and a half to three times what they had been. AECI's new plant was starting up, though, and the prices from that were two and a half to three times what South African prices had been. The oil-based ammonia production from refinery gases saw its cost soaring to totally uneconomic levels.

Once again we became a threat. In fact, of course, once they succeeded in having a tariff imposed on ammonia, which effectively set a floor price on imports, we happily sold, duty paid, to all customers, including ourselves, at this floor price. We made a pile of money offshore as a result. This was through our Liechtenstein Anstalt set-up, courtesy of the Reserve Bank, to conduct our ammonia trading. Whenever we wanted to use our offshore funds to invest onshore, we tried to utilise the good old blocked rand route. We had a different regime from Nic van der Westhuizen, though. The Reserve Bank consisted of a humourless lot of bastards with the mentality of traffic cops. Offshore money must come back through the commercial rand route. They insisted. Well, as our funds were legally beyond any control they had, I was damned if I was going to accept that. We therefore did the first cash shell deal by buying OVCON, using blocked rands, with the Investec Group, and selling the assets to the controlling shareholders, who held 98% of the shares. The minorities went home in a daze with a totally staggering profit! We divided up the goodies from this deal.

Then came the Hanhill deal. A small motor trading company, Capital-Cartoria Motors, was being bought out by McCarthy – our old friends Anglo. They had offered to take the company out at 80c per share. I got to hear of it, and said to Martin Glatt, their finance boss: "You sell the underlying assets for 80c and I will give you 91c for the cash shell and delist it. We will then just use the cash for our interests." The economics were roughly this: we could buy the 91c for about 55c and land up with 80c. We would therefore be able to get most of the blocked rand discount.

Senekal at the Reserve Bank went berserk over this one, but, as described elsewhere, we did it anyway. The De Kock Commission then turned round and allowed the use of finrands specifically for financing operations like Swaziland.

We now had to consider our marketing approach in full. All the thoughts and ideas had been thoroughly discussed, and it was time to put them into effect.

We had by now achieved a 15% penetration of the market. Nothing daunted, Philip decided to double our capacity. By now we had a serious shortage of product, as our high-grade mixtures were sweeping the market. And the world suppliers at large knew of this success, as they were well aware of the way DAP would sweep the market. So Philip was able to get 180 days' credit direct from overseas. This gave us, in effect, a cash float of 90 days, which was used to spend on new plant. Also, as we had a monopoly on ammonia, Philip insisted on being paid up front for ammonia. This meant he had the money for, say, 50,000 tons, but had only 15,000 tons in storage. After all, he argued, the banks don't keep your money in the bank. But they have got it when you want it. And our Russian contract meant that we could always get a shipment within about 60 days. I found a second Hamilton 180-ton nitric acid plant and we erected it as an extension to No 1 plant. De-bottlenecking the downstream units was easy. And we built a blending plant in Richards Bay. The sugar cane industry use basically only nitrogen and potash. Having a blending plant in Richards Bay meant we did not have to rail our potash to Swaziland and then back again.

At last we had arrived. We were actually invited to join the Fertiliser Society.

IN WITH A BANG

Neil Steyn and I were battling with the fact that we had a large capacity for ammonium nitrate production, with, at that time, a very small share of the fertiliser market. The Amcor promise had turned out to be a total frost, so we had a lot of ammonium nitrate to sell.

According to the Fertiliser Act, straight ammonium nitrate could not be sold, but had to be admixed with limestone. There was no definition of how this was to be done, so we bulk-blended our ammonium nitrate granules with similar-sized limestone chips, to achieve the required degree of dilution. This blend actually became quite popular with farmers, because the abrasive chips acted as a scouring medium in their planters, and prevented blockages, which were the curse of the fertiliser-spreading operation.

The "friendly" fertiliser cartel, however, seized upon this mechanism, and went to the authorities with dire stories of how we were putting out a product that was dangerous, and that provided a ready source of raw material for all the terrorists involved in the total onslaught on South Africa. It was all a dark plot by a black state to provide a large source of explosives for terrorists. This twaddle was accepted at its face value, of course, as the Department of Industries was hell bent on the destruction of SCI. The result was that we had a lot of difficulty in selling our ammonium nitrate in the fertiliser market.

It was clear that we needed other outlets. The obvious one was in the explosives industry. Here, South Africa's tightest monopoly had a total hammerlock on the market. It had bought off the other producers of ammonium nitrate, who were banned from offering either explosives or ammonium nitrate for explosives purposes to anyone. The market was regulated by the infamous Chamber of Mines Agreement, which gave, in effect, an evergreen monopoly to African Explosives. This monopoly had established a pricing policy to discourage the use of ammonium nitrate fuel-oil explosives in order to protect its explosives position in dynamite. In effect, this monopoly subsidised its dynamite production by charging wholly extortionate prices for ammonium nitrate.

This, of course, made the sale of ammonium nitrate to the explosives market an extremely lucrative one. The price was at least double that in the fertiliser market. The market was not seasonal, and the customers were well-heeled mining companies, so that credit risks were virtually non-existent. All in all, a good market to be in. We started in a quiet way, by employing a man to go out into the market, and to start selling. The man was Steve Middleton, who played a major role in the eventual destruction of the explosives monopoly. With hindsight, I wonder if we would ever have entered what we now embarked upon if we had known the forces that were arrayed against us.

Steve, Neil and I decided that we would go to the Swazi Iron Ore Mining Company first. Although this was walking into the lions' den, as the company was a wholly owned subsidiary of Anglo, we judged that it would pose a political problem for Anglo to be seen to not support a local industry. It was well known that Anglo's affiliate, AECI, was the ringleader of the companies trying to smash the Swazi industry, but whether Anglo in the circumstances would overtly support this policy in Swaziland was a question which had to be tested – especially as we were offering a much lower price.

Our guess proved right. The mine management acted in accordance with what we thought the political requirements dictated, and we started selling ammonium nitrate to the mine. AECI was not slow to react to this, and swiftly dispatched one of their men to the mine. They told the mine that, while they understood the problem, they had a very simple solution from their point of view. The mine used a special pack of 5-inch dynamite for special applications, and unfortunately, with the loss of the ammonium nitrate business, the price of this would have to be raised enough to compensate for the entire loss of profits on the ammonium nitrate business. We were back to square one.

I therefore decided to look into the possibilities of making dynamite. It was clear that this was not an easy option. The back-up chemical facilities needed, and the scale that these needed to be in order to be competitive, were formidable. The ability to use vast quantities of spent acid in fertiliser manufacture was critical. All in all, dynamite manufacture seemed a very unattractive option, and quite beyond our limited financial resources.

One of the markets for ammonium nitrate was the Palabora Mining Company. This company made its own explosives, using technology from America, called slurry explosives. We had tried many times to sell to them, but they never used us as more than a stick to beat their regular suppliers into shape, so we had abandoned talking to them. It was one of the really good lessons we learned in South Africa. We never asked anyone for a price without fully intending to purchase from them if we got the best deal from them. This attitude on the part of South African buyers is, I believe, one of the main reasons for the deep-rooted, persistent and endemic inflation.

The American technology seemed to offer a possible way out. Neil and I sent Steve off to the USA to see what everyone was doing. Steve visited all the major players, and when he returned, he brought back what had to be the most revolutionary document for the history of the explosives industry in the past 20 years. America was going off dynamite. The reason had nothing to do with the problems that we faced, but was rather due to the increasing problems of safety and health, which were causing enormous awards to be made by juries in the

United States. The American manufacturers were closing down their dynamite plants, and were going for these new water gel technologies.

The ace in the hole as far as I was concerned, however, was that this technology seemed to offer a low cost of entry to the equivalent of the dynamite business. For a mere 2 million dollars, one could get a plant.

I discussed the matter with Neil. We were of the same opinion that, in what we might be about to undertake, it would be of paramount importance for us to have an unimpeachable name to come to the market with. Whilst Hercules were offering technology which looked superficially cheaper, Neil and I decided that Du Pont would be better for our purposes. Du Pont was a household word, even in South Africa. It was one of the most admired companies for its commitment to research and development, and the array of inventions spawned from its labyrinthine labs. We believed that, whether or not the Du Pont technology was better or worse than Hercules, to break the Chamber of Mines monopoly we would need a household name to push our way in. We believed, and still do, that without the advent of an exciting new technology, we would never break up the monopoly with a "me too" product.

The decision was that Du Pont was our first prize, and in October I went to America. In America I met the two men who were to have the most profound influence on me, and the explosives industry, and with whom we were to have one of the happiest and most fruitful collaborations we had ever enjoyed as a company. The first was Ward Kissell, who was the licensing manager, and the other was his boss, Al Luft, who was Director of International Operations, both from Du Pont. Ward gave me the standard Du Pont sales pitch and showed me what their new technology was all about. I was electrified. It was the answer to the cracking of the market. There were problems, however, and these would have to be solved. Ward took me to lunch that first day with Al Luft. I did not want to waste any time if the promise which I saw was going to, at the last minute, be snatched away. Luft knew

Wapenaar and Tony Heugh, the twosome who were responsible for AECI's explosives, very well indeed. It transpired at the lunch that they had visited Du Pont the previous month, but were put off because the cost of the technology seemed out of reach. I was convinced that this was not the case. At the lunch, I told Al Luft what had transpired at my meeting with Mostofi in Iran five years before, whereby, whilst I was in his office, a telex came from ICI to state that any deals he did on investment with NPI would severely prejudice ICI's attitude towards investment in Iran. As Mostofi was trying to interest ICI in Iran, he was forced to drop the investment proposals I had made.

I told Luft that it was inevitable that he would get nasty telexes from AECI and no doubt from ICI as well, with similar threats. I wanted to pursue the relationship I could see developing, but it would all be to no avail if Du Pont were going to react as Mostofi had been forced to do. Al had a simple, straight and direct reply: "Into the wastepaper basket!" As I later came to appreciate, there were not two more direct, straight and honest men in that company. Unfortunately, in the later years, after they had left, the persons who replaced them were not of the same calibre!

I believed Luft. His reply was spontaneous and direct. He *was* spontaneous and direct. He was without guile. I believed at that lunch that I was about to embark upon one of the most exciting journeys in business ever. To me it had now become a race against time to get the technology before AECI realised what was going on. I knew that if they thought someone was about to do the kind of deal I had in mind, they would do what they had done with the Ireco technology. This was the technology being used by Palabora Mining Company. AECI took a licence for the rights outside PMC, paid a minimum of $400,000 a year, and sold nary an ounce of product for years. It would pay them to do the same with this.

The sole gap that existed was that AECI were apparently not too interested, as Du Pont told me that when AECI saw the cost data, they were not interested. Neil Steyn's parting words to me were the following: "I don't care whether they think that their technology is competitive in South Africa. What matters is whether they are price competitive with dynamite in America. If they are, then we must be able to compete with AECI in SA."

The whole problem seemed to revolve around the pixie juice that was the stuff that made Tovex tick – monomethylamine nitrate. This product was made only for explosives, and there was no market for the stuff. Du Pont quoted me a price which, translated into SA terms, meant that the price of the MMAN alone in the product exceeded the selling price of the product. On this basis it was clear that we could never compete. I became very curious about this pixie juice, and, following Neil's theory, came to the conclusion that there was a lot more to this stuff than met the eye.

Over dinner in the evening, Ward gave me the leads I was looking for. He told me not to believe everything that the technical people had to say about MMAN. He took me to an MMAN plant being built for Australia, and he made an appointment for me to see Mr Methylamines himself, an ex-Du Pont man (who isn't?), in New York, who made his living selling amine technology.

Mr Leonard was a revelation. He convinced me that there was a huge amount of myth surrounding MMAN, and that Du Pont wanted to keep it that way. They had had two disastrous explosions with MMAN, and were scared of their own shadows as a result. I proposed to deal with the stuff as we dealt with ammonium nitrate. It seemed to be so analogous and, as it would always be a solution in water, I felt that there was indeed too much mystique about the product.

The problem that I faced was that we needed an 86% solution of the stuff in water. We only had fertiliser-grade acid available to us, and to concentrate this acid would need a very expensive plant. I believed that I could concentrate the pixie juice in a thin film evaporator, as we did with ammonium nitrate. The whole point of a falling film evaporator is that in the case of ammonium nitrate at 100% concentration the liquid never reached its critical diameter and therefore could not detonate. Leonard agreed with me that he could see no good reason why this shouldn't be a safe technology. I left his office convinced that this was now one option open to me.

The other factor that emerged from my meeting with Leonard was that, in the manufacture of these amines, the process produced three amines: namely mono-, di- and tri-methylamine. There was a good and diversified market for the latter two, but for mono the only market was in explosives. Du Pont was the only amines producer which had a balanced market for all three, and most other producers simply had to recycle the mono product through their plant. That meant that anything they could get above the raw material cost for the mono was a plus for them. Thus it should, according to Leonard, have been possible for us in a distant market to actually enjoy a better price for mono product than Du Pont had to pay its own Chemicals Division. This proved to be the case.

From Leonard I went to Washington, where a very old friend from Harvard was now the Chief Financial Officer of the IFC, part of the World Bank Group. He agreed that it would be possible to get IFC finance through the Swazi IDC if the project had the blessing of Du Pont and the IDC.

I returned to SA via Paraguay, where we had a contract to do a study for an ammonium nitrate plant similar to what we had done in Rhodesia. Paraguay was building, with Brazil, on the Parana River, the greatest hydro project the world had ever seen. The power in the first phase was a mind-boggling 12,500 megawatts, ten times the capacity of Kariba North and South combined! Of this, Paraguay was entitled to half! The power consumption in the country was 150 megawatts, so they were looking for power-intensive industries. The fertiliser market could not carry the extent of the bribes required to get the project off the ground, however.

The Government took me on a tour of the project. It was quite stupendous. The river at the Itaipu dam site was 600 metres wide and 200 metres deep. The river flowed at 5 to 6 knots. The diversion canal was the largest open-cast mine in the world at the time, using, I noticed, 100 tons a day of Du Pont dynamite!

Truly a great project.

On the way back from Paraguay, I had to pick up a flight from Rio to Johannesburg. Surprise, surprise. Who should be catching the same plane, but my old friends Wapenaar and Heugh. I carefully ducked meeting them as we boarded the plane, but found that we were the only three passengers in First Class. They were sitting two seats in front of me. As we got airborne, the stewardess brought a Manhattan cocktail to Wapie. I thought it was time to have a little fun, so I said in a very loud voice: "Who on earth starts drinking Manhattans at 8 o'clock in the morning?"

When the seat belt lights went off, I got up and strolled forward, and said in great surprise: "Why, it's Wapie!" Wapie glowered up at me. He was totally smashed out of his mind. I discovered that he and Tony had come directly from a party to the plane, and were both decidedly the worse for wear. Wapie said: "Oliver – fuck you, fuck you, fuck you!!"

I thought Tony would crawl under the seat from embarrassment. This was hardly the language to be expected from an Executive Director of AECI. I thought it was hugely funny. Wapie proceeded to launch forth a torrent of abuse against me, telling me that he would give away explosives to anyone who he thought I would sell to, and that the price of dynamite would be used to compensate for any losses on ammonium nitrate sales. He ended his tirade by telling me that I would not sell one box of explosives – ever!

I asked him what he was doing in Brazil. He told me proudly that they were coming from important meetings in America and Brazil, where AECI and Du Pont shared the market. From the tone of his language, I was led to understand that he was bosom buddies with Du Pont, and that together they would carve up the world. I refrained from mentioning my meetings in Wilmington!

This chance encounter made up my mind. I thought on a remark that Al Luft had made over lunch. We were discussing Wapie, and Al's comment had been: "With enemies like that, you don't need friends!"

In South Africa I went into the costs of making Tovex very thoroughly, with, as ever, the valuable input from Neil – truly a man with insight and craft. To make the product competitively in South Africa, we had to be competitive with AECI's Dynagel. We started with the selling price, deducted all costs, and came up with a cost we had to achieve for MMAN to be in the game.

The only way that it could be done was to radically change the whole approach I had seen at Du Pont. Du Pont shipped mono-methylamine in pressure containers to Australia, and bought expensive concentrated nitric acid to make the MMAN at 86% concentration. I was by now totally convinced that it was possible to concentrate the MMAN, so there was no reason in particular to use anhydrous MMA as a raw material. We found that we could achieve the best shipment economics by far, as long as we shipped it as a 40% solution in water in 1,000 ton lots in a parcel tanker. To make the product then at a competitive price, we would have to make at least 50 tons a day of MMAN. This costing determined the size parameters of the project, for if we did not build a plant to that size, we were admitting from the start that the whole idea was a loser from the word go. This size implied a 25% market share of the dynamite market. We felt that that was not out of reach.

Based on those parameters, I prepared a presentation for Du Pont, and made arrangements to meet them again in November. I was terrified that Wapie would hear of our plans, and I wanted to forestall him at all costs. Back to Wilmington I went, armed with my figures, to show what I thought we could do, given that we achieved a reasonable degree of market penetration. I had a pleasant dinner with Ward Kissell, and bright and early the next morning, I sat down with Paul Egerton-Vernon, our London in-house lawyer. I gave them a three-hour presentation of the market as we saw it, how we planned to tackle it, how we would deal with the Chamber of Mines Contract, and the technical route we proposed to follow of concentrating MMAN, as well as why we thought that it would work, and why the economics were in our favour, in spite of the very low prices we had to compete against. Du Pont had a full technical, marketing and legal team at the meeting, and at the end they spent an hour grilling me on my presentation. We broke for lunch, and after lunch I was expecting to start in again, but Du Pont asked to be excused for a while before resuming. When we resumed, they walked into the room with a document and said: "We have decided to offer you a licence. Here is our proposed agreement, which we would like you to study. Call us when you are ready to discuss it." Well!!

Paul and I went through the document. I thought it was one of the fairest documents I had ever seen. They were asking me for a lousy $150,000 for the package, together with a 4% royalty on sales. Knowing what AECI were paying to IRECO, I couldn't wait to sign before someone changed their minds. We finally had Tovex.

I went back to South Africa in triumph. One of the interesting sidelights was that, before I left for America, I made an appointment to see Dr Taute and Ernie Atkinson at Goldfields. These two gentlemen had expressed strong views to me in the past about the way the monopolies were raping the mining industry. I revealed to them that there was this new explosive and asked them what they thought. Their reaction was immediate: "Tie up the technology!" I didn't tell them that I was leaving almost immediately to do just that, but on my return, some ten days after I had originally spoken to them, I told them that I now had what they had suggested I get. I hoped that they would be as good as their word, and support us in our endeavours to break the Chamber of Mines contract. Shortly thereafter, I had a telex from Al Luft. He had had an angry telex from Wapie saying that someone in SA was claiming to have the Tovex licence. As, according to Wapie, this was not possible, as AECI had an agreement with Du Pont for the licence, Wapie wanted to know what was going on. We asked Al Luft to hold off a reply until we had Board approval in Du Pont. This he did, and then told Wapie that not only had he granted a licence, but the licensee was that *bête noire* – Oliver Hill!

Wapie hit the roof. I had a series of abusive phone calls, *inter alia* ordering me to relinquish any right to the licence. According to Wapie, I had absolutely no right to interfere in the explosive market. He reiterated the threats I had got on the plane from Brazil, and warned me of the wrath of Harry Oppenheimer, God, and a lot of other people.

We were happily riding the crest of the new ammonia wave, and could easily ignore his threats. AECI were already doing their best to smash us anyway, so one new threat more or less made little difference. It was hard to believe, but we were now in the ring with the most powerful explosives monopoly in the world.

MORE BANG

Now that we had the entry to the real explosives market that we sought, we had to plan our strategy for manufacture. We had persuaded the Swazi IDC to lend us the necessary money to build an MMAN plant in Swaziland, so we set about doing just that. At the same time, we tried to convince the Chief Inspector of Explosives that we could safely transport liquid solutions of MMAN from Swaziland to South Africa by road tanker. After an initial favourable reaction, we had an input from AECI to the inspector, which basically said that he was virtually condemning to death any person who might be in the path of this transport. Accordingly, he classified the solution as a ZZ Explosive, the worst category in which it could be put. The US authorities and the International Maritime Organisation had classified the product as a flammable solid, but he was unmoved by this. We consequently faced the problem of having to handle the product in drums, in an explosive vehicle. This was our first setback, brought about by the friendly intervention of AECI.

We then built an explosive lab in Swaziland and started making the explosive for trial purposes by lab production. For political reasons we had to have a site in South Africa, so I set about trying to find an appropriate manufacturing site.

The problem with the manufacture of explosives is that a very large area of land is required by law, as there are required spaces between buildings, magazines, etc, and for the large magazines which are a necessity for a factory you need kilometres of space around the plant. Also, of course, this land is not being used, but is sterile. It was therefore necessary to seek land which was useless, but which could be used for the manufacture of explosives. Industrial land in an area of hundreds of hectares was simply not on, in our budget.

The obvious answer was in land owned by a mining company with a mining title. You did not need land with industrial rights as you could, on mining property, conduct manufacturing operations directly concerned with mining. We certainly qualified for that! The more messed-up the land was, the better it would suit our purpose.

As we had had encouragement from Goldfields, I approached them first. They had tens of thousands of hectares on the West Rand, mostly condemned, as they had de-watered the dolomitic compartments and this land was basically unusable, except for the likes of us. I found a beautiful site at East Driefontein, and we were in the process of finalising the arrangements, when the word came from above: "Goldfields is not in the business of providing manufacturing sites for explosive manufacturers." The long hand of Anglo was at work.

I then found a beautiful manufacturing site on Durban Roodepoort Deep, ironically a mine on which I had lived for some years when my father was the mine manager there. I approached Rand Mines, who, at the time, were enthusiastically supporting the idea of some competition, and they agreed that we could lease a beautiful mine dump from them. Once again, just before signature of the contract, a similar word came down from above.

Thus thwarted, I tried a third time. Rand Leases, next door to Durban Deep, was a defunct mine but with an intact mining title, and the land, being proclaimed, could be used for little else. The company was surviving by renting out its mine offices and sundry bits of land. This time I presented my case to Clive Menell first. There was no point in dealing with the mine if AngloVaal were going to buckle under the power of Anglo. I put to him essentially the same point I had made to Al Luft: "If AngloVaal are going to kow-tow to Anglo, let's stop now." Well, in the end, the first plant was indeed erected on the Rand Leases site.

Whilst this was going on, we were negotiating with Rand Mines to get the bulk supply contract at their joint venture mine with Shell. The management were young and enthusiastic and visited a Du Pont bulk site in America, coming back convinced that this was the way for them to go. They wrote the toughest bulk supply contract I have ever seen, giving themselves a service that existed nowhere else in the world, and at an unbeatable price. We, in order to meet the deadline, were forced to build a pump truck to meet our agreed dates, as AECI clearly had plenty of pump trucks available and this was not of concern to them. Being totally green in the matter, we built the truck strictly according to the Du Pont of Canada designs. It cost us a fortune we could ill afford, but we had to do it. The day before the signing of the contract, I had a call from the mine manager designate. AECI had gone to Shell, their mining partner, who had guaranteed Rand Mines a fixed profit on the mine. Shell was AECI's supplier of fuels and oils. Shell was bluntly told that AECI wanted the explosives contract on the mine, and Shell were to see that they got it. The mine manager had had a call from Shell, who told him that an AECI man was arriving that day with a contract which he would sign as is. This contract was hardly at the price or the service terms he had negotiated with us, but that was that.

Breaking into the market was not easy.

We now had to design and lay out our factory at the Rand Leases site. Polly (Mr Cruywagen, the Chief Inspector of Explosives) and Herman (Mr van Dijk, the deputy) were not enamoured with our plans. They claimed that in the USA you could just buy dynamite over the counter, and America had a totally irresponsible attitude towards explosives manufacture. Polly's attitude was that if he classified everything as a ZZ explosive and said no to everything, then he could never be blamed if there was an accident. Our Du Pont designs for the plants were rejected out of hand, and all the savings in manufacturing costs this implied were cast on the scrap heap. We struggled to find an acceptable way of getting the benefit of the low inherent labour cost designs of the Americans, without offending Polly and Herman, who regarded everything we did as being potentially lethal. (It must be remembered that they did have access to the largest manufacturer of dynamite in the world who gladly provided input to them when they were unsure of a problem. That input was, however, hardly disinterested.) We battled along with these bureaucrats, and finally arrived at some kind of a dog's breakfast of a plant which made everyone happy (except us!), and we built it.

The problem, of course, was the lack of finance.

Making the explosive itself was relatively easy. The plant was reasonably inexpensive, but the main problem was in the packaging. The machine we had set our hearts on was a thing called a Kartridge Pak machine. This machine made plastic sausages out of film and polythene beads, and clipped the sausages with clips that the machine made from coils of wire. Du Pont estimated each machine would cost, with modifications and installation, $250,000. This was far beyond our reach. We therefore had to start life with a thing called a Universal machine, which was very cheap, but was a horror story. It had a bar sealer on the sausages, and used pre-formed clips. The cost of the clips alone was 25% of the selling price of a box of 25mm product! We did not have a business at all using a Universal machine. The only reason for having it was to produce sufficient product to test in the market. No-one would even look at us if we didn't have a factory. We had to show them we actually had a fully-fledged factory producing explosive, and then they might test the product. (This was the only thing they were allowed to do, in terms of the Chamber of Mines contract).

In Swaziland we built the MMAN plant. In spite of all the hysterics, I had been to the Potomac River Works to put forward my ideas. I considered, from all the available data on the product, that it was not at all dissimilar from ammonium nitrate when it was in solution. The fact that we would only be dealing with solutions and never with solids was a bonus factor. Also, once the technology was changed to allow the use of 73% liquor instead of 86%, it was clear, to me at least, that this material could be handled and dealt with very much as 99% ammonium nitrate liquor. All this sounds trite now, as this has been the procedure for some 35 years, but at that time we were very much on our own, and were doing it entirely at our own risk. That plant cost R2,500,000. Today, we could build such a plant for less than R1,000,000. I suppose the only saving grace of the whole affair was that in the aftermath of the liquidation we got to sell our half of it for well over a million rand to AECI!

Apart from the fact that MMAN appeared to act as a universal solvent for all aluminium alloys, the plant ran like a dream, and vastly exceeded its design capacity. When they bought it, AECI at least got a beautiful plant which ran like a Swiss watch. We now had an MMAN plant, we had built an MMA terminal in Maputo, and we had a site and a small explosives plant at Rand Leases which was functional and able to produce the product for trials. We now had to get members of the South African mining industry to ask to test the product. This was to be the beginning of our five-year struggle with the Chamber of Mines to get the explosives market opened up.

TOVEX

Explosives were sold to the mining industry in terms of the infamous Chamber of Mines contract. This was an evergreen contract which could only be cancelled once every 10 years on 10 years' notice. Anyone who acceded to the contract to get the benefit of the contract price was bound in, in the same way, for 20 years. Thus, theoretically, it was utterly impossible to break in. There was one small loophole: the Chamber could test other explosives. That was one thing that the Du Pont explosive gave us. We were something new which could be tested. AECI could, however, observe the tests and then offer a "technically equivalent explosive". Just what the hell this was, no-one knew. AECI claimed their SINEX was technically equivalent. At least the Chamber reluctantly agreed that, if there were mines that wanted to, they could test the explosive.

I went first to Syd Newman. He was not only an old family friend, but an old fishing companion from Mozambique days. Syd agreed that Western Platinum would test TOVEX. The problem was, he wanted it at the price of ANFO. He wouldn't listen when I kept saying that our price was competitive with dynagel and couldn't be compared to ANFO. Anyway, he let it go. He made his own ANFO at the mine by buying prills from AECI and mixing them with diesel oil. He told me that, as soon as his request for trials took place, he got sent the floor sweepings from AECI. Thank God for someone with guts. He phoned AECI and blew them out of the water. They were buggering around an important strategic mine, earning valuable foreign exchange, and if he closed down, he was going straight to the Minister of Mines and the Minister of Finance and get AECI's balls into a wringer.

The result was that we got our Western Platinum trial under way. If it hadn't been for Syd, we never would have got going. No-one else in the industry would dare to get tough with AECI. They were all too shit-scared of what Harry might do, so it was vital that someone should be seen to do trials and not suffer retaliation from AECI. That was the importance of Western Plats.

I also got Lucas Pourolis to try it. He didn't belong to the Chamber and was independent. And once again, the AECI blackmail approach met a man who wouldn't take their shit. They did promise to cut off his accessories, though.

That was the battle on the one front. We had to get people to try our explosives. We needed to actually find out what we had and how it worked. We needed a number of guinea pigs who would be sold on the product. It was to be the same old story as DAP: get the product in the market. Another front was to be the legal battle. We actually had to find a way to break into the market in the face of the Chamber of Mines contract.

Yet another battle was the fight on the marketing/PR front. We had to achieve success on all of these fronts to break the monopoly. We needed the ozone of publicity. I never expected to achieve penetration of more than 5% of the market, to start, but I needed that small number of people to read my message and to be willing to try something new. I needed people who would take attacks on me as a sign that I must have something good. After all, if the product was rubbish, it would not survive. We had to be noticed. If we could get the monopoly to attack us, that reaction would in the end be the best endorsement of the product we could get.

Sometimes you have to be very devious. Al Luft told me that in America, Atlas Powder Company had run an advertisement called

"We're not going to the funeral", which had a picture of a Western town (actually the OK Corral) with a funeral procession going to Boothill Cemetery. There was a sign saying "BOOTHILL". When I saw this, I knew that William and Wapie would love to run an ad which, in effect, said: "Boot Hill into the Cemetery". Somehow we had to get them to react to us. We started dishing out licence holders saying: "DYNAMITE IS DEAD". We made bumper stickers with: "DYNAMITE IS DEAD". All our efforts were directed to getting AECI to respond. And, being them, inevitably they did. They ran the Atlas Powder ad in the *Financial Mail*. And it achieved the reaction I was looking for. I had a call from Max Borkum, one of the doyennes of the Johannesburg Stock Exchange. Max said to me: "If AECI have to start running ads in the *Financial Mail* against you, then I know they are in trouble." He asked to visit our plant, which he did, with Henry Hare. When they saw the tiny little plant I told them that, with the additional packaging machines, I could supply 20% of the market, and Max said: "Now I know that AECI is in serious trouble." He was, of course, absolutely right. AECI had momentum, though, and fought a rearguard action which took a hell of a time to break. If you look at the pale shadow of its former self AECI is now, it all started back there. It was all because technology had made their whole method of manufacture obsolete.

We were, anyway, pleased with our promising start. We had a violent and vicious campaign against us, and, of course, most of the people at whom it was directed responded in the intended way. Enough people, though, noticed the fundamental point that Max Borkum had picked up: we had something that was a serious threat to AECI, and, of course, we were a cheeky lot who said what we thought. I won't say that any publicity is good publicity, but AECI fell for attacking our product and our motivations and anything they could think of. Most of it was, in the end, exactly what we needed. We were noticed and everyone in the mining industry had heard of us. We even managed to get into "The Villagers", a local soap about a mining community, which was *de rigeur* for the whole mining community to watch.

You had to be cheeky. When we had the ELECTRA MINING EXHIBITION, we chose the site opposite AECI. I got in Peter McColl, our brilliant interior designer. I told him that we had to have a stand which would make us look slick and modern and new. With it. With advanced technology. We wanted AECI to look the way they actually were – living in the past. Well, it was really very amusing. The show opened on a Monday. On the Sunday, Dave Mather of AECI visited the show. AECI had a tent with a small picket fence and poles with little flags. Next to our slick modern creation, it had exactly the impact we had wanted. They had a major panic and turned out the whole Modderfontein maintenance department to build a wooden structure around their tent. It looked even more of a dog's breakfast. They were promoting their water gel – Sinex. This was what we had wanted and hoped for. It was a very unfortunate move on their part.

In England, Vicks made a product called Sinex. It was a nasal spray to clear your sinuses. I assumed that AECI would be promoting Sinex at the show. So we bought a couple of cases of VICKS Sinex. We dished them out to all engineers who asked us what the difference was between Sinex and Tovex. We told them: "If you really want to blow up rocks – use Tovex. If all you want to do is blow the snot out of your nose – well, we have a product for that as well." We also issued T-shirts with "TOVEX" on the front and "THE BEST BANG IN TOWN" on the back. They went like hot cakes. We were succeeding in getting what we wanted. We were getting AECI to sweat, and it was that fact, more than anything else, which meant that some people started to take us seriously.

When I was at Harvard, one of the things I studied in-depth was Business History. I was particularly fascinated by the Robber Baron era, and the techniques which were used to establish and perpetuate the great trusts of the nineteenth century. In particular, the Rockefellers and the Standard Oil Trust. The irony was that, a hundred years later, AECI used the same tactics, and they thought that they were so clever for innovating them!

We were, after all, up against the power of the Anglo-American Corporation. Whilst AECI was mostly using every means they had to block us, Anglo really never got involved much. They didn't have to. This is why the debate in South Africa is so sterile. Monopolies are OK if they don't abuse their power. I have never understood the difference between the use and misuse of power. I think the average person's concept is that the "abuse of power" is, in some way, hitting you on the head with a club! Power exists to be used, and it is. The greater the power, the less overt its use has to be. It's the old story of the gorilla in the restaurant. When massive power exists, most people do what they perceive the top of the pile – in this one, Harry Oppenheimer – would want. It may or may not be what he would want, but no-one is going to blight their career by doing something that he perceives will be against the wishes of HFO. Of course, when one small branch of the Empire is screaming blue murder about how "Harry wouldn't like it", it has a salutary effect on all concerned.

We had to start a campaign on the merits of what we were offering. The South African mining industry used to put out a huge propaganda campaign about its concern over safety and health. The big reason Du Pont had gone out of dynamite was safety. If anyone was killed or injured in a dynamite accident, it affected the consumer sales of Du Pont products, and if Du Pont dynamite was involved, it was fair game for American lawyers. So the game wasn't worth the risk.

The South African industry had 250 people killed or maimed, on average, every year in explosive accidents. We thought this would be a pretty fair starting point. We got Tommy Gibbs, the ex-Government Mining Engineer, to do a report on health and safety of our explosive. He was very enthusiastic, and came up with a number of suggestions which he said he would have proposed if he had been GME. Due to the safety record of our explosive, he suggested that all explosives could be taken underground on a Sunday, because he would have allowed a mine to store a week's explosives underground as compared to a day's! This meant that shaft time during the week would be fully available for productive purposes. Also, he would have allowed, because of the fine characteristics of Tovex, re-entry into the detonated area to be cut from two hours to half an hour, or less. He made the point that it was an open secret in the industry that re-entry times were totally ignored anyway, and that miners on high-speed development were retired after five years due to total destruction of their health, because they ignored re-entry times.

So health and safety were big selling points. The whole point about water gels was that, in making them, you were coming from the side where your whole technology was geared to trying to get them to explode at all, whereas with nitro-glycerine explosives the whole problem was to control its tendency to detonate. Tovex was very safe, and dynamite was very touchy stuff. From a health point of view, there were two aspects. The first was the fume characteristics. Dynamite, apart from nitro-glycerine fumes, gave off loads of carbon monoxide, but worse, high values of oxides of nitrogen. These, of course, turned into nitric acid in the lungs. Tovex fume levels were less than 10% of those of dynamite, and this was the primary reason Tommy Gibbs wanted re-entry periods relaxed. For me, though, the big factor was the nitro-glycerine headache. Anyone who has ever had a nitro-glycerine headache knows what I mean. I felt like hell for three days after being in a badly ventilated development end with nitro-glycerine fumes. When people are expected to work in an environment like that, their productivity has to be abysmal. That was the actual point. Safety and health were worth money, but were very difficult to actually quantify. Anyway, to me it was pretty clear that, if the mining industry was serious about health and safety, this would be our major platform.

Of course, as it turned out, nothing could have been further from the truth. The utter hypocrisy of the industry took one's breath away. That, in the end, is the greatest criticism I have, not only of the mining industry, but the whole of South African white society. No-one really gave a damn about the health and safety of the workers. At the top level of the mining houses, the attitude was that it was only Afrikaners and Kaffirs who got headaches, and that was a bloody good thing for them. When talking about cutting the death rate, one mine manager actually said to Steve: "The more of these black bastards that die, the better off we whites will be." These were the people who thought the Nats were "beastly to Kaffirs!".

Even my father, who really took the whole issue of safety and health very seriously, thought I was going too far. He had never thought that headaches were a problem. But one day, playing golf at ERPM, he asked the mine manager whether headaches were a problem. When the mine manager phoned him and told him that the mine issued 100,000 aspirin tablets a month, he got quite a shock and started to take it very seriously.

It's actually no good ducking the issue. The difference between the public posture and the real feelings could not have been more different. The campaign for health and safety went down like a lead balloon, but anyway, I had one or two connections. One of mine was a fishing fanatic friend, Dr Nick Strydom. Nick had actually got me to quit smoking by giving me the most graphic description of what went on in your lungs and bronchial tubes when one smoked. He worked for the Human Sciences Research Lab of the Chamber of Mines – ironically one of the things my father had been instrumental in getting off the ground.

I went to see Nick with the data I had at my disposal. Nick's office had a shiny sign up: "SMOKE-FREE ZONE" – quite something in those days. Anyway, I showed him all the fume data, and he waxed ecstatic. He had two MSc students who had just finished his big project, and they were short of good projects to work on. He told me that his researches into pneumoconiosis indicated that the effect of oxides of nitrogen accelerated the onset of the disease, and may even have been the major factor, rather than dust, in causing it, because of the dust-suppression legislation (for which my grandfather had been instrumental in setting up, and for which he had also been knighted). Nick thought that it was important to ascertain the effect of oxides of nitrogen. He had mountains of statistics which would enable them, for starters, to come up with statistical correlations. He would also start in on the physiology of fumes and their effects on miners' health.

The other thing which I brought Nick was the information about the effects of nitro-glycerine. In a small town in Sweden where the sole employer was a dynamite factory, deaths from heart disease were extraordinarily high. The reason, of course, is that nitro-glycerine is a powerful vasco-dilator, and people who are exposed to it on a daily basis develop an ability to suppress the dilatory effects of it, so that their bodies act to reverse it. When the nitro-glycerine is withdrawn, the same contraction of their blood vessels leads to heart attacks. It was pretty clear to us that long-term exposure to dynamite had severe implications for heart disease. There was also a more ribald side to it. It would clearly have a hell of a weekend effect on miners trying to get it up!

Anyway, we had a first-class serious research programme, initiated by someone who could really give some cold scientific answers to what, to me, was a pretty logically assessed health hazard. About a month later I phoned Nick to find out how he was going. He ducked the whole question and suggested I drop in for a quiet drink. He told me that Salomon, the head of the Chamber of Mines Research Organisation, had called him in and asked him, point blank, whether he was carrying out any research which investigated any relationship between dynamite and miners' health. When he replied that he most definitely was, and that it was a very fruitful field, he told me that Salomon told him that on pain of instant dismissal if he disobeyed, the Chamber of Mines would not be investigating anything to do with dynamite and miners' health. Salomon was not going to do anything which would offend (in his mind) the Anglo-American Corporation. Nick had been warned to toe the line – or else. Nick told me that, regretfully, he could do nothing.

It was this all-pervasive power of Anglo that got to us. Actually, I don't believe that Anglo lifted a finger to do anything to us. They actually didn't have to, but didn't, of course, stop AECI threatening all and sundry with the wrath of Anglo. Keith Douglas, the head of Northern Lime Company, was really keen on trying our product, and on getting rid of the explosives monopoly. As he told us years later, on safer reflection, 50% of their sales went to Anglo. The Board couldn't let him rock the boat.

There was one small chink in the armour. There was no way that anyone in public was going to stand up and say that, because of Anglo, our explosive would never be used. We would be undermined and screwed behind the scenes, but a totally brutal flattening was not what was in the mind of Anglo. Anglo knew what we were up against and they didn't have to soil their hands. There were even people in Anglo who thought we had a case. So, whilst there was no substitute for making an attack on the Chamber of Mines contract in terms of the pathetic cartel trust legislation which existed, we had to use the opening given to us to get our explosive tested.

We had succeeded with Syd Newman in Western Platinum, and found someone who not only would not take the flak that AECI gave him, but threatened to sue them. We managed, as a result, to persuade Durban Deep, West Rand Consolidated, President Steyn (!!), apart from Western Plats, to do "Chamber of Mines" trials. The urgent problem, apart from just getting the right to do trials, was actually to make the technology work in South African conditions. If we fell flat on our noses, then AECI would really be laughing all the way to the bank. And even just to get started on trials, we had to build a plant costing millions! Truly, no sane investment company would have invested in view of the legal fortifications AECI had constructed around its market. It was an insane investment decision, but you get sucked into these things a little bit at a time. In the end, it cost a fortune, but each step was not too bad, and I had devised some crafty financing techniques, which meant we were able to do a lot of the Capital Expenditure almost for free.

Due to the fact that the whole entry to the business was really costing money in Swaziland and South Africa, we were building up gigantic tax losses in both countries. These losses might one day be worth something to us, but we turned them effectively into cash. Our profits were all made effectively in tax havens (from ammonia) and everything else lost money. What I devised was the old concept of adding soft cost onto our capital plant. We would invoice from an operating company for engineering services to our construction company. This, of course, would reduce the tax loss in that company, but we weren't concerned about that, as it did not result at that point in having to pay tax. The construction company would then invoice out at four or five times the hard cost for explosives plant. We would then package up the plant for sale as a leveraged lease. The lease would be done over, say, seven years, and all the interest would be capitalised front end on the lease. We could then claim investment allowance of 30%, initial allowance of 25% and wear and tear of 25%, all in the first year! We sold the package typically through an avaricious bank like Rand Merchant Bank, to a consortium of investors, and with the right package we paid for the equipment and had some cash over.

This happy game was played throughout the late seventies and early eighties. Unfortunately, some other people went even further than us, and eventually it was stopped. I did, however, manage to finance most of Natex by this means.

Now we started trying our explosive out. Fortunately, we had South Roodepoort (Lucas Pourolis), who was furious with AECI as they had tried to blackmail him over accessories when he started buying from us. If blackmail works, that's fine, but when it backfires on you, you have a mega problem for a long, long time. And so was it there.

Fortunately, in Steve Middleton we had the best hands-on explosives engineer in the country. Du Pont suggested we try their simpler product, Tovex 100, first. They claimed it was the workhorse in America.

Mining in South Africa is unique in the number of operations which stope at about a 1 to 1/1.2 metre stoping width. The geometry is tight, and the rock is hard. The condition ranges from the hard competent norite at Western Plats to the fractured quartzites at great depth in Durban Deep. Tovex was a high-velocity product which got its efficaciousness from its high brisance (compared to dynagel). Where dynagel had a velocity of about 2300m/sec, we were looking at more like 4000m/sec. But in tight geometry, you needed more heave and not necessarily such high brissance.

Also, when you went underground and supervised operations closely, you got results. You have to drill typically about 100/120 holes 1.2 metres deep at an angle of 70° spread at 30cm in a stope panel. With careful supervision, the holes are all parallel at the correct spacing, but if the holes deviate, when you get to the bottom of the hole the burden can easily vary from 10cm to 50cm instead of 30. If 10, then there tends to be a waste of explosive; but if 50, you need a big reserve of power to pull to the full 1.2 metre depth.

Well, we went up to Tovex 200, which contained 2% of fuel-grade aluminium. The extra heave this gave us meant that Steve was able to get the same results as Dynagel when he supervised; but when he pulled out, results became variable. We had to go up to the then top-of-the-line Tovex 220 to get the right results in actual unsupervised mining conditions. These were the practical problems we found. We had all kinds of problems which we found out the hard way.

All other things being equal, the lower the density of the explosive, the more sensitive it was. Under confined conditions, the velocity of the shock wave in air could exceed that in the explosive. This shock move could desensitise the explosive ahead of the detonating front, and cause it to fizzle. The problem was that it went off, but didn't pull properly. We had tried, to keep our costs down, to increase the density of Tovex 200, so as to get more in the hole. Without realising it, though, we were getting transient pressure desensitisation. This was difficult to detect because the explosive had actually gone off, but failed to pull. On a much more practical level, we had one really pissed-off miner, because he was paid on fathoms broken. When you had explosive which was wrong, it was a hell of a thing to make a new batch and get it out to the mine and replace the stuff that wasn't working. Transport permits were always a problem, and we had, until we had a continuous transport permit, the problem of getting a permit every time we wanted to move trial quantities. Truly, everything was rigged against us in trying to find out what worked, before our official trials started.

I must say the thing that really, in the end, sold me on our product was a visit to West Rand Consolidated. I asked Steve to show me how the trials were going, so we went out to the mine. When I arrived, the Underground Manager was just emerging. When Steve introduced me, he said: "Come, I'm taking you underground." When we reached the level where they were stoping, he said to me: "Smell the Tovex atmosphere!" It was a beautiful fresh environment, and, speaking to the miners and machine boys, they were all ecstatic about Tovex. No-one had any headaches. The stopes were all poorly ventilated back stopes, the same as I had suffered in, in South Roodepoort. The big difference was that they were fresh-smelling, with no NG fumes.

The face was white spotted. No sockets. The Underground Manager told me that they couldn't thank us enough for the environment we had created. On surface, he showed me the absenteeism graphs. As soon as Tovex appeared in the stope, 2½% more people were at work. He told me the productivity had risen sharply. His estimate was that we had cut their overall mining cost by 10%. As the cost of the explosive was only 1% of his operating cost, he claimed he was enjoying free explosives, and didn't care what he paid. This was a big emotional boost to me, because the fight was starting to get me down. Sometimes, when you see the odds against you, you just wonder if you will ever fight your way out. You need some boost to your spirits. One got precious little from one's partners. I tried to get Max Hahn to work on the whole health thing. After all, he was supposed to be a doctor. He felt that he was much too grand, as a shareholder, to soil his hands and get down to some honest work. John had decided that he should join the company and I didn't really see that I could object. But he was pretty useless to us, especially as he could have brought professionalism to bear on the health fight.

Another revealing incident was at Western Plats. Steve was out there doing figures with the mine management on the consumption of explosives compared with Dynagel. The mine manager claimed they used twice as much Tovex as Dynagel for the same advance. Steve didn't believe it and went underground. Scouting around, he found a disused end. In it were 250 boxes of Tovex. When he challenged the miner, the miner told him that he knew that when the trial was over he would have to go back to Dynagel, and he was just building up a little personal supply to keep himself on Tovex as long as possible!

At Harmony, they put half a shaft on Tovex for a month, and then the other half. When they switched them over, the half that had been on Tovex stole the Tovex allotted to the other half, and there was a major fight underground. The miners were voting the only way they knew. It was clear that we had a winning product. When, many years later, I met Peter Clinch of ICI, and went into his office, he held up his hands in mock surrender, and said: "The war's over. Dynamite is dead!" But, of course, he was Australian and not full of the arrogance of the ICI clan.

It took 15 years. The cost of this to the mining industry in South Africa has been in the billions of rands. The great all-powerful monopoly that was AECI is a pathetic shadow of the colossus that bestrode the South African chemical industry 20 years ago. I told them that, in the end, they might destroy me and force me out, but the fire I had lit would then have the result that they were up against SASOL. This is exactly what happened, with the visible results that we see today.

Despite all that we were up against, we started getting some dedicated followers. The biggest psychological impact came in Lesotho. We had taken on another ex-AECI explosives engineer in the form of Peter Malpage. Peter was well connected (especially within Anglo) and he told me he could get De Beers. This was a startling proposition. De Beers was the actual owner of half of AECI until it was put into AMIC. I didn't believe him for one minute. But I let him try. Peter went to De Beers Lesotho. This was a mine high up in the Maluti Mountains. The only access, apart from air, was up the Moteng Pass, one of the hairiest roads in Africa. Dynamite freezes at about -2 deg C. The mine management was concerned about the transport of explosives up this route in a frozen condition, and considered that an accident was inevitable sooner or later. They wanted to use a water gel. Water gels get less sensitive as the temperature goes down, in contrast to dynamite. It is possible to make special low-temperature dynamite using glycol instead of glycerine, but that is a special – not done in SA. So the Letsing mine had a problem.

AECI was supplying a Sinex slurry which was sensitised with paint-grade aluminium. It suffered all the problems of water gels. At the low temperatures of Letsing, in confinement, it often deflagrated. Anyway, Peter went up there and kept saying he would get a trial at Letsing. Eventually, I had a telex from Keith Whitelock, the manager, while Peter was up there. The gist was that he was willing to do a trial, but he wanted to know who would pay if it was a failure. I replied that I would answer that when he told me what the response would be if it were a success, because I frankly doubted that we would get any business as a result of a success. I got a very sharp telex back saying that was a slur on his integrity. He suggested that I go up to Letsing and discuss it, if we were interested; so up I went.

Whitelock was absolutely straight up and down. He told me that the Lesotho Government held 25% of the shares in the company. They had wanted De Beers to buy everything locally for the mine. De Beers had refused and said that they would buy competitively; and only if the local suppliers were competitive would they buy locally. How could De Beers then insist on competitive purchasing but buy in-house from themselves? He made it clear. He had major safety concerns and wanted to go over to a water gel. Sinex was a failure mostly, though, and caused major blockage problems in his crushers because of the poor fragmentation. The last blast had flung silver cowpats of Sinex all over the pit, and stuffed up the blast. It had to be re-drilled, and, because it was fractured, fragmentation was very poor. If we would pay for a stuff-up, he would give us business if we were a success.

Well, we bust our guts. Letsing used a 3-inch product which we could hand pack in lay-flat tubing and we didn't have to use the Universal packers. Our first trial using Tovex 800 was a dream. We got a beautiful order, and we decided to supply it in a special sexy red plastic. This was a disaster. We had a terrible time, as the red plastic split in transport and we got a gory mess at the mine end. To keep the mine going, we had to send staff up there to re-package, and, because of the purchasing pipeline length, we could not readily stop with the red film. It seemed that, by dyeing it, we weakened the plastic. After a few weeks of hysterical trauma, we sorted out the problem.

The mine was very patient. Actually, the point was that it was obvious to them that we were busting our guts to sort out the problem. They were used to total indifference from AECI, who hated drag-arsing up into the mountains, and took weeks to respond to any complaints. They were patient because we were trying to solve the problem, and acknowledging that we had one! This was a real turn up for them. It did not happen in the explosives industry.

Finally, De Beers Lesotho became the first mine in Southern Africa to go 100% on Tovex. Many things flowed from that. I heard the inside story many moons later from Keith Whitelock. Apparently, JOT (Julian Ogilvie Thompson of Anglo) asked the question of

AECI at an AECI Board meeting why, if Sinex was just as good as Tovex, which was what Wapie and Tony had told the AECI Board when the whole thing started, it was that they couldn't get into De Beers Lesotho? The response was that the manager was a difficult sod and might have some reasons of his own for buying from us, ie maybe there was some corruption involved. Well, that did it. JOT didn't get where he was by letting this kind of thing slip.

The chief consulting engineer of De Beers was ordered to do a full investigation into why the mine used Tovex instead of Sinex. The implications were pretty clear. The most detailed report ever done on the comparison of one explosive against another was carried out. I got a clandestine copy myself, but had to promise never to publicise it. (It didn't come from Keith Whitelock, although he was so straight in his dealings, I think he probably would have given me one.)

If we could have used it, it would have been the best testimonial ever. The mine output had risen by 25% against virtually no increase in cost because of the excellent fragmentation. The powder factor was far superior to anything that AECI could produce, and because of the density and filling of the hole, drill patterns could be expanded, with a concomitant decrease in drilling costs as well as improved breakage. The greatly reduced fly rock meant all the equipment could be left in the pit during blasting, which saved a phenomenal amount of time during the mucking-out cycle. The shelf life of the explosive was far superior to AECI's product, which had a shelf life of little better than 28 days. As the delivery cycle from factory could easily reach 28 days, this was a major factor.

The report was dazzling. Keith Whitelock was sent for by JOT himself. He arrived to find Wapie and Tony in the office with JOT. He was expecting to get shat on from a dizzy height, but found himself on the receiving end of an abject apology from Wapie and Tony in front of JOT for the insinuation that he was not using Sinex because he was taking a back-hander from us.

When I tried later to sell to De Beers Botswana, when Keith Whitelock moved there as a manager, he told me that I would have to give that one a miss. JOT had said to him it was pretty difficult to get someone to go up into the mountains of Lesotho, but not so difficult in Botswana, so his freedom of action was more constrained. All this goes to show that, at the top of Anglo, if the facts were made known truthfully, the reaction was logical and did not reflect the general amount of hysteria lower down. Wapie retired early and Tony was never made an executive director of the company – the first time ever that the head of explosives was treated thus.

In spite of our increasing technical success, though, we still had the insurmountable obstacle of the Chamber of Mines contract. I had been struggling with the Board of Trade, but finally a new Competition Act came into being, and I started to work on the whole concept of free competition in the Explosives Industry.

The whole problem in South Africa was and is a total lack of understanding of and belief in a free market system. South African law even today is based on a faulty philosophy. That philosophy is that a monopoly *per se* is not wrong, it is only the abuse of it. This, of course, flies in the face of all world experience, especially in the USA, but, in the usual South African xenophobic fashion, they thought they knew better. We had a much more difficult task, because we were up against people who inherently didn't understand the moral corruption of monopolies and the stultifying effect on an economy that they have. I was at a cocktail party talking to a certain Kuschke, who was head of the IDC. I mentioned to him that the South African mining industry was exceptionally backward. He absolutely bristled and said we had the most advanced deep land mining industry in the world – we mined more rock from greater depths than all the rest of the world put together. I pointed out that I was well aware of our technical skills, as my father and grandfather had both been among the foremost mining engineers of the country and I was well aware of the technical achievements.

When it came to the technology of production, though, we were woefully behind the world.

This was the problem in South Africa. The attitude was: "We know it all. If it hasn't been invented here, it may as well not have been invented." It took the industry 25 years to adopt tungsten carbide universally. When my father had been mine manager of Durban Deep, he decided to try tungsten carbide. After a very careful scientific trial, he put the whole mine on tungsten carbide. His report was widely circulated within the Rand Mines group. It took 10 years for the whole Rand Mines group to go onto tungsten carbide. Explosives were to be no different. Peter Harris, one of the consulting engineers at Gencor, who was personally sympathetic and supportive, told me, a week before the final publication of the Competition Board enquiry into the explosives industry, that I was crazy to think that the Chamber of Mines contract would be set aside. The Chamber had unanimously given evidence to the Board that the contract and the explosives monopoly was in the best interests of the mining industry. When I asked him if he and Gencor really believed it, his answer was: "No, but we belong to a club. The club wants to keep the monopoly, and we, as good club members, must go along with them. It is quite impossible that the Competition Board can rule against a contract that both parties want."

That, then, was what we were up against. Everyone was terrified of Anglo and no-one was going to buck the perceived interest of Anglo. In a small way, we were a microcosm of all that is completely rotten about South African industry, and why, in the brave new world it faces, South Africa is found wanting as one of the least productive industrial states on the planet. I actually believe in the ingenuity and ability of South Africans and have never subscribed to the philosophy which is inherent in the structure, which is that South Africans need protection from competition. The managements that rise in the companies may need protection, but the real guys in the front line don't. The problem is that the capable people aren't the people running the show, because, when you set up an oligarchic structure, politicians rise to lead companies, not industrialists. Even Anglo came to this realisation eventually and its industrial successes are run by really capable industrial people – not political chocolate farmers.

As things were, though, we had to embark upon a long battle with the Competition Board. Sometimes you have to get a lucky break, and for once we did. The whole Board was new, so the front-line soldiers had to be found from somewhere. If we had got the old guard from the Board of Trade, we would have been doomed. They were creatures of the Department of Industries, who saw themselves as bastions against the "total onslaught" on South Africa. This belief, of course, was assiduously fostered by South Africans, particularly the likes of Francis Le Riche of Sentrachem, who turned protection of the chemical industry into an art form of its own. They were even worse than AECI, perhaps because they had even more dubiously viable chemical manufacturing projects.

We got Bert Pienaar as the man assigned to do all the legwork on our case. He didn't have a job because he was an economic attaché working for the Department of Foreign Affairs and was between assignments. The great advantage for us was that he was uncontaminated by the Department of Industries, and had spent his life in the big real world outside South Africa. The result was that he brought a relatively unbiased view to his task.

To me, the issue was one of crystal clarity. It was about a free market. It was that free competition would result in lower mining costs. My view, summarised in a nutshell, was put to the Board when it asked me the question: "What will happen to the price of explosives in a free market?"

The answer I gave was that I expected the *price* of some explosives to fall (such as ANFO) and the price of some to rise (such as dynamite and water gels). I expected that the costs of *mining* would decline across the board, though, as explosives were sold as a tool for breaking rock, and that competition would bring about a drive to lower mining costs as a selling tool, rather than just discounting explosives, although the lower the technology, such as with ANFO, the more price would come into play.

I gave two concrete examples. One was ISCOR Thabazimbi, where, because of the nature of the geology, it had to be drilled and could not be jet-pierced. The cost of drilling exceeded by a very wide margin the cost of explosives in the hole. To reduce the overall cost, you could increase the power of the explosive in the hole and thus open the drilling pattern and drill fewer holes. Although the more powerful explosive was more expensive, the overall cost could be dropped. The second was West Rand Cons, where, by the effective use of a non-nitro-glycerine explosive, productivity had soared and brought about a big cut in mining costs overall. For me, this was the issue. I contended that Harry Oppenheimer had more to gain as a miner than he ever had to lose as an explosives manufacturer by the loss of market we would bring about. Dr Graaff, one of the Board members and an economist, stated that he had come to the same conclusion by a factor of 20!

Most of the fighting seemed to be addressed to irrelevant issues. Was Tovex as good or better than Sinex or dynamite? This seemed to be the main thrust of AECI's case. They could make whatever we did, so, in view of the control of their profits by the Chamber, there was no need for competition. It should have been noted that there was no control of their costs! How could there be?

The arguments raged on and on for years, but seemed to me to mostly miss the whole point. At the end of the day, Bert Pienaar did not allow himself to be bamboozled, and his report to the Board was a model of what the issue really was. To anyone used to free competitive markets, it sounds almost too fantastic to be true, that in the end the Competition Board decided that a free competitive market was in the best interests of the country. The report, however, which mostly condemned the monopoly and the "awesome barriers to entry", created a major sensational shock when published. Both the Chamber and AECI were incommunicado for three days.

The Chamber then said that the report was a mistake and not in the interests of the industry. AECI never made a public statement. The whole question then was what the minister would do. Would the Cabinet have the guts to tackle Anglo? Well, it did, and declared the contract an unlawful restraint of trade. That should have meant an open market. It didn't, of course, but in the aftermath the Government undermined its whole credibility in Competition Policy. Bert also did the report on the liquor industry and really condemned the Afrikaner control. He told me that he had been anxious to show even-handedness. He had shot Anglo, and the Afrikaner establishment, to pieces, but when the Government gratefully carried out sentence on Anglo, it ducked on the Afrikaners. He reckoned that that fact had destroyed the whole credibility and effectiveness of the Board (which it had). It never again came to tackle the major competition issues in the South African economy, because the political will to bring free competition in a significant way simply didn't exist. The establishment had too much political power. It is interesting, in view of my experiences, to see the current developments taking place in South Africa. The mood is to co-opt a black elite into sharing the goodies which came from this exclusive little oligarchy. The reformers are trying to bring competition in the only way possible – via imports. It remains to be seen whether their nerve will hold in the face of the job losses an effective policy will bring about. While there will be short-term losses, the long-term gains will be incalculable.

There is, in fact, only one solution. A free market with a free *currency*. The Reserve Bank has been rigging the currency for decades, with little understanding of the effective economic devastation its policies have wrought. The truth of the matter is that South African wage rates relative to productivity in world terms are out of line. The only way to bring this into line is for the currency to fall down to the level at which these inefficient industries can survive. At the same time, export industries which are competitive will now become boomingly competitive, and will suck in investment.

It is so obvious that it sounds trite to say it, but a cretaceous cretin like Chris Stals does not, and never will, understand the working of a free market. He will never understand the fact that you have to release the energies and abilities of people to *compete*. He, being a bureaucrat anyway, does not know what it takes to earn a living in the real world. The establishment mechanism is that foreign confidence in South Africa would erode if he departed. The truth is that foreign confidence in South Africa is not deceived by window dressing and transient beings. Everyone knew that Stals was a lame duck. The ANC have put their own men in his place, eventually. It's *Mandela's* policies they are interested in, not Chris Stals's. Until the shape of South Africa is seen clearly, post-Mandela, no-one is going to invest in serious bricks and mortar. It will all be liquid portfolio stuff – short-term and volatile.

Once the Chamber contract was struck down, AECI developed what they thought were imaginative ideas to keep the monopoly. We, of course, were marketing on the easiest basis of all – having two suppliers. If you have two suppliers, you are less vulnerable to disruptions in supply. You can also play them off against each other to get a better service. To counter this, AECI stated their 95% scheme. If you buy 100% of your needs from us, the last 5% is free. This was the ultimate in predatory pricing.

The problem that this posed, of course, was that we had to be able to credibly offer to supply the requirements of an entire mining house. What with the clever leverage lease financing and, courtesy of Reuben Sive, who had been at Harvard doing an AMP course while I was there, we had found some old Kartridge Pak machines from Melrose Cheese, we were in a position to credibly do this. In the end, the whole strategy blew up in AECI's face. As I had predicted, the OMNIAs and the SASOLs are into the ANFO market and price pressure came on ammonium nitrate. To compensate for this, AECI were raising prices on whatever they kept a monopoly of. It was a short-term fix because it opened up other sources, finally, for other predators.

I had a meeting with Chris von Solms, who was now running the show. We were old antagonists, as he had dealt with me in Sable. In a way, his heart was in the right place, but AECI could not quite bring itself to make peace. Their best solution would, in the end, have been to keep up a little competition with, say, 15% of the market (on which we would have been very rich). My form of competition would actually have increased profitability.

The decision, however, was taken to try and wipe us out. I pointed out that it was too late. Pandora's box was open, and, for AECI, the spectre they should fear was SASOL. SASOL, with our technology, would be the worst possible news that could ever hit AECI. That in the end is precisely what they got, with the end product of their policy. That once great company is a pale shadow of its former self. ICI bought its explosives (now bought back by AECI), and SASOL runs its plastics. All it has itself is a hodge-podge of the rest, with an utterly demoralised staff looking at SASOL triumphant.

In the meantime, we had the hard struggle of the breakthrough. At last everyone now knew that we had the best product. De Beers Lesotho closed down, but Anglo was quite crafty. We got LTA. Actually, LTA was smart because they got the best explosives service in the country. I was sitting next to Zac de Beer at dinner one evening and tackled him head on about the in-house buying of Anglo. I did acknowledge that he was the wrong person to tackle because he was the only Anglo outfit buying from us. Crafty Zac pointed out that, by LTA's action, Anglo could utterly deny that it practised in-house buying. Of course, it enabled him to make better profits in LTA as a consequence as well.

PHASE II

Explosives accessories had never been part of the Chamber of Mines contract. AECI were too greedy for that. Early on, we came to the conclusion that we would be dealing with the contractor market and people like Iscor, who were open-cast miners. Courtesy of my friend Ward Kissel at Du Pont, who suggested we go to Peru where, in their opinion, the best detonating cord plant in the world was. Du Pont itself, by agreement, left the detonating cord business to Ensign Bickford. I sent off Manie Coopmans, one of our engineers, to Peru and report back. They were very happy to sell us a plant and licence to make detonating cord. We then had to source PETN (Penta Erithrytol Tetra Nitrate), which is the active explosive ingredient. We finally bought it from Societe Suisse des Explosives, courtesy again of my friend Ward. Of course, AECI also manufactured PETN, but we first did not want them to know what we were going to do, and, in view of the way they had supplied crap to Western Plats, we thought that they might well supply us with rubbish so that our cord would fail due to holidays in the explosives column. The technique of manufacture was to pour the PETN powder into a core made with two paper tapes, and spin a cotton braiding, followed by an extruded covering of polythene. We had a disaster when we started when someone had the bright idea of using plastic instead of paper. This did cause holidays and failure of the cord. We found out about it very early on, before any damage was done in the market place; however, we were stuck with tens of thousands of metres of suspect cord which we couldn't sell.

The army came to our rescue and bought the lot, as they spun it into a rope which they called a "plofadder", which they would shoot across a minefield and detonate it to set off any mines in its path and thus give a quick and convenient way of clearing a path through a minefield. You couldn't be too careful, which is why we never ever gave any PETN business to AECI.

Of course, with detonating cord you had to be able to supply detonating relays to introduce millisecond delays in the blasting pattern. We had to buy these from AECI, who made a so-called "dogbone" relay. You put detonating cord in each end and when a detonation came down the line, the dogbone introduced a delay before setting of the detonating cord installed at the other end. These things were ferociously expensive and I was determined to first be independent and secondly to make them more cheaply.

In its simplest terms a detonating relay converted a detonation into a flame, which entered a burning component which burned for the time delay required and then converted the flame back into a detonation. These things were custom-built and multi-directional. I saw no reason why they should be multi-directional. If they were uni-directional, it was an easy job to make the plastic casing in an arrow shape instead of a dogbone, and make it uni-directional. That meant that you needed three components to make a relay. Something to convert a detonation into a flame. I found that a .22 primed cartridge case did the job just fine. These things were mass produced for a couple of cents. To convert the flame back into a detonation, a 6-D detonator did the job. These were also mass produced. The problem was the centre portion, which carried the delay element. The best people in the world for this were ICI, who put the burning compound, which did not give off fumes, into a lead pipe, which was then extruded to the required small diameter. Other people made simpler delay elements, but by all odds the ICI method gave the most accurate results. So I had a programme started to ascertain how we could make a cheap but acceptable delay element. And patented the idea.

I was also becoming unhappy with the rather primitive way of making cord. The Bickford fuse was invented in 1831 and was essentially unchanged in 150 years. It used the same technique of pouring powder into a pair of paper tapes. It seemed that this technology was ripe for some innovation. At the time, certain specialist techniques were being done by Du Pont with plasticised PETN. They were extruding it into flat sheets for explosive cladding and hardening processes. So I went to see Al Luft. I told him I wanted to buy some technology from them on plastic explosive. I explained to him I wanted to make a detonating cord by extruding plastic explosive and extruding a plastic cover with a Dacron strengthening cord inside it. I felt this would be far more reliable than what we were doing. It would need a lot less PETN and would not suffer from any "holiday" problems. Al listened to my sales pitch for about half an hour. Then he opened his desk drawer and pulled out a secrecy agreement. He said: "Sign this". I signed it. He then opened another desk drawer and pulled out a coil of plastic. He said: "Is this what you mean?"

I looked at it and there was exactly what I had been describing for the last half hour! He said this was a new development which they were going to start. There was a very good system on the market in the form of Nonel, which the Swedes had developed. It used a shock tube to propagate an explosion and was the latest and hottest thing around. Du Pont supplied the plastic which was extruded into a hollow tube coated with explosive. The plastic was Surlyn. Its biggest use was for golf ball covers, as it was virtually indestructible. The problem for mines using it was that the Surlyn tubes were not destroyed in the blast and clogged the screens. So, although the mines got a beautifully controlled blast, they had a "garbage" problem. Du Pont's new product, Detaline, would obviate that. Surlyn was also incredibly expensive.

In reading the history of the Du Pont company, one of the interesting points was the discovery of nylon by Carothers. Du Pont wanted to replace silk. When they came up with nylon, one of the reasons why it made even more money for Du Pont than had smokeless powder in World War One, was the fact that nylon was so much cheaper to manufacture. The whole secret was to find a cheap way. When they tried to replace the looming leather shorter as they saw it with Corfam, they crashed and burned. Corfam, a so-called poromeric material, could breathe just like leather. But it was very expensive to make and eventually Du Pont gave up and sold the whole sheboosch to Poland (where they still make it!).

The exciting thing about Detaline was that it was fundamentally cheap to make. Yes, it used PETN, but only one quarter to one fifth of what we used in detonating cord, cheap polythene and Dacron. It had what we needed to make a cheap system.

The whole point about initiating systems was the quite extraordinary quantity of accessories. Because of the tens of thousands of narrow stopes which used typically half a kilo of powder and one set of accessories per hole, South Africa was the greatest market for holes in the world. On average, 40% of a hole cost was accessories.

Having got Al Luft to agree that we could get a licence to make Detaline, I sent off an engineer to Pompton Lakes to ask about my idea for a new detonating relay which I figured we could make for less than 10% of AECI's cost. He came back with the news that they thought it was feasible.

To my absolute astonishment, about ten months later someone brought me Du Pont's new detonating relay for Detaline. It was my invention! To cap it all, they patented it as well. Their problem was that I had patented it a year before them, so I had precedence world-wide. It was my invention. "Well, if you want Detaline, you will withdraw your patent." No debate. Big companies are pretty rough sometimes. I had no choice.

As we had with fertilisers, our superior product started to penetrate. One of the real ironies was that when AECI had a major strike and there was a looming shortage of explosives, we had a call from Goldfields. It will be remembered that it was Goldfields who egged me on in the first instance to get Tovex, and then, in sheer terror of what HFO would do to them, pulled out the rug.

Goldfields phoned and demanded that we immediately give them their fair share of our explosives production! That's chutzhpah for you! There were now too many people in the industry who were aware of just how good our product was and we picked up market share apace. After all, it is the easiest sell in the world to ask for 10 per cent of someone's business as a second source. This was mightily helped by the AECI strike. And Anglo took something of a back seat and did nothing to interfere with the workings of the market. They knew from the De Beers report just how good our product was. And they were starting to enjoy a better service from AECI as well

I had lunch with Dave Mather, who was one of the chief people in AECI. I nearly fell on my back when he told me that he could not thank me enough for what I had done for them. In the past they got no recognition from the Board, although they were the great profit centre. It was like being in a backwater. Now, the pressure was on from the Board to jack things up. Unlimited amounts of money were being made available and he was the busiest he had ever been and was having a rewarding life. Even he understood finally about my philosophy that we were selling broken rock – not just a box that went bang.

Then I had an invitation to meet with HFO himself. Well, it was a private one-on-one meeting and was interesting. Harry, of course, was an Oxford gentleman to his fingertips. He opened by saying that, as Chairman of African Explosives, he could hardly be expected to welcome a competitor. I responded by saying that, as the Chairman of Anglo-American, he should welcome it! He asked for elaboration on this and I replied that so far in the trials we had achieved demonstrated cost savings in mining of up to 10%. This had to be worth more to him as the premier miner in South Africa, and it was not the cost of explosives I was talking about. I was not coming to indulge in a price war. I told him that I took the view that what we were selling was broken rock – not explosives. I said that, although the guys at AECI had told me that De Beers had a billion dollars in the bank and would happily spend it in a price war ... I took the view, however, that those funds were there to support the diamond market and were not for the frivolity of a pointless price war.

At this point, Harry reacted that nothing could be more irresponsible than to think that the De Beers cash stockpile could ever be used for such a purpose. He had noted the great success we had had at Letsing-la-Terai and hoped that we had galvanised his company into improving its services and products. We parted on the best of terms and he wished me well.

Much later, my mother was sitting next to him at one of the Witwatersrand University functions (my father was Chairman of the University Council). He, of course, had known her well from her father's days as a Director of De Beers, etc, and, of course, he had offered my father the job of running the Copperbelt. He said to her: "I have the greatest admiration for your son. It is a great pity that we were on opposite sides of the fence, because we should have been exploiting his talents for our mutual benefit!"

He had told me that he made a habit of asking mine managers when he visited their mines what their service was like from AECI. They all told him it was excellent. Here was the old syndrome at work and I told him about General Somoza and how everyone around him told him what they thought he wanted to hear. I doubted that any mine manager would risk blighting his career by telling him that he got a lousy service from his company.

Thus all was finally beginning to set fair, until the South African Government decided that the time had come to flatten poor little Swaziland Chemical Industries. That story belongs to another book.

STRATALOC AND KEVLAR

During my many visits to chemical giant Du Pont in Wilmington, they kept urging me to look at a new product that was going very well, and was being used extensively by the international mining industry.

Mining and tunnelling had come to the use of roof bolts to support the strata and prevent roof collapses. Conventionally, this had been done by drilling holes in the roof and putting in pieces of reinforcing bar or destranded old hoisting cables and filling the hole with grout. Another means was to use a type of rawl bolt.

Du Pont developed a resin cartridge with two compartments, which, on insertion in the hole and then spun with a special roof bolt made from rebar, would set in 60 seconds and the bolt would be supported through its whole length. This gave a much-improved performance.

At first, I was reluctant to divert funds from our main struggles, and there was a competing product on the market, but not anywhere near as good.

Eventually, when we had some spare funds, I decided to go ahead. I hired new staff and decided that we would rise to the luxury of buying a plant off the shelf from Du Pont. It cost us a couple of million dollars, but had the huge advantage of being rather like our Sable airplant project. It started up flawlessly and we never had any serious technical problems.

To penetrate the market, it was obvious that we should go for the customers who were already using resin. I knew from my discussions with the technical folks in Wilmington that the secret of Du Pont's product was that we needed only 17% resin, whereas most competing products used 30% resin. Part of the secret was that the catalyst compartment accounted for 30% of the volume, because it also had filler in it.

The big question was: how to tackle the market? With the cost advantage we had, one could clearly see that a lower price was possible, but this could start a price war. I was loathe to institute this, because I felt our competitor would have no choice but to match us, and that would in the long term have a downside effect in that, when the price war was over, there would be a tremendous resistance to increasing the price, and a low price image was not good for the product image.

So we went the route of setting the price at a level which, at a reasonable volume, would give us an excellent return. And to sell the product on its superior qualities, to which I assigned Eric Fluke. I had hired him as an explosives salesman and he came to us from selling tungsten carbide – a rough, tough competitive business. He was a typical salesman, but would not take no for an answer. The key thing in the mining industry was to get people to listen to you. Mostly, salesmen were chased away. Eric was persistent and succeeded.

So, although it was a slow start, after a year we were breaking even and selling well. Part of the selling job was to pinch existing resin customers. Another part, by far and away the largest, was to convert people from the cement and destranded cable which, in the interests of economy, the mining managements tended to favour.

However, we were entering an era where the low cost of migratory labour was starting to rise sharply, and the use of proper roof bolts and resin had tremendous advantages in labour terms. So logically, the richer mines became much more receptive. The mindset, as we had found in the explosives industry, was to focus on the cost of a box of product. It took a sea-change to get people who were not used to costing their labour to see the improvement in overall efficiency. Also, roof collapses, fortunately not frequent, were rarely assigned to the roof bolting system failing. People were too busy digging out the mess to really look at the reasons for the collapse. Once again, the brighter managers appreciated the hugely improved safety from an improved system. But it was a long, slow process.

I remain convinced that our strategy had been correct. Our main problem was overcoming the resistance to change in the mining industry I have referred to earlier.

But slowly and surely we were winning and had a nice little business going.

Today, of course, it is the industry standard, as are the explosives we introduced.

Again, while in Wilmington, I came across a new product which seemed to have enormous promise. Kevlar was a so-called "gold fibre".

It had, weight for weight, five times the strength of steel. New applications were arising every day: bullet-proof vests, tyre cords, boat building (instead of fibreglass), mooring lines for drill rigs. I asked them if they had considered using it for hoisting ropes. I pointed out that there were 70-plus major mines with probably an average of three shafts with, say, six compartments each – a lot of hoisting ropes. The whole problem with deep-level mines, which we had dozens of in South Africa, was the weight of rope which effectively restricted the depth of a shaft to about 2,000 metres. Also, the weight of the cable at that depth exceeded the weight of the skip and rock. If you were doing a new mine, a rope with only one-fifth of the weight would dramatically increase the depth of a shaft. For existing shafts, a much greater payload was possible, such that one could almost double the hoisting capacity of that shaft. Because the weight of the skip being hoisted was counterbalanced by the skip being lowered, the power demand got less and less as the skip was hoisted. If a new skip was being hoisted with double the payload, this decrease would be less, and the power demand curve would be flatter. This would make more efficient use of the power curve and would cost less to hoist. So there was a double benefit. And, Du Pont claimed 10 million stress reversals without loss of strength. The rope should, therefore, have a much longer life. This was important, because the cost of a Kevlar rope was about three times as much as a steel rope. But the life of a steel rope was only nine months. This was a huge business, carried out, largely, by Haggie Rand – owned by Gencor and Anglo.

Anyway, I got the mine management at Blyvoor to agree to do a trial in a shaft dedicated to rock, as we had to solve the problem of non-destructive testing of the rope in service for safety reasons. One of the ironies was told to me by the Government Mining Engineers Department, which pointed out that a similar problem had arisen when hemp ropes were replaced by steel. We now wanted to go back 80 years or so! We agreed to finance the surplus cost and be paid out on power savings and every nine months for the equivalent cost of a new steel rope.

At the Electra Mining Exhibition, we had a wonderful example of these technologies. We suspended a five-ton boulder from a tripod by drilling into it and inserting a roof bolt anchored with Strataloc. The whole was then hung from a Kevlar rope which was thinner than a washing line. Quite spectacular! It generated huge interest.

Alas, the internal politics of Du Pont then came into play from the fibres division. It was their prerogative to do the marketing of fibres. Their nose had been put firmly out of joint by the explosives division pointing out this application. Unlike Al Luft, who in explosives saw clearly that AECI had little interest in developing slurry explosives, whereas we had every incentive to do so, and therefore gave us the licence, the man from the fibres division came out and spoke *inter alia* to Haggie Rand. I had told him it was the kiss of death to Haggie and that they would not push it. Anyway, they gave it to Haggie, who gave them a 10-year development programme!!

No Kevlar ropes have ever been used. I noticed on a website that Krupp have developed Kevlar for lifts, so, clearly, whatever problems there were have been solved. But not for the South African mining industry.

INTO THE BLEACH

Whilst we were working on the electrolysis of water to make hydrogen and oxygen, I told John I had seen an electrolysis plant at Simonstown making margarine. John mentioned that he had a friend, Lance Japhet, who was managing director of Epic Oil Mills, who made a lot of margarine. Lance had given us a lot of insight into the whole thing. Later, at a dinner given by John, he mentioned that the Government had finally given up on protecting the dairy industry from margarine competition, and that they could now make yellow margarine which looked and tasted much closer to butter. As a result, he expected that demand for margarine would sky-rocket and he would be looking for more hydrogen. Margarine is made by hydrogenating a variety of unsaturated fats and oils with a Raney Nickel catalyst.

"Did we have any ideas?"

I had been looking at other sources of electrolytic hydrogen, and one source seemed really interesting. Hydrogen peroxide. We all knew that it had been a big factor in German rocket motors and submarine propulsion during the war, so we decided to investigate. Lurgi advised us to talk to a certain Dr Schmidt in Germany. We duly landed up there to find Dr Schmidt was responsible for the 70% hydrogen peroxide used in V-2 rockets and other such items. We were sent off to Sweden to inspect an electrolysis plant which he had built for the manufacture of hydrogen peroxide. While we were there, the Swedes mentioned that they had a newer plant which was not based on electrolysis, but it was a secret. Anyway, we came away and proposed to Epic that we should build a hydrogen peroxide plant adjacent to their margarine plant and supply the hydrogen to them.

Lance immediately took to the idea and set up a meeting with Joe Bloom, chairman of Premier Milling, the owners of Epic. It was quite a meeting. To break the ice, I pointed to a picture of Tony Bloom on his desk and asked if it was his son. He grunted and said: "Yes – do you know him?"

I said no, but we had been together at Harvard, where he went to the Law School and I to the Business School.

He grunted again and said: "Well, I went to the best university."

"Oh, which was that, Mr Bloom?"

"Newtown." (One of the toughest districts in Johannesburg.)

Joe had to be one of the toughest guys around. John gave him the nickname "Flintstone". It suited.

Anyway, he was enthusiastic about the project, but wanted to go right away. We would have problems to get away quickly, so it was suggested that we get away with a small hydrogen/oxygen unit. This was agreed, and we put together a project. One of the key factors was to get an outlet for the oxygen, so I got in touch with our old friend at Afrox, Beau Sutherland, the chairman. He agreed to buy the oxygen at R1.20/'000SCF (Standard Cubic Feet).

So we duly signed up with Joe. Lance had agreed to buy the hydrogen at R1.80/SCF, but then Joe came to the party and demanded that all gas should be R1.20/SCF. In vain, I tried to point out that hydrogen and oxygen were totally different, but Joe was adamant.

This upset the economics of the project, and, after the new figures sank in, I had a surprise phone call from Joe. He didn't want an unhappy partner in a bad project, so, although he had a contract, if we wanted out, he would agree to cancel. I decided that that would be a better option and so the deal was off.

Crafty Joe. He didn't tell me that he had phoned Sentrachem and told them that he had a deal for hydrogen at R1.20 from Oliver Hill, and they must meet it or he would get his hydrogen from me. They met the price and it was years before I found out why they hated my guts. (Their hydrogen was a by-product of chlorine/caustic soda production.)

Years later, an acquaintance who had shared a study with me at Bishops, one John Bewsey, appeared on the scene with one Eriksen in tow. Eriksen had worked for the company in Sweden we had visited years before, and wanted someone to finance a hydrogen peroxide plant. He claimed to have all the drawings and know-how.

After much discussion and investigation, we agreed to finance a plant. Eriksen wanted to keep the rights outside South Africa, to which I reluctantly agreed. John was very against Eriksen and these rights, but reluctantly agreed to go ahead.

Bewsey was put in charge of engineering the plant, locating a site and finding the feedstocks and so on. The process was a totally different low-energy process compared to the old electrolysis process we had looked at. We knew it was working well in Sweden from our visit there, so we happily went ahead.

We set up the plant at Chloorkop, on land leased from Sentrachem, and agreed to buy feedstocks from them. When we tried to get the plant going, it soon became clear that Eriksen had little idea of running the plant. John was humungously pissed off and flatly refused to tinker with the plant. Eriksen had sold us the plant and it must work as he had specified. We were not going to be his guinea pigs and work it all out for him to sell it around the world. So he was kicked off the plant and I went to our old friends at Wilmington. Ward introduced me to their peroxide specialist and in an afternoon I got the necessary lowdown on the critical elements of know-how necessary. Unfortunately, we fell into arrears with Sentrachem on our lease payments, and, as they bitterly resented any chemical process being performed by other than themselves, they quickly liquidated the company. Unfortunately for them, I bought the plant in bankruptcy for R150,000 (we were, of course, the largest creditor, as we had funded it by loan account. As we were owed about 4 million, we were bidding with 10 cent rands, so, at the end of the day, less the fees and commissions, Sentrachem got about R5,000, and we got about R120,000 back.

By now, with the input from Du Pont, I knew what we had to do and the plant was taken to my new explosives plant at Bronkhorstspruit. Unfortunately, as will be detailed in a later book, I was forced to sell the explosives plant to Sasol. They did not buy the peroxide plant which was stored there. But when I returned to South Africa, Sasol refused to give me the plant back. Typical of the dishonest way in which they conduct business! You can only fight so many lawsuits!

Whilst engaged with Bewsey, he brought along another entrepreneur, one Brent Becker. Becker was a specialist in high-performance urethanes. I knew about these products as they were made by Du Pont and I had been considering getting a licence from them. The problem, as always, was to find someone to run the business. So we agreed to finance the company, National Urethane Industries, and took 50% of the shares. This turned out to be a highly successful company, as its major market was the mining industry, where these products, which had 20 times the wear resistance of steel, found ready application. In exiting the business from the Hahns, they swopped their shares in *Finance Week* for the shares in National Urethanes, and so landed up with 50% of it. Presumably since sold.

LLOYDS

Lloyds of London was always synonymous with insurance.

To be a "Name" at Lloyds showed you had *arrived*. So, enter Robert Enthoven. Robert was a many-times-over millionaire and was said to be the doyen of insurance brokers. We had done quite a lot of business with Robert, as he had accumulated substantial funds in Mozambique which had little or no prospect of ever seeing the light of day in South Africa. We always needed funds in Mozambique and were able, by virtue of some clever insurance deals, to buy these funds at a huge discount.

Robert at one stage proposed to John and me that we should join Lloyds. He extolled the virtues and showed us the very attractive returns he had been making. I remember him saying that his share of the Darwin disaster had been one hundred pounds. There was no way, although you were liable down to the shirt on your back, that you could or would be bankrupted by Lloyds. All this sounded too good to be true. And the people who were enjoying this were all the doyens of the community. But in the end there is the old adage that if it sounds too good to be, it probably is.

So we looked into it. You had to "show wealth" first and then put up a bank guarantee for half of the wealth you had shown. You were then allowed to underwrite business through various syndicates. I took the decision that I would divest myself of all my assets except that which I was required to put up. So the most they could ever get was your "funds at Lloyds". This was a wise precaution.

Initially, Robert was right. My money was in the bank earning interest and on average I made 10/15% per year on my "funds at Lloyds". So my money worked twice. I finally put up £300,000 at Lloyds, and for a time enjoyed an income around £60,000 a year from this source. You were, of course, taxed both in England and America, but it was a nice nest egg for retirement.

However, that old hairy syndrome reared its ugly head. When you joined Lloyds you were paraded before the Committee of Lloyds. There you were told: "You have arrived. The select few permitted to become a name is a total of 10,000 people representing the crème de la crème of society." Only gentlemen could apply. You sat under the portrait of Lord Nelson in the Nelson Room while this sales pitch went on. So I was inducted into this exclusive club, and, I have to say, fell for most of the bullshit.

You had a so-called "Lloyds agent" who managed your portfolio.

He allotted you shares in various syndicates. You would have a spread to reduce your risk, and, it was pointed out, you were largely covered by re-insurance, so that, according to him, you had virtually no risk.

What I found out later was that the happy members of my agent (Sedgwick Lloyds) eschewed many of the syndicates which later crashed and burned spectacularly. Good enough for the external names, but not for the smart insiders. Each syndicate was run by an individual owner. There was a three-year accounting period. At the end of three years, the year was closed by taking out a "re-insurance to close". This meant that, after this had been determined, the profit could be declared. The happy syndicate owner could then collect his 20% of profit. But, of course, the "re-insurance to close" was written by your syndicate. The larger this was, the less profit was available.

So the happy syndicate owner could be forgiven if, when looking at the re-insurance to close, he had rose-tinted spectacles. Any problems could be swept under the rug, to be dealt with in the next year. There, once again, the problems could be rolled forward, and so on. Certain types of insurance had virtually indeterminate life spans. The most insidious of these was asbestos.

For years and years the asbestos problem was swept under the carpet by just rolling it forward with the pious hope it would go away and all the afflicted people would just die. Eventually, the smart people at Lloyds decided that the only way forward was to vastly expand the number of suckers to help. The membership was trebled to 30,000 names. And all these unsuspecting suckers were given the same sales pitch about the integrity of this ancient institution, etc, etc, etc. They joined in their droves. After a decent interval, the re-insurances to close had to be raised. But some years went by, as the new members were fully inducted into their share of this horror story.

To aggravate this, one of the syndicates I was on specialised in "excess of risk". Thus, typically, they underwrote any loss greater than $100 million. Being greedy, they did very little re-insurance. We had a succession of disasters: Piper Alpha, *Exxon Valdez*, Phillips Petroleum, hurricanes and various matters. These losses were all in the billions. It effectively wiped out all the capital of the syndicates involved, which meant that we all had to pony up our share of the losses, which was done by cashing our bank guarantees.

The Names formed action committees which sued Lloyds. Most of these actions were successful, and Lloyds had to pay up. But the huge losses eventually forced Lloyds to form a new re-insurance company called Equitas, which re-insured all the stricken syndicates. We, of course, had to pay up. Basically, they took my £300,000. It was said that in 10 to 20 years we might even see a return of our re-insurance. But, after some 12 years, Warren Buffet appeared on the scene. He offered to buy the re-insurance to close. The management, although reluctant to give up the vastly overpaid jobs they were holding, succumbed, so that if a profit is to be made, Warren Buffet will collect it. I always took the view that if someone as smart as Warren Buffet thought there was a large hidden profit, maybe we should just ride with it. But, it was sold off. We were told: "You are now off the hook. You cannot be asked to pay in. Your estates can have certainty. Go for it."

Thus ended the sorry saga. It is a prime example of the huge greed which has unfortunately become a feature of the modern institutions which run our lives. The losses of Lloyds at the time exceeded £10 billion. Twenty years ago, that was a lot of money. It is dwarfed by the banking disaster of 2009. The root cause is the same – greed. I always think of Gordon Gekko in "Wall Street": Greed is good.

That became the philosophy of the age.

REVOLUTION

In the midst of all the struggles with Swaziland and explosives, Salazar, the long-time dictator of Portugal, died. In the turmoil, the socialists assumed the ascendency in Portugal. It did not take long for the chaos in Portugal to lead to the total abandonment of their two colonies of Angola and Mozambique. This led to 20 years of wars and chaos in those countries.

We had the difficult situation that, in extricating ourselves out of Rhodesia, we had agreed to build a new terminal on land we had purchased in the port of Lourenço Marques, the capital of Mozambique. We had acquired a 100-hectare site on the waterfront, with a couple of kilometres of access to the Maputo river. In fact, the water depth at our Matola site was better than 11 metres.

It was, in fact, a key element in the negotiation with Sable, as, at the end of the five-year lease I had negotiated with Champalimaud, they would be faced with one of three options: they could sell the terminal for $400,000, they could give Champalimaud a half-interest, or they could remove it.

This last option was not ever thought to be a realistic one. But I had discovered that the hovercraft people had developed a hover system for moving tanks. I visited a guy called Al Hake in the USA, who had made a fortune relocating a tank farm for Shell in Deer Park, Texas. He confirmed that it was a piece of cake to do the move we envisaged.

So I took a licence from the hovercraft people and we bought the hover skirt and the blowers necessary for a move. In order to build a new terminal, we had to keep the show on the road by using the old tank. We also had to build an embankment linking the Quimica Geral site to our new site – a 70 metre wide by one and a half kilometre long embankment. In the meantime, we set about building a new terminal.

Quimica Geral did not really interfere much. Antonio Champalimaud had decamped to Brazil as most of his Portuguese holdings were seized. The socialists were hell bent on dispossessing the rich. The robber baron era in Portugal was over!

We were in the throes of doing this when Mozambique fell apart. It added immeasurably to our problems. The majority of the Portuguese population were in the process of fleeing with whatever goods and chattels they could get out. Law and order disintegrated. Our crane driver was summarily hauled out of his car at a roadblock and murdered. My staff in Johannesburg were very unhappy at being asked to travel to Mozambique, as no-one felt safe. I had to go down to Mozambique a lot during this time as I felt I could not ask staff to risk their lives unless I was prepared to set an example. It was certainly nerve-racking to go through the myriad of roadblocks manned by children waving PPSH 41 tommy guns into your car and screaming at you. Bearing in mind the fate of our crane driver, it made for a lot of tension. And John, in spite of his DFC, flatly refused to go to the country.

Things slowly settled down as Frelimo assumed control with a ragtag bag of illiterate and untrained terrorists. Being a movement of the people, there was a strike a week in the port demanding a doubling of wages. Eventually, it reached the point where the wages were so high that the people holding the jobs simply subcontracted the work to those without work. We had our own share of labour troubles. Our plant was plastered with "A Luta Continua", "Viva Marxismo Leninismo" and similar slogans.

I was asked to have a formal meeting with the staff, which I approached with no little trepidation. I expected a real Donnybrook in the meeting with the staff. So I spent two hours inspecting the terminal and eventually Rudi Bossard, our local manager, asked when I was going to meet the staff. He told me they had been waiting for two hours!!

So I hastily repaired to the meeting room. At the one end a dais had been erected with a kind of pyramidal structure, headed by what I could only describe as a throne. As we entered the room, one of the senior staff acted as a sort of major-domo and shouted "Attention! Padrone!". Everyone in the room (about 50 of them) stood to attention. I waved them to sit down as I ascended the throne. I had no idea of how to address them. I was not prepared to call anyone "comrade". I decided that it would be a fair compromise to address them as "fellow workers". I told them that they obviously knew that times were difficult and that I valued the way in which they were loading the tank cars to keep the factories running. They were also helping Mozambique by keeping the terminal producing annual revenues of $1.5 million to the port authorities, besides the railway revenue. We, for our part, would do whatever was reasonable to make their lives better. Were there any questions or problems? The major-domo immediately came forward and asked those who wanted to speak to tell him their problem, which he would then translate for me.

I was actually surprised how unradical their polite requests were. The one which sticks in my mind was the request that we would supply them with raincoats, as it was very uncomfortable to load in the torrential rain during the rainy season. I thought about it, and, feeling a bit like Solomon, I said: "Yes – we will issue everyone with a raincoat. However, if they lost their raincoats, it was fair that they buy a new one." I have actually never been cheered like that in my life before or since.

The final request was that they would like a Christmas party. In a communist state? I said to them that not only would we have a

Christmas party, but I would personally fly down with the food and drink for the party and host it myself. I also agreed privately through our major-domo to pay each member of staff R100 per month of their pay in rands cash. This enabled them to purchase staples like mealie meal, oil, sugar, etc, at the foreign exchange shop, which was the only place where these goods could be purchased at a normal price. On the open market they cost up to 10 times the price.

We took the whole restaurant "Zambi" for the Christmas party. With the food brought down, we were able to lay on a spread the likes of which the staff and their wives had never seen before. At the party I made a short speech to the staff, thanking them for their efforts through the year. Reuben Da Silva, our terminal manager, came to me and said: "You know, there is not one member of staff who would not die for you."

So much for communism!

The new terminal we built was a model of efficiency. We were accustomed to budget a 2.5 per cent loss from ammonia purchased to delivered to customer. The new terminal was designed at a pressure of 0.2 bar, which meant that the tank had to be strapped down with stainless steel straps to the foundation, which had now to be piled to resist the up-thrust of an empty tank on the foundations. We put in a 12-inch line to the tank to cut pressure drop and to be able to handle 600 tons per hour. To avoid any flaring, we had a gas return line which we used to pre-chill the line, so that as soon as we were coupled up we could pump flat out with no flare loss. As mostly the charter party provided for us to receive 400 tons per hour, we could usually avoid any demurrage, and could sometimes earn dispatch.

We also made provision to provide nitrogen to purge the ships' tanks if they were planning to change grades in the Persian Gulf. This meant that the ammonia gas in the ships was sent to us, and we quickly liquefied it, and so, mostly, we actually got more ammonia than we had purchased. We also arranged for their propane tanks to be filled so that the change of grade could be made on the Persian Gulf voyage. The effect of all this was that, even if there was sloppy loading or warming of the cargo, we did not flare a drop. Our new standard became 0.5% loss! This may not sound much, but two per cent of 150,000 tons per year at $200 was $600,000 per year.

So, after much trouble, we finally built the new terminal and hovered the old one across to our new site, thus putting it out of action as a possible competitor.

In fact, the Minister who became in charge was actually extremely grateful that we had continued to build the new terminal, when most companies were closing down and fleeing the country. So we settled down to an uneasy peace with the new regime. I bought a boat from a South African who couldn't go down there, a beautiful 26-foot Bertram, for all of R5,000, into which I put new engines and we spent many happy weekends camping on Portuguese Island and fishing. As I commented to my guests: "There is nothing as nice as being a capitalist in a communist state." Absolute hedonism!

We had bought a floor in the new Rennies headquarters overlooking the port, as well as a couple of houses to keep our staff, and where we stayed when we came down. Theoretically, all land was nationalised, but we were not interfered with.

This did not stop our competitors in South Africa from trying everything they could to get the Government to seize the terminal and let them use it. The leader of the pack was George Mrkusic, a Serbo-Croat who was the boss of Fedmis, the fertiliser arm of the Afrikaner-controlled Federale Volksbeleggings Group. The Federale Group mercilessly exploited the paranoia of the SA Government with respect to sanctions, and they steadfastly declined to look at the possibility of building a terminal in Richards Bay. But if they could mastermind a snatch of our terminal, that would be OK. But it has to be said that they were very inept plotters.

And at the time that we were all riding high, Sentrachem, also in the Federale Group, decided that Fedmis was getting out of hand, and absorbed it into Sentrachem. Dave Marlow, the new managing director after George Mrkusic retired, then negotiated with Philip and myself to purchase the whole sheboosh. Dave Marlow did not have the chip on his shoulder of most of the Sentrachem boys. He saw a fine opportunity to rationalise the fertiliser business and to avoid the price controller by moving profits out of SA via our Liechtenstein activities, thus boosting his bottom line. So we agreed to sell. $65 million. I went to Mozambique that weekend. On my return from Portuguese Island, Reuben da Silva, the terminal manager, met us at the Clube Naval. The shit had hit the fan. South African Special Forces had attacked the ANC headquarters in Maputo. He was sure that we were about to be arrested. So we repaired to our house, packed up and decided that the only thing to do was to go to the airport. It was eerily quiet. There were no roadblocks on the road. The airport was a morgue. No-one there. We were cleared out faster than ever before. We took off happily and went home. The Sentrachem deal fell through.

The next thing which arose was that somehow the Mozambique Government induced someone to put up a couple of million dollars to do a study for an ammonia project, as they wanted to exploit the gas at Pande. I offered to do a small project based on two of Hamilton's ammopacs, which I found in the USA for $3 million each. Although they would use 40,000 SCF (Standard Cubic Feet) of gas per ton, at a gas price of 25c per 1,000 SCF, this was no big deal. A big modern plant used 30,000 SCF per ton, but the project, according to their consultants, would cost $250 million. They needed at least two hundred dollars a ton to make it viable.

They asked me about using the terminal, to which I obviously assented, pointing out, though, that they would have to have a dedicated fleet of small tankers which would probably be at high pressure and we would have to beef up our refrigeration capacity. Although the price of ammonia per ton at the time was high, over $200, I was never sold on these prices. They wanted me to insist that the customers would have to be made to pay their $200, as otherwise they could not finance the project. I pointed out that, although the Rhodesian market had very little option but to pay our prices, it was inevitable that, if the South African trade was held to ransom, they would just build their own terminal. I was then considered by Mario Marques, the head of the Mozambique gas company, as being a roadblock to his ambitions. He was not interested in the ammopac project. "Toys." We must bring a project for a proper ammonia plant. I talked to our old friend Cordell Hull at American Express. He had put together a nearly $200 million package for Pertamina, and, if anyone could put together financing, it was him. He had the advantage of knowing Mozambique well from when we did the original project.

His view was short and to the point.

Mozambique does not exist in the international banking world. To raise money for ammopacs was maybe feasible, from AMEX as a special favour, but a quarter of a billion was just a joke.

That did not stop our friend Mario Marques. He really believed that they could raise the money to build a plant and run it. So he brewed up a scheme to grab the terminal.

There were a number of Chileans who had fled the embraces of friend Augusto Pinochet and found a salubrious clime in Mozambique. One of these bright sparks came up with a scheme. In spite of the fact that our arms-length contract with Quimica Geral provided for a terminal charge of $6 per ton (pretty much a world standard at that time), he decided in his wisdom that we had undercharged. Ten dollars was what we should have charged. This would have resulted in a profit tax of 50 million escudos. Because we had evaded tax, he was treble taxing us! We owed 150 million escudos. We had 10 days to appeal, which we did. He rejected our appeal summarily and demanded that we pay by the month-end or he was seizing the terminal.

We pointed out that the terminal was not owned by Terminal De Armazenagem, but by NPI in South Africa. This dated back to a meeting which Tim Jooste had arranged with Brand Fourie, the Director General of Foreign Affairs. He told us that we were, in fact, the only South African company who had approached him. It seemed to him that most people had not shared with the Reserve Bank the facts of their Mozambique holdings. The SA Government's attitude was that, if a foreign company had a company in South Africa, and the assets were nationalised, the SA Government would, of course, pay compensation to the company. But the Reserve Bank would deny the right to repatriate the money. Following this logic, they could not lift a finger. But, if the asset in question belonged to an SA company, they would insist on compensation being paid and would withhold all payments to Mozambique until this was done. Thus, his advice was to leave the asset in NPI's hands as the contractor and we would have the protection of the SA Government.

So we told our happy tax man that if he looked at the tax returns of TAL, there was no terminal contained therein. And the land was owned by EMPIL. After this fiasco, they backed off.

But finally, in 1989, the Mozambique Government just seized it. They then tried to approach the South African trade. I told all the members of the trade they were free to do what they wanted. But I would sue them in South Africa for $100 per ton for the use of our terminal. So they all backed off and the terminal collapsed. All the movable assets were stolen and there are four tanks standing forlornly on the site and have done no business since then. To all would-be investors, two words: "Caveat Investor". Anything Mozambique wants, it will help itself to!!!

FINANCE WEEK

While I was involved in the various scraps with the establishment, I had a fairly (justifiably) negative view of the press, which was controlled by the two respective establishments to whom I was the worst possible news. I still remember the anguished remark made to me by Steve Anderson of AECI: "But you have no right to be in the fertiliser business!"

Well, others may have thought that we lived in a free country!

OWNER-IN-CHIEF: Hill, whose wife Dominique owns 82% of *Finance Week*, pictured with the magazine's publisher and editor, Stuart Murray, at the Hills' cottage in Wiltshire, August 1995. While Dominique holds the shares, her ownership of the magazine is legal nicety; she may act as proprieter but it is Oliver who is generally supposed to exercise the sanction of ownership.

I had a call from a certain Stuart Murray from the *Financial Mail*. Could he come and see me to write an article on what we were up to? With the usual cynicism, I agreed to give him an interview. Well, he was different. He opened by saying that he had spent three months studying the motor industry before he started writing about it. He now wanted to understand what made the chemical industry tick. Would I give him a complete "off-the-record" briefing, telling him what was really going on – who were the villains and heroes, and what was the real nature of the industry, because there was so much propaganda put out by the ring that he needed to understand the industry in depth.

Well, I treated this with a good deal of suspicion, as virtually every journalist simply wants you to say something rather rash or off the cuff and then plaster you. Especially someone like me. But, what the hell. Nothing ventured, nothing won. Well, the man was as good as his word. I gave him the unbridled story of what was going on, most of which was highly defamatory (but true). But he was scrupulous about observing his promise. He published only what would be allowed for publication, and did not try to distort what one was trying to say. He also never used the trick of sending you an article and asking for a response within an hour as they were going to press! In short, he was a rara avis – an honest journalist.

Over the next few years I got to know Stuart rather well, as he used me as a source of information on the industry even where I was not directly concerned. One day, he arrived at my office with a story. He had been asked by two colleagues, Richard Rolfe and Allan Greenblo, to put together a study for the feasibility of a competitive magazine to the *Financial Mail*. They had been a bit hesitant to involve him as he was the senior assistant editor and was considered "too near management". Their fears were unfounded.

During the trio's discussions, Murray had pointed out the difficulties in starting any greenfields publication, but he had an idea. At that time the newspaper publishing group Perskor produced a weekly broadsheet newspaper, the *Financial Gazette*. It was more or less ridiculed as a serious business publication and its circulation had dwindled to five or six thousand copies. Murray's suggestion was that the conspirators approach Perskor with a plan to can the FG (known to hacks as "Fairy Glen") and turn it into a magazine. Thus, the new magazine would have a head start in terms of circulation – and would have the power of Perskor behind it. From a cash requirement point of view, it was a much better proposition.

However, negotiations with Perskor's lugubrious boss, Marius Jooste, broke down when the journalists had the "temerity" to suggest a shareholding split (who had ever heard of journalists being owners?). Word of the revolution leaked (by whom, it is not clear to this day) and an angry management at SA Associated Newspapers, owners of the *Financial Mail*, sacked Murray and Rolfe in a very public manner. That day was a Jewish holiday, so Allan Greenblo had to turn up the next day to get the boot!

The editorial coverage which SAAN, the Anglo-controlled group which owned the *Financial Mail*, indignantly gave to the issue backfired. A great number of prominent businessmen (the majority friends of Murray) rang the journalists offering to help back the publication. Murray approached me privately to help with finance; so, with support from around 16 businessmen, the team decided to go ahead and start what was eventually named *Finance Week*.

The joke was on SAAN and its boss Clive Kinsley. After the Jooste fiasco, the journalists had pretty much thrown in the towel in terms of raising the capital required and getting the show off the ground. The fuss and opprobrium thrown at them by the establishment got them the support needed to go ahead.

Once again the old adage, we had found, held true. Your enemies can afford all the publicity and have the means to publicise their views;

but it shows that they are taking you seriously, and to persuade some people out there to support you!

With high hopes, they started their venture, based on the slogan "The facts without the waffle". They also took a very irreverent line with the companies they reviewed. In short, they did not use the magazine to lionise the establishment and flatter their egos, as was *de rigeur* with the *Financial Mail*. They managed to turn the magazine into almost a kind of cult status, especially when their **Piker** column started. You had not arrived unless Piker had a crack at you. The essential is that the magazine was not nasty or vindictive, but rather irreverent, and was funny. It won a reputation for facts and understanding, and its circulation started to build.

The original capital projections turned out to be inadequate. So it was back to the shareholders for more money (none of which was forthcoming from the founders!).

My wife had had a small inheritance from her father, which she had put jointly with me into a plot at Plettenberg Bay. We sold the plot at a huge profit and she wanted to know what she should do with her share. I suggested *Finance Week*. So she became a shareholder in the company. The largest number of shares we held through NPI, but some time before the manure hit the fan she and Max Hahn bought the company's shares in *Finance Week*, as well as the shares in National Urethane Industries. In a later settlement, the Hahns swopped the shares in *Finance Week* for the Urethane shares, leaving my wife as the largest shareholder outside the original founders.

People think that being a shareholder in the magazine would have been helpful to us. In fact, the only helpful thing was that the magazine was not an active enemy, but Stuart was harder on us than anyone else. He insisted that it was to maintain the reputation of the magazine, and he had his fair share of digs at me in Piker. But, when we caught our enemies with their fingers in the cookie jar, he was not afraid to exploit it. On one occasion, just before the Electra Mining Exhibition, I was looking at AECI's in-house rag, which carried an article purporting to show how wonderful Sinex was in comparison with dynamite. It had a photograph of two piles of rocks, and explained that one was shattered by dynamite and the other by Sinex. I was puzzled by the photographs, because the one was much grainier than the other. Studying them idly, I noticed a peculiarly shaped rock in the one photo, which also appeared in the other, only twice the size. Slowly it dawned that it was the same photograph, only blown up.

I took it to Stuart, and said I was not going to make any remarks, just let him draw his own conclusions. Well, he soon spotted it, showed it to Richard Rolfe, the editor, who ran a lovely Piker article about how at AECI it was the boys in the darkroom who did the blowing up. An absolutely furious AECI phoned up and told Murray it was cancelling the 12 back-page advertisement contract it had booked for the year. Stuart was quite unrepentant, and remarked how next week Piker would just *have* to comment on how AECI had attempted to blackmail the magazine. We, of course, had a lovely display of this lot in our stand at Electra with the caption: "We blow up rocks – not photographs!"

But the magazine became reasonably successful and, of course, with success comes the usual problems. First, Stuart and Greenblo became increasingly incompatible. The magazine was still on shaky ground, being attacked and harassed by the Anglo-owned press and finding it impossible to get advertising support from Anglo-influenced companies and from independent ad agencies who didn't want to be seen supporting a failure, since the market was being fuelled by rumours of *FW*'s impending demise.

At the desire of his wife, Richard Rolfe decided to return to the UK. Murray was worried that that news of Rolfe's leaving so soon after the launch would be taken as proof that *FW* was going down the drain. Being a good spin doctor, he decided to put a positive slant on it by announcing the opening of a London office. As a result, Greenblo became editor. Murray carried on as managing director responsible for operations and advertising revenue.

Stuart eventually found a very congenial way to sell advertising by having a yacht in Cape Town (and an office with a couple of bedrooms as well).

Clever Stuart decided that a good way to finance his lifestyle was to sell some of his shares back to the Finance Week Trust to help establish a staff share scheme. Lucky man. He got a price never realised before or since for his shares.

Profits zonked out because of the recession and the rand's collapse. The company had a cash crisis.

Stuart came to see me to explain that they needed "re-capitalisation". I responded that, whilst I didn't have cash in hand, it would take a few weeks to find. He obviously didn't take me seriously (he had no idea of the cascade of cash we were getting from our round-tripping!), and I was up to my eyeballs in a fight with the Hahns and gave no more thought to this, until about two months later, when Richard Rolfe arrived on my doorstep. His story was that the company was in trouble, and Greenblo was organising a rights issue to raise R600,000 to be underwritten by Rand Merchant Bank. Rand Merchant Bank had bought out Stuart, and were backing Greenblo to take over as managing editor. He proposed that he should return from London to take that post. I made it quite clear to him that, actually, my wife favoured supporting Greenblo because, as far as she could see, he was the one who had been left to do all the work, while he had enjoyed the London living. She reluctantly accepted my support for Rolfe's plan and we agreed with Rolfe.

It soon became apparent that there was, in fact, a conspiracy between Greenblo and Rand Merchant Bank to seize control, to the detriment of the other shareholders. RMB saw a nice juicy flotation, and an in-house magazine which they could use as an in-house propaganda organ. Which, of course, it ultimately became, and its articles about the wonderful Rand Merchant Bank were enough to make anyone puke.

Well, at that point I had the R600,000 in the bank available and so made a counter-offer. We even offered to buy out Greenblo on the same basis as Stuart Murray and RMB. We thought Rolfe should be the managing editor, Greenblo the editor and Murray could be a part-time consultant. Greenblo just wanted control. At that time I had not paid too much attention to the Memorandum and Articles of the company and later, of course, found that Rand Merchant Bank had unlawfully acquired control as part of Greenblo's conspiracy.

Ronnie Taurog (the Chairman of *FW*) called a meeting with the parties, messrs Greenblo, himself, Dippenaar of RMB, Rolfe and myself. Rolfe tabled his proposal, which I supported, saying that I was prepared to underwrite the R600,000 necessary for the company and that, subject to proper financial controls, Rolfe should be managing editor and Greenblo editor.

Dippenaar and Taurog were highly abusive and told me in effect to go and get stuffed, with Rand Merchant Bank assiduously backing Greenblo.

There was nothing for it but a proxy fight. In this, they succeeded in winning by two votes. In the course of the fight we bought out most of the other minority shareholders. The net effect was that Rolfe and my wife became a very large minority (over 49%).

After the proxy fight I had better things to do than involve myself in *Finance Week* and took the view that Greenblo had won, and if Rand Merchant Bank were to carry out the policy that Dippenaar stated, it would be to the benefit of minorities, and that Dippenaar would understand the fiduciary position as a merchant bank.

In effect, Rolfe's contract was cancelled and he instituted a claim for compensation, as had been agreed with Stuart Murray when he ran the company.

However, in the course of Rolfe's action, we discovered that RMB, as part of their support for Greenblo, had extracted an indemnity from Greenblo for any and all costs and claims by Rolfe against the company. So, if Rolfe brought action against the company, Greenblo would be responsible for all the costs of the action, and for any award by the court. When the case finally came to court, it was a shoe-in. Rolfe got full settlement and costs. Then it was that the real acrimony started. I discovered that the company had picked up the full tab of the action. My wife asked our lawyers to attend the shareholders' meeting and to ask why RMB had not enforced the indemnity and instead left the shareholders to pick up the tab. At the meeting, Ronnie Taurog, the *Finance Week* chairman, was evasive. And RMB quickly ducked as well, suggesting that "it would de-incentivise the management [ie Greenblo] to enforce the indemnity". One would have expected no less from Greenblo and Taurog, especially in view of the later court judgement. But for a merchant bank to fail in the enforcement of a condition of its takeover is a much grosser breach of its fiduciary duty.

Because of our support for Rolfe, Greenblo embarked upon a campaign in the paper of being as defamatory about me as he possibly could. He was responsible for painting me in the worst possible light, and, because at the time I was constrained from coming back from London, there was nothing I could do about it. I did consult Britain's top libel lawyer, Peter Carter Ruck, who agreed that it was some of the worst libel he had ever seen. Should Greenblo publish in England, we would have been able to plaster him. But in the meantime Greenblo was able to defame me to his heart's content.

Then I was approached by a lawyer I had known through Loucas Pourolis. He told me that, because of our effective blocking minority,

Greenblo could do nothing with the magazine. Under his tutelage it had languished, and RMB's dream of a flotation on the Stock Exchange had not materialised. In fact, he told me that Greenblo had sworn that our shares would forever be worthless.

Greenblo, we then discovered, had hatched a plot to sell out the assets from under the company to Euromoney, and he would be given shares in the new company. Because the holding company only owned shares, he was advised that he would not have to get his greater than 26% minority shareholders to approve the sale. My lawyer tipster told me he thought that it was probably pushing it and it was a moot point.

I was very pissed off and consulted with my lawyer, Oshy Tugendhaft. The one thing in my life that is almost a fetish is to listen to your lawyers. On Oshy's advice, I had dropped a number of cases in which he advised that our prospects were not good. He said that he thought that there was not a good history of minorities trying to prove oppression. It was difficult and he advised against it.

This time I did not follow his advice. I was so angry that we went ahead anyway. So my wife and Rolfe sued.

Mr Justice Plewman was on the bench for the case. I had crossed swords with him when AECI tried to cancel our Tovex patent and I was a little worried that AECI's vituperative affidavits may have given some preconceived ideas. We had had Sydney Kentridge in that case on our side and had butchered AECI, however.

Mr Plewman's judgement established a new landmark case for oppressed minorities. Greenblo and Taurog were found by him to be in breach of their fiduciary duties as directors and were ordered not to pursue the Euromoney deal. They, of course, appealed the judgement, but one of the orders we had sought was to stop them from using *Finance Week*'s money to fund the case. So Greenblo's lawyers went to bed on a fat debt and they were ordered to put up R400,000 guarantee of our costs to be allowed to appeal. Then a very large conglomerate, of which Taurog was a director, told him that if he did not settle he would have to step down, as they could not have a director on the Board who had been found in breach of his fiduciary duties.

The upshot was that the unhappy pair had to surrender their shares in *Finance Week* to my wife, who thus became the controlling shareholder in *Finance Week*. Greenblo did not wait to be "de-hired" but quit immediately and has been consigned to the dustbin of journalistic history. But he took the trouble to contact many of *Finance Week*'s advertisers and implored them to cut their advertising. Never in history has there been a more sanctimonious hypocrite than Greenblo in running a financial magazine.

Dominique asked Stuart Murray to come back from Cape Town to take over the magazine, and, in spite of Greenblo's efforts in persuading staff to leave and for advertising contracts to be shelved, he managed to keep the show on the road – no mean feat with a weekly magazine.

With my monumental struggle with the Reserve Bank, my wife in the end had to sell her shares to finance my cases. We sold to Nigel Bruce and David Gleason, who took over with a flourish and a big budget, apparently financed by Brett Kebble. They then sold to Nasoers, the owners of Finansies and Tecniek, who still own it – now renamed *Finweek*.

RIDING HIGH

When Neil departed for the fleshpots of Sentrachem, and learned that Philip Clarke had forsaken Triomf to join me, he coined a nickname for Clarke and I: the awesome twosome. Philip and I did, in fact, make a good team. As had been my habit with Neil, I used to meet with Philip for a short time every morning and we then got on with the rest of the day.

Before Philip joined, Phillipe Angostures had persuaded me that we should look seriously at Russia as a source of ammonia. After all, our terminal was in a quasi-communist country whose security was run by the Stasi, and Swaziland was a black state. So, politically, we were acceptable to Russia. The fact that Swaziland Chemicals was run by us was glossed over.

So I flew to Brussels to meet the Russians. To us, in those days, Russia was definitely another planet. We all saw them as hell bent on installing a black Communist state in South Africa and getting their hands on those strategic minerals. After all, America allowed the import of Rhodesian ore on the grounds that Russia was the only other supplier of metallurgical-grade ore. If Russia could get its hands on SA, then Rhodesia would fall into their hands like a ripe apple and Russia would have the world over a barrel for the strategic resources of southern Africa.

So there was a certain paranoia about Russia. We had not forgotten Angola, where the Russian surrogates, Cuba, were giving us a run-around. So going to meet the Russians was to be quite an experience.

To export chemicals, the Russians had set up a company in Paris in partnership with the French Communist Party. This company was, of course, extremely rich, as we found out as we went along. But I didn't have a clue as to what their negotiating strategy would be. They may as well have come from Mars.

So Phillipe set up a preliminary meeting with Roskin, who ran the Paris office. Roskin was a white Russian, a refugee from the communists, but, of course, was fluent in Russian. He had a Russian minder, one Smirnoff. Smirnoff's greatest fear in his life was that he would be sent back to Russia. One could understand his position. But I could hardly stop giggling when I met him. He was every South African's caricature of what a Russian was.

Anyway, we met with Roskin for a drink. I asked Roskin about his bosses. What made them tick? When you deal commercially with Westerners, you understand where they are coming from. They have the same commercial approach as you. But Communists?

Roskin said he didn't understand me at all. So I said to him: "Well, for a start, these guys are coming to the West. How does that work?"

So he said, well when they come to the West they are on a per diem of $45 per day. So I said to Roskin that that wouldn't go very far. After this clip joint (Brussels Hilton), we are ensconced in costs a hundred bucks for a bed. No food in that.

"No, no, no. I pay the hotel costs from our Paris account."

"Oh," I said. "How far does that extend? After all, there are some pretty fancy shops in this place."

"Well, since they arrived yesterday they have spent $10,000."

"God. On what?"

"Oh, video machines, clothes, other electronic gear."

So I said to Roskin: "At last I am starting to get a handle on these guys. But surely, when they go back to Russia, the Customs will climb into them?"

"No. If you are of the privileged few allowed to go to the West, when you return you are untouchable."

"OK, so the Russians have pretty much the same motivations personally as we do."

"Much, much more so. Russia is such an awful place for the consumer that when they come here they go mad."

So we sat down with the Russian delegation and started our talks with Abashkin, the leader of Soyuzchimexport.

He said to me he would like me to give him a memorandum on Swaziland Chemical Industries and Terminal De Armazenagem. He could ask the KGB to do it, but that would take years. Years.

What an eye opener. Here we viewed this monolithic organisation as having eyes and ears everywhere and ready to pounce on the slightest infractions. And here was a senior Russian in effect saying that the KGB was a vast and completely incompetent bureaucracy!

Anyway, we got down to business. It was agreed that we would effectively contract through Geogas for 100,000 tons a year of ammonia and we were permitted to deliver the ammonia to Tanzania, Mauritius and Maputo. We also got the right to send it to Brazil. We wanted this in case we were embarrassed by being overstocked. The price would be fixed every November for the coming year. This was a vital point for us, as the price of ammonia started to go up for the American spring planting season in about February. November was the time of seasonal lows. All other things being equal, therefore, we had a ten to twenty dollar advantage in a normal year.

Into this merry scene Philip was pitchforked. He told me that the trade had never been able to understand how it was we had survived financially. They had mercilessly piled on the pressure through the banks and whatever means came to mind. It was to him reminiscent of the time when Triomf was in shit and the simple answer as far as AECI were concerned was that each partner would just put in another million or two. Which Louis succeeded in doing. Where he got it from, AECI could not understand. When the Info scandal broke, it was obvious. From Eschel Roodie!

He said that the view was that Hill could walk on water financially. Once he understood the ramifications of the finrand system and our little games with RMB in financing our plant, he was in with gusto. He invented a few of his own.

The main reason Neil departed was that our ammonia trade had dried up. But then AECI closed its Durban plant, which used naphtha as a feedstock and which made that stuff quite expensive, and Philip knew that there was going to be a tremendous shortage of ammonia. Of course, the trade eschewed imports. The Rhodesian experience was very fresh in everyone's minds and the fear of sanctions was assiduously preyed upon the Government's minds, particularly by Sentrachem. Everything had to be locally made and import control would protect the local industry.

Of course, because of the total technical incompetence of Sentrachem, the industries it set up cost the country an unbelievable amount of money. So the trade could hardly at that stage consider building its own terminal, as that would have given the lie to the self-sufficiency policy.

And Philip knew how to exploit the monopoly. Covered by our Russian contract, we knew the price we had to pay for the next year. Philip insisted that all the South African buyers and the Rhodesians had to pay cash up front for their ammonia on the grounds that we had to finance the cargoes. We knew the rate at which it was physically possible to take ammonia out of the tank, so, if our average stock in the tanks was, say, 15,000 tons, we were paid up front for 50,000 tons. In addition, we got 30 days from Geogas. We knew the draw-down rate and knew that there was no logistical possibility of suddenly drawing all the ammonia out. After all, we were just a bank. The bank doesn't keep everyone's money there. They lend it out! So we had free working capital of millions of dollars from our bitterest enemies, which Philip used to great advantage by buying DAP in proper quantities, which gave us sharp shipping rates and very low input costs.

Our tough sledding of the early years had now started to bear fruit. Our product, in spite of the attacks by the competition, was becoming recognised as by far and away the best product on the market. We achieved a market penetration of over 15%. Finally, wonder of wonders, we were asked to join the Fertiliser Society. Of course, we had to reveal our market share at that point, as were all members. And we actually started to make money in fertiliser.

The characteristic of the trade and the banks in those days was that they were a lot of sheep. Neil had often quoted to me aphorisms from Milne, a former MD of AECI. Two were: "Greed is the enemy of policy" and "Good business never lasts". While business was booming, everyone wanted to get on the band wagon. Gone were the days when they all wanted letters of credit. Philip asked for and got 90 and 180 days' terms from our overseas suppliers. The banks in Swaziland fell over themselves to lend to us. We were awash with cash. We could even afford the endless swanning around the world by John with his entourage in tow.

In fact, we even had an amusing run-in with the Standard Bank of Swaziland. We had got a very low special rate from them for cashing our South African cheques. We found that it took two weeks for SA cheques to clear. So we deposited our money in South Africa and put it on call. When the cheque was presented, the money was immediately taken off call. In the meantime, the bank allowed us to use the money in Swaziland, ie they cleared the cheque. This was set against our overdraft. So we scored. Eventually, the Bank Manager called in Philip and accused him of kiting. Once he understood what we were doing, he said that what we were doing was borrowing from the banking system at 5% and placing it on call at 10%. No way. So he increased the cost, which meant that if we borrowed from the banking system, it would cost us 10%. But for a couple of years we made good money.

With booming fertiliser sales and ammonia sales, Philip decided that he wanted to double the plant capacity. We had already started building a prilling tower. All the lessons learned at Sable were applied. To save cost, the Americans jacketed the ammonium nitrate lines with carbon steel. The trouble is that ammonium nitrate gets in everywhere. As the lines are jacketed with 200lb steam, they are stressed. And you get stress corrosion cracking. The result was that we had to re-jacket the lines in stainless, whilst keeping up production. It was a nightmare. I insisted that everywhere in our plant we would use stainless. People tend to dodge it, but when you are doing the fabrication yourself there is only a marginal increase in fabrication costs, and the extra expense of the stainless. If you go to a contractor, he tends to add all his overhead and profit margins to the total cost, and thus a contractor price for stainless compared to mild steel is significant. Do it yourself and it is a lot cheaper.

The only problem with the prill tower was that we did not have a proper foundation where we were adding it. For better or worse, our C&I Girdler design manual called for the design to withstand 125mph winds. That's fine in the hurricane belts of America, but I doubt that it would ever be necessary in the midlands of Swaziland. But our bitter experience with fighting with insurers made me very cautious, so we kept with that specification.

At Sable, we had had to dig down quite a few metres to put in a massive block of concrete to resist the overturning moment of a 125-mile-an-hour wind. We ended up with a very strange structure to meet this requirement. And, at Sable, wherever we had not put in acid-proof tiling, the foundation had corroded away with time, necessitating extremely costly repair efforts. So the whole plant was done in acid-proof tiles.

Another problem which reared its head at Sable was in process storage. The neutraliser capacity was for only 8 minutes of hold-up. So the slightest hold-up downstream meant shutting down the neutraliser. The problem was that the fancy pH controllers did not work, so you had to carefully adjust your flows of acid and ammonia. This could take up to half an hour. The obvious solution was to build a large storage tank for ammonium nitrate liquor and to do final pH adjustment there. These innovations gave us unparalleled on-stream time. And I put the fans of the prill tower back where they belonged. There is always a wind at that height and control of the airflow in the tower was easier with four sets of fans.

So we finally had a state-of-the-art prilling system in operation. At Philip's behest, I went out looking for another nitric acid plant. We, of course, wanted to get one of Hamilton's standard 180 ton plants so that we could reduce our spares problem. Luckily, Hamilton had sold around 50 of those units and we quickly found one at a Monsanto plant in the USA and bought it for around $250,000. They had substantially upgraded the plant over the years and it was a real buy. So, once again we had acquired the heart of our new plant for a song.

During this period I was talking to Francis Le Riche of Sentrachem at one of Neil's birthday parties. I was expounding to him my theory of how South Africa should develop its chemical industry. There is a well-known fact about chemical plants known as the two-thirds factor. That is, the capacity of a plant goes up as the cube of the dimensions, whereas the size goes up as the square of the dimensions.

So a plant which produces twice as much as another one does not cost double, but around 1.6 times as much. So the problem in South Africa is that we have to build small plants because of the small size of the market. I argued with Francis that Europe and the US was littered with small plants which could not compete in those markets and were closing, and as a result were available for essentially scrap value. And I had proved it.

Francis looked at me pityingly. What did I know about the chemical industry? When I eventually learnt something, I would learn that putting up cast-off junk was not the way to go. You had to build *new*. Well, I figured that we were building secondhand at around 15 to 20% of the cost of new. I admit that process efficiency was not quite up to a modern plant, but it was possible to tweak the plants to improve it. So I was much sneered at by Sentrachem as a secondhand merchant. But these plants are built of stainless steel, high-pressure components. The plant we bought in France is still going strong, 70 years after it was first built.

The real problem with our expansion was that we lost our local engineering genius – Mike Mcguigan. On one of his rare return trips to South Africa, John decided to visit Swaziland. He thought he would go down and raise a bit of hell. Well, he certainly did. He accused Mike of running a time-clocking scam, which really got Mike's Irish up. He quit.

So Philip got some of the people he had worked with in Triomf to come in. My approach was scorned as being "not proper engineering". Money flowed like water on the construction of engineering monuments costing three or four times what Mike would have spent. In no time we were in for 20 million. As long as the music was playing, it was fine. But if the music stopped, the penalty of using short-term money to finance long-term assets would rear its ugly head. And we had broken our unshakeable rule of financing fixed assets with our money.

And the trouble with the Triomf people was that they knew nothing about ammonium nitrate. It has to be handled in either heated spaces or dehumidified spaces, because the fine ammonium nitrate is so hygroscopic. So the whole of the buildings they designed were dripping with ammonium nitrate liquor, which wreaks havoc with your machinery.

Then we started having real difficulties with the Swaziland Government. Swaziland was a difficult place to work in. No-one wanted to live there. You tended to get the dropouts from the chemical industry. We were lucky in having a few really top-notch people, but really skilled people were very short. And then Mugabe came to power. We were flooded with applications from Sable. All good people. Mugabe got hold of Swaziland and told them not to hire these racist Rhodesians. They were all white supremacists. History has shown how right they were to seek another life, but that is not for my comment. We had work permits refused for a number of them. So Philip and I sought a meeting with the Deputy Prime Minister. In particular, we had one individual we desperately needed. He was a turbine fitter. As we had gas and steam turbines on the plant, we needed this man.

The Deputy Prime Minister was adamant. The man had standard eight, and there were thousands of Swazis with standard eight. I told him I was utterly unaware of his academic qualifications. He was a turbine fitter and there were precious few in South Africa, let alone Swaziland. With 10 to 15 years' experience, we could eventually train a Swazi, but not now.

Well, as far as the DPM was concerned, Philip was an English racist who only wanted to employ whites and not blacks. He was not stupid. A Swazi could do the job. Permit refused. Well, Philip hit the roof. He told the Deputy Prime Minister that, if he could not employ the people he needed to run the plant, he would close it down. He was leaving to issue that instruction. And we left. Philip notified the banks he was closing the plant because of the Government's attitude. We returned to Johannesburg. Well, the banks went ape. How could we pay them back. Answer – ask the Government for money, because they had closed the plant. They put up a tremendous howl to the Government, who grudgingly gave way. So we got a fine team to come and run the plant.

Of course, this attitude was a disastrous forerunner of what was to come in South Africa. The policy of ethnic cleansing has led to a massive exodus of highly skilled, technical, financial and legal people, to the huge detriment of the country. I alone, within my family, have four people with advanced technical degrees who have departed to get a much better life overseas, and who will never return. It is said that you can tell where a country is going by looking at the migration statistics of skilled people. Those who are losing them are going down. The more that go, the faster the decline. And that comment had nothing to do with colour.

However, our smart Rhodesians wrote another chapter on how not to do things. It had become apparent that ammonia spheres around the world were becoming subject to stress corrosion cracking. The sphere I had built at Sable was closed down and they built a new one in stainless steel. So our boytjies decided that a pressure test was necessary. To do this the sphere had to be drained, purged and filled with water. No trouble to our guys. They drained the sphere and pumped in water. Well, as everyone in the business knows, ammonia is incredibly soluble in water. Our bright guys left a small 2-inch opening to let in air. This was grossly inadequate, so the whole sphere imploded on itself as the ammonia dissolved in the water. I was phoned the day after Christmas and given the glad news. If I had been the insurer, I would have refused to pay. This was the one time we actually got a settlement without having to go to war. New storage, which was high-pressure, cost 1.2 million rands.

Philip's approach to marketing was, to say the least, rather brutal. He hired Piet Uys, a rather well-known Springbok rugby player, and it was not long before half our sales staff were rugby players. Clever.

Their entree to farmers was immediate. So, although the epithet that particularly Fedmis chucked around was that I was a "kaffir-loving communist", we penetrated the market. We were all making piles of money; so much so that Sentrachem was becoming alarmed at the way Fedmis was chucking money at all sorts of investments, that they took it over. Francis considered he could spend their money better on far more desirable projects.

So eventually, when Dave Marlow took over from Francis, we had a much-improved atmosphere. Philip and I were invited to a meeting with him. He politely enquired how things were going. Philip admitted that things were indeed going quite well, thank you. Dave Marlow sat back and said to us: "Let's face it, guys, we have never had it so good." He offered to buy the whole sheboosh. Well, the price was pretty substantial, as I recall it. Something like $65 million. We accepted. The day before we signed, the South Africans launched a major attack on Maputo. I was actually in Maputo, fishing off Portuguese Island, and was returning that day. When we got back to the Clube Naval, where I kept my boat, an ashen-faced Reuben Da Silva, our terminal manager, met us with the glad news. We had no idea what would happen, but we went to the airport anyway, expecting to find thousands of soldiers and to be arrested as South African spies. The airport was eerily quiet. No flights were coming in or out. But we hopped on our plane and flew out.

Sentrachem did not buy the business.

One of the ironies of the attack was that there was a panic about security in Matola. As I mentioned, it was run by the Stasi. We were considered as a strategic company in the place, so the head of security came to meet with my terminal management. What only three people in our company knew was that the man running the terminal physically was in fact a member of the Rhodesian special forces, who had been their lead paratrooper and had been on many raids into Mozambique, shooting up terrorist camps. He had been landed a number of times by submarine to take out terrorist camps and walking back to Rhodesia. The head of Rhodesian security had come to me with a problem. Although they had aerial reconnaissance of Mozambique, they sometimes needed intelligence on the ground. They needed a man on the spot and we had one of the few credible operations there. Could he put a couple of his boys there.

It was obviously of some concern to us as, if it ever came out, we would probably lose our whole investment. I was also concerned about how the guys would be treated if caught. I was told not to worry about that. There would be a trail of bodies and they would be sprung. So I agreed, provided we set up a proper front. We advertised for two people to come and work in Mozambique at pretty minute salaries. Everyone in the company was pretty amazed when two strapping great guys pitched and applied for the jobs. They were, of course, the only applicants and duly went down. Their names were Rob Garmany and Bruce Spargo, and were two of the top SAS people in Rhodesia.

Bruce didn't last long, as he was picked up with "car trouble" in a place he shouldn't have been. He was quickly pulled out, which left Rob. And Rob became the big consultant to the Stasi. The whole security of the area was discussed and the measures which were being taken to keep those wicked Rhodesians out of the place. So Salisbury had, from the horse's mouth, all the details of the security measures being taken against them. It was a little delicious, but I couldn't share the joke as our own security had to be absolute.

It is one of the great ironies of history that twice Rob was sitting with a dirty great bomb to send friend Mugabe up to heaven. But he had to get the final go-ahead from Salisbury to press the button. They chickened out at the last moment. How different subsequent history might have been!

In retrospect, of course, those were the halcyon days. Philip and his wife and I with Dominique used to attend the annual bean-feast of the International Fertiliser Association. They always chose rather nice watering holes to hold this annual conference. And the host nation usually bent over backwards to lay on extra-mural activities for all the aangelastes. We had conferences in London, Monaco, Nice, Vienna, Copenhagen, Singapore and a few others. Dominique and I used to arrive a week before the conference to take in the sights and sounds.

The Russians always attended the conference and we used to meet them to discuss the next year's contract. I remember in Majorca where Rudnev, the head of Soyuzchimexport, had a beautiful suite right above the sea. We used to always try and get an early meeting, because they were usually quite sozzled by late afternoon. Well, we got the first meeting one morning and when we got there the table was bare, except for glasses and a gallon apiece of whisky, brandy and vodka.

"You will have a drink – ja?"

Philip had a liver problem and said that he couldn't, but would take a Coke.

"Then we too will drink Coke!"

They certainly enjoyed the fleshpots. Some years later, Phillipe Angostures phoned me and asked if I had a handy £15 million. Well, never in good old NPI. But what was the story? It appeared that auditors were arriving from Moscow the next day and our Russian pals had diverted some 15 million into buying some rather nice real estate on Cap Ferrat and Antibes. The villas were now worth nearly three times that, but our pals had to find the 15 mill in a hurry to stay out of a Siberian Gulag. Phillipe's Turkish partners came up with the money and did a hell of a deal.

At that meeting, Abashkin tackled me about South Africa. What were we going to do when the revolution hit us? I said we would deal with it the way Joe Stalin would. Simple.

When we were in Vienna, the last night was a ball in the ballroom of the Hofburg Palace. Real Belle Epoque stuff. The Russians were there in force and I introduced Dominique to them. Fortunately, I had warned her not to giggle when she met Smirnoff, who clicked his heels, bowed and kissed her hand.

The joy of having Philip was that the whole running of the fertiliser business was taken care of and it allowed me to pursue the explosives business. It was important to push up ammonium nitrate consumption, as there was no seasonality in the business, and we were still a nitrogen-rich company.

Our peak year with Philip reached a profit of over $9 million and that after financing all John's wild expenditures on swanning around the world trying to sell ever increasingly larger projects. I was relieved with Philip running the day-to-day affairs, which took a huge burden off me, as I was fully taken up with the quite monumental struggle to break the explosives monopoly. We now had an unstoppable momentum as our superior product based on Di-Ammonium Phosphate was sweeping the fertiliser market.

The shift to this product was momentous. It was the closest thing to a magic bullet, and we could not keep up with the demand. It was pretty clear to all that this product had rendered the fertiliser ring's products obsolete. Screams arose to stop these imports. In the end, Louis bit the bullet and built a DAP plant in Richards Bay. Imitation is, after all, the sincerest form of flattery.

This gave our old enemy Joep Steyn, the Secretary for Commerce and Industry, the excuse he had been looking for, and he imposed swingeing duties on DAP. The duties imposed were enough to effectively stop the sales in South Africa.

But finally, with the decision of the Competition Board declaring the Chamber of Mines contract to be an unlawful restraint of trade, some of the Chamber members cautiously began to buy from us.

To counter this, AECI devised a stratagem. The mines would pay for 95% of their explosives. The last 5% was free. This was to force us, as they saw it, to give a mine the explosives for free.

Fortunately, when this happened we were able, because of our capacity to offer to supply the entire requirements of a mine. The Rand Mines Group then turned to AECI and said that, in the event of AECI penalising them, they would accept our offer. The floodgates opened and both Rand Mines and General Mining gave us substantial business. The holdouts were, of course, Anglo and Goldfields. Anglo owned 30% of Goldfields and they were all terrorised as to what "Harry would do to them!"; but when there was a major strike at AECI, the first company on the phone was Goldfields, who demanded their fair share of our production!! In my eyes, that was zero, but, knowing what happened when miners got to use our product, we agreed to supply them.

But there was very little doubt in the minds of the mining industry that we now had a far superior product to dynamite. We had solved all earlier problems with breakage in tight stopes, and in bulk explosives we were saving most opencast operations a fortune in drilling costs. So we were soon riding the crest of the wave.

We had also, courtesy of Du Pont, acquired a licence to make detonating cord from a company in Peru. I then designed a detonating relay to use with the cord, which was based on mass-produced components. By making the cord mono-directional instead of multi-directional, and putting it in an arrow-shaped plastic holder, we could make a relay at a cost of something like 10 cents, instead of one rand.

I sent an engineer over to Du Pont to ask them what they thought of the idea. The basic concept was to use a .22 cartridge to convert a detonation into a flame, and then the lead tube with the time fuse in it followed by a 6-d detonator. They thought it was quite a good idea. About a year later, it transpired that they had developed a new initiation system called Detaline. And for relays they had copied my idea, not knowing that I had, in fact, patented the relay! They had also patented it, but their patent was pre-dated by mine, which was a year earlier! This gave rise to a big problem.

Many years later, when in exile in England, I had a meeting with Peter Clinch, a really switched-on Australian, who was head of ICI Explosives. He obviously phoned South Africa to find out who I was, because when I walked into his office he pushed his chair back and raised his hands in mock surrender, and said: "I surrender. Dynamite is dead." An auspicious beginning. He confirmed the fact. Dynamite had, to all intents and purposes, ceased to exist as an explosive around the world.

All good things come to an end. I always think of Alan Milne's aphorism: "Good business never lasts." And we had broken our own rules. After all, after hubris comes nemesis. That is the story for another time.

Our great enemy, the Director General of Industries, Joep Steyn, finally got swingeing tariffs imposed on our imports. At the same time, we had a devastating drought, and, due to the Reserve Bank monetising the Government debt, the rand collapsed to half its value. Although by now our explosives business was making good profits, the result of all of this was catastrophic for us. That struggle is the subject of another story. The net effect was our enforced refugee status from South Africa.

But eventually, when we returned to South Africa after some 15 years of exile, we were pitchforked into a new scenario. Like most South Africans, we had queued at Trafalgar Square to vote on a new dispensation. Dominique had had a long meeting with Mandela in South Africa, who told her he was anxious to avoid what had happened in Mozambique and Zambia. He urged her that I should return to a new South Africa to devote my energies in building a new non-racial democracy. He assured my lawyer who was at the meeting that his Government would be dealing with matters like Exchange Control and clearing the decks so that the country could get on with development.

Like most of us at the time, we voted "yes".

Unfortunately, the high hopes with which we had entered this bold new enterprise and had voted for did not materialise.

The ANC has turned out to be even more racist than their predecessors. Revolutionaries seldom turn out to be good governors and the same is true of the ANC. Mandela said to Dominique that there were thousands of his supporters who had stood behind him in the dark years; he could not desert them when he came to power. While this may be an admirable sentiment of loyalty to your supporters, in practice it means that jobs will be given to the ANC cadres – regardless of qualifications or experience.

One of the few things preached at Harvard was that, in tackling any business problem, the first thing to do is to define the problem! They emphasised that this was not always obvious. If you defined the problem correctly, the solution usually stared you in the face. After all, if a doctor diagnoses your malady incorrectly, he is most unlikely to cure you!

One only has to think of one of the most controversial politicians in Britain – the late Enoch Powell. If you listened carefully to what he said, he brought powerful intellectual capacity to Britain's problems. 95% of what he said was cogent and to the point. 5% was sometimes way out of political correctness. As a result, everything he espoused was tarred with the brush of the 5% and all the sensible things he was promoting were all considered the ravings of a lunatic. So was it with apartheid. Everything was treated as a problem of apartheid. So, if you define South Africa's problem as being apartheid, you haven't a hope in hell of getting it right.

One has to study the facts and stay away from emotional issues. One of the best programmes aired in recent years by the BBC was on genetics. The last episode was titled "Genetics and Intelligence". At the outset, the presenter said that they had been unable to find a single anthropologist who was prepared to say that the theory of evolution did not apply to intelligence as it did to all other factors which enhanced the survival characteristics of a species. It is completely politically incorrect to assert that races in different parts of the globe may have, as a result of the "survival of the fittest", different physical and mental abilities brought about by the environment in which they have been forced to survive over many millennia. This, however, flies in the face of some startling and obvious facts. If you look at a 100-metre final of the Olympic Games, the number of black competitors is by far and away greater than whites. In fact, a white finalist is a rara avis indeed. Could this just be because survival in Africa needed the endowment of the tremendous physical ability so evident in blacks?

On the other hand, if you look at the lists of Nobel Prize winners in the intellectual pursuits such as Physics, Chemistry and Medicine, one is struck by the total absence of any blacks at all!

In their excellent book, *IQ and the Wealth of Nations*, the authors, Canadian professor Dr Richard Lynn and Dr Tatu Vanhanen, have attempted to correlate the wealth of countries with the average IQ of those countries. There is a remarkable correlation, but there are also anomalies. One such anomaly is Qatar. However, they point out that the national product of Qatar is produced by the international oil companies and has nothing to do with the rather low average intelligence of its citizens.

Another is China, which has the second highest IQ in the world (after Israel) at 106. It should be the richest. However, this can be explained by the repressive system which prevented the citizens from achievements. Now that a relative degree of economic freedom has been achieved, the Chinese are growing at a terrifying rate, and certainly within the next two decades will be the richest nation on earth.

Another anomaly is South Africa. South Africa has a miserable mean IQ of 72, but its actual income is far above the predicted amount. Lynn and Vanhanen point out that this is undoubtedly due to the fact that whites with a mean IQ of 94 are running the economy.

Unfortunately, the authors' view of sub-Saharan Africa with a mean IQ of 65 means, in their opinion, that sub-Saharan Africa will remain a basket case for the rest of time.

These simple facts are, of course, ferociously attacked as being racist. As the BBC said in its programme, it would be attacked as being racist. Facts are facts.

I have alluded to the whole question of employment equity. This is fundamentally based upon the premise that all people are endowed with the same inherent intelligence. To espouse any other theory is racist in the extreme. If the BBC and Drs Lynn and Vanhanen are correct, this is simply not true. Accordingly, to insist on so-called "transformation" means dropping standards in order to give "qualifications" to people who are not capable of doing the job. Hence the dumbing-down of matric. Hence the fact that my old university has fallen off the radar in world rankings. When I was there, the pressure was on us at all times. The world is advancing at a huge rate and we must keep up. Now our degrees are no longer acceptable – for good reason.

A professor of mining at Pretoria told me that he had been put under huge pressure from the Government to make his degree course "easier". His reply was that, if you wanted a degree from him, you must meet his standards and not set your own. He said the pressure was to allow a diploma in mining to be good enough to qualify for mine manager. He made the point to me that they estimated that a diploma was worth about 6% of a degree!

It makes me think back to when we in the Harvard Business School Club of South Africa decided to raise funds to send black candidates to the MBA programme. Unfortunately, after two years of searching without finding a candidate, Harvard proposed an alternative. They were of the view that to send a black candidate who flunked out would be counter-productive to what we were trying to achieve. They were sure that all our prospective candidates would flunk out. There was no way that Harvard would in any way relax its standards and award a degree to someone who, in their opinion, was not worthy of a degree. So they suggested that, as our objective was to expose black citizens to the economic freedom of the West, and its democratic institutions, we should send them on three-month courses. These did not have examinations, but were heavily orientated to class participation, and this became a howling success.

This whole programme of affirmative action can be seen in concrete examples of the behaviour of this ANC Government. A prime example is the disaster of Eskom. It is crystal clear that, from being a utility which succeeded under the old apartheid regime in achieving annual reductions in the real cost of power, the new Eskom has achieved swingeing real increases in the cost of power which is now in the process of putting many of our power-intensive industries out of business. I had quite a lot to do with Eskom whilst in exile.

Whilst we were in exile in England, I became interested in Zambia. One of the obvious things of interest was power, as I had been for obvious reasons very concerned with power in Zimbabwe. I soon became a consultant to Edith Nawakwe, the Zambian Minister of Power. A study had been done of the Batoka Gorge project, which, for obvious political reasons, Zambia did not wish to support. However, it was not protocol to just can the project, and she needed proper reasons as to why Zambia should not support the project. From my reading of the feasibility study, it was obvious that this run-of-river project had a serious defect in that, in the low-water season, the output would fall from a high of 1,600MW to a low of as little as 200MW.

I pointed out to Edith that this fact made the Katombora Barrage above the Victoria Falls a virtual requirement of the project for full viability. This project would flood a large area of Chobe – one of the greatest game reserve sites – and would be an act of ecological vandalism. There were other lesser objections, and the Zambian Government was keen to rather see the Lower Kafue Project go ahead instead. Whilst smaller than Batoka Gorge, it had a far lower cost per installed KW. So I duly wrote a speech for her in Parliament. For the first time in my life, I got a big kiss from a black woman!

In the midst of all this, I spent quite a lot of time with Pierre Rubbers, who was Eskom's roving representative in Africa and had been responsible for the wheeling agreements for the sub-continental movement and trading of power. In looking at the Lower Kafue project and Eskom's plans for the electrification of the townships, it became obvious that the shape of the power demand curve for Eskom would necessitate dealing with the power peaks which would result from this. Eskom's strategy of massive 700MW coal-fired sets simply was not suited to the new demands. I wrote an article for *International Water Power* magazine called "Peak Power on the Horizon", which argued that the growing regionalisation now being pushed by Eskom meant that this so-called "mid-merit power" was best supplied by using the vast water-storage capacity of central Africa, and which would in the long term mean that the dream of future power from the mighty rapids of Inga in the Congo would come closer to reality. After all, if you wanted more power from a hydro station, you just opened the tap! Mr Rubbers of Eskom embraced this idea and took the article to Eskom for study.

Thus encouraged, I had lengthy meetings with Knight-Piesold in England, who had authored the Batoka Gorge study. I took with me the Harza Engineering study of Lower Kafue.

What was obvious was that power was in the hands of bureaucrats who were totally uncommercial. Power was arranged by engineers deciding what was going to be done and then doing it. Whatever the final cost, this was simply passed on to the consumer. What made power investment unattractive was the typical seven-year development period, with the attendant interest costs and inflation over the period, and with all the uncertainty attached. I had been involved in the Pascua River Project in Chile – a 2,000MW project in the far south. The Japanese had done the studies and typically had come up with a seven-year programme. I radically redesigned the project to give a three-year cycle, which improved the economics out of all recognition.

So, in looking at Lower Kafue, it was necessary to cut the seven-year cycle, and to make the project as a more regionally designed project, in line with my discussions with Eskom and the whole idea of using water power for doing peak duties. Harza, in their study, had decided to put a small weir at the outfall of Upper Kafue and to take a 9km tunnel down the valley to a power station, where the river emerged into the Zambezi valley. I disliked it for a number of reasons. First, the lower station would be a "slave" station. Whatever Upper Kafue, in its wisdom, was generating had to be generated at the lower station or the water spilled and the power lost. You could only generate what was done above you, which hamstrung your plant operationally. At most, you had about half an hour of storage.

Then a 9km tunnel. Contracts down there involving underground powerhouses and tunnels had some bad history of poor geology and tremendous unanticipated costs. With the long construction period, the project would be difficult to finance. So, after much discussion, it was decided to move the dam site to one which had been studied by the Swedes in their earlier report. This site called for a simple roller compacted concrete dam 100 metres high, a short tunnel of 400 metres and a 3.5 kilometre-long canal. The advantage was that the tunnel, dam and canal could be done within the time horizon of the delivery of the mechanical and electrical equipment, and there were no geological surprises. With the gentle slope along the canal portion, it was possible to build a large canal to increase the water supply and not sacrifice too much head, at a very modest increase in costs.

The whole point about hydropower is that you are stuck with civil work costs. The mechanical and electrical equipment is pretty much fixed, although it follows the inexorable law of the two-thirds factor. So, having paid for the civils, you can double the size of your generating equipment for a 50% increase in costs. So we decided to increase the project to 1,250MW instead of the 650MW proposed by Harza. With a five-metre penalty in head, we could comfortably store 24 hours of water, and so be virtually independent of Upper Kafue and be a true mid-merit power station. Our capital cost, allowing for interest during construction and escalation, meant that a finished price of $600 per kw was our pretty firm estimate of costs. One of my associates in this venture had been my best friend at Harvard, Kurt Eckrich. Kurt had gone on to become the CFO of the International Finance Corporation (a private enterprise arm of the World Bank). Through his connections, they advised that any hydro project at less than $2,000 per kw was of interest. At $1,000/kw, it was a shoe-in. At $600/kw, it was a humdinger.

So, after this, we bit the bullet and offered Eskom a 10-year contract at $140/kw/year.

Whilst we were busy with this, another opportunity arose. We were offered two pumped storage units from Northern Ireland. These units had been ordered for a 350MW pumped storage facility in Ireland and the project was cancelled. 4,000 tons of equipment were offered to us for one million pounds – less than £3 per kw! And the design head was the same as Kariba.

As it happened, when Kariba North Bank was built, the powerhouse which had 4 X 150MW sets had actually been partially excavated to provide for two additional sets. The roof and crane were in place and half of the hall had been excavated. All that was needed was an intake works and tunnel for 100 metres, and a tailrace tunnel. We estimated the civil works at $15 million. So we came up with less than $20 million for a 350MW power station – less than $60/kw!! We added this in our offer to Eskom, with the proviso that the kwhs would have to be provided by Eskom in off-peak hours, as Zambia's water allocation was taken up by the existing 600MW station. It was actually a sensational deal, as power could be obtained from The Congo through the Likasi link for less than $0.0125 per unit, if Eskom had a shortage of off-peak power.

The response we got from Eskom was typical. They stated that, as far as pumped storage was concerned, they had identified seven sites in South Africa for 1,250MW of pumped storage at an overnight cost of $450/kw. They argued with our estimate for a coal-fired station of $1,700/kw and stated that they could build a coal-fired unit for $1,200/kw. Our offer was unattractive. All they would pay would be half a cent per kwh!

In 2008, I went back to Eskom with revised figures. We had up-to-date costings, which meant that our cost of Lower Kafue was now $850/kw, so that we would be looking for a figure of more like $200 per kw per year. We were never troubled with a reply. When you look at the cost of their pumped storage plant, together with the fact that you have to generate the power in a coal-fired unit, and return it to the grid at around an 80% efficiency, compared to the offer from Lower Kafue it is just a joke.

The point of this dissertation is to look at what Eskom has wrought. The first thing done by the ANC Government was to ethnically cleanse Eskom by sacking 600 senior white executives and replace them with unqualified executives whose only qualification was their black faces. The pumped storage plant being built by Eskom at Nqula is now estimated at 26 billion rands – $2,300 per kw. This is five times what the old regime would have spent. It is nearly three times the capital cost of Lower Kafue, and you still have to pay the generating cost of your power stations! When one gets to the new coal-fired stations being built, the figures are even more staggering. We are looking at $5,000 per kw. Even allowing for inflation, this figure is beyond belief. Clearly, some staggering profits are lining the pockets of well-connected ANC cadres, and total incompetence reigns in the running of Eskom. You only have to look at the mean 5.5 gigawatts of unplanned outages in the system to realise that the affirmative actions of the ANC have sounded the death knell for the most promising future industry in South Africa – smelting. It is pretty safe to say that Eskom has killed a million future jobs by this single act of racist stupidity. And the ANC in its recent conference has decided in its wisdom not to nationalise the mines. Just to tax them virtually out of existence.

Further, I am advised that the running of the Koeberg nuclear station is being done by effectively unqualified staff. Imagine the consequences of even a Three Mile Island accident when the Northwester is blowing over Cape Town!

Another wonderful example is PetroSa. When I returned from England, I saw an ad for a chief executive. We had been involved, as much earlier we had taken a licence from Sasol to propose a GTL on the North Slope of Alaska. A great deal of gas was being produced and there was no effective way to get this to market. We proposed a GTL plant, as is discussed elsewhere. But when Mossgas came up, we gave our feasibility study to Sasol, as they had not done any work at that time on GTL. The result was PetroSa. When I saw the ad for a chief executive, I thought that, with all my experience with chemical plants, Pertamina, etc, I should take a look at it. After all, I had sold the explosives business to Sasol, who were doing pretty nicely out of it – thank you very much.

Well, I applied for the job. I thought I would be a pretty prime candidate. I never even got an acknowledgement.

But the bright people selected to run Mossgas came up with their own unique piece of chemical engineering. The boiler feed plant broke down. Well, any idiot could see that all you did was to put water into the boiler plants. Which they did. And destroyed all the boilers on the plant. The cost? Three months down at a cost of half a billion dollars. And what was said about it? Nothing.

As an observer of the field – no longer being involved, but having cut my teeth in states which were black-run long before South Africa – one has to make observations based upon facts – not emotions. There's plenty of that to go round! An excellent article in The Economist made the observation that, before making serious investments, one should carefully check the emigration statistics of a country to see if it was going forward or backwards. High emigration of the professional classes – engineers, scientists, accountants, lawyers – is a powerful indication of a country going backwards, not forwards. South Africa has lost at least 500,000 people in this category – six of them from my own family!

It has been estimated that every such professional, in fact, supports 10 other jobs. On this basis, the ANC has destroyed five million jobs! Is it any wonder that anything run by this Government has all but collapsed? The only thing being done competently is the wholesale theft of money from Government by ANC cadres, by every means of corruption devised by man. Once again, *The Economist* has hit the nail on the head with a well-researched article, "Cry the Beloved Country". South Africa is not a place to invest in.

This is unlikely to change. When Mbeki was inaugurated at the Union Buildings, the loudest cheer was reserved for Comrade Mugabe. He, after all, had put the white man firmly in his place by seizing all his assets. The fact that this entirely destroyed the economy of his country was beside the point. When Julius Malema advocated confiscating all white assets, as these have been stolen from the black majority, he, too, was cheered from the rooftops. When the whole unhappy situation collapses into a mess, it will become the excuse to seize the assets of those greedy whites. And by then the Constitutional Court will have been packed and will bow to the will of the people.

The problem, of course, starts at the top. Schabir Shaik was convicted of bribing Jacob Zuma. No such fate for Zuma. Through some devious means, his prosecution is "politically motivated". Although Shaik got 15 years, after a small interval it was decided some years ago that he had but a few months to live. Let him out. He appears to have got a new lease of life! It has been estimated that at least 30% of all tax revenues are syphoned-off into the pockets of the well-heeled ANC cadres. It is positively obscene to see the wealth being garnered by the black elite in the name of black economic empowerment. Every company is blackmailed into handing over great swathes of the economy to these oligarchs. Lest you think that this enhances tax revenues, an associate of mine was in a very private bank in Switzerland. Who should pop out of the private wealth section: Cyril Ramaphosa! Soon to be the next President.

The so-called Black Economic Empowerment has done little more than allow well-connected blacks to extort a portion of the wealth possessed by the white community. It is instructive to note how this works. Tokyo Sexwale was financed to buy a big chunk of Goldfields. As the shares soared, he baled out, with profits in the hundreds of millions. Goldfields were then told they were no longer empowered. So a hastily stitched together sordid deal was done with convicted criminals to give back the empowered status. Another stalwart, Mzi Khumalo, was financed by the IDC to buy at a huge discount the BEE stake in Harmony. The Harmony shares soared and Mzi got out with a billion rand profit. Nice if you can get it. And poor old Harmony is no longer empowered.

As an entrepreneur, one tries to start projects. In these projects the driving force is what I call the "entrepreneuring margin". This gives the entrepreneur his profit and shareholding. Now he is in effect forced to hand over his margin to a black empowerment partner, who will contribute little or nothing to the business, unless he wants to join the corrupt queues. Many have been forced to accept this as the price of getting a project. But a very good friend of mine in Zambia, Nonny Mwanyungwi, who runs a very successful Farm Chemicals business, told me that he avoided like the plague getting politically connected folks involved with business. He reckoned that one day these well-connected individuals would find a change in regime and they would be in deep trouble. So, at your peril you accept the inevitable corruption associated, as you have to make out of the hide of the customers the excess profits needed to finance your BEE venture. A number of people I have come across have just given up. The stress of being involved in projects with people whose only connection is with politics, and who need to fatten these folks' pockets, finally wears you down. A far more salubrious climate exists in other areas of southern Africa.

So, not only do we live in a totally corrupt society, but a totally incompetent one. The only place in the world I know where your local radio station tells which traffic lights are out of action is Johannesburg. This is symptomatic of every municipality in the country, where all the rates revenue goes into fat-cat black pockets and all services are slowly collapsing. The roads are slowly becoming potholed, the town is filthy – in truth, a fine example of a third world country. At least twice a month we have a power failure.

The Government embarked upon a policy of wholesale ethnic cleansing, thus forcing an unparalled brain drain from the country. All whites know they are living on borrowed time. The brightest and best have left, and the rest are departing in droves. In an interesting recent programme on "The Justice Factor", Moeletsie Mbeki, Thabo Mbeki's brother, gave us his analysis of the problem. He singled out BEE as a major problem. Another is education and how affirmative action in the Statal sector had brought about a collapse in service delivery. His prediction was that eventually there would be a huge explosion of dissatisfaction from the black masses who have seen little benefit from the ANC Government. The scale of corruption in the country is legendary. The fact that Zuma can spend R270 million on his private residence sets a fine example for the rest. Probably 30% of Government revenue is wasted by being syphoned-off into black pockets. One only has to look at the sale of Julius Malema's assets to see the scale of misappropriation of state funds. Apart from the fact that the mean IQ of sub-Saharan Africa is 65, South African education is the second worst in the world. And even though universities have been ordered to dumb down their degrees so as to pass more blacks, the resultant output is becoming less and less likely to handle modern technology, which is becoming more and more sophisticated, not less.

And the ANC finally showed its hand. The premier of Gauteng declared that she was getting rid of all the "pale males" working for her Government. She described them as the "White Gevaar". No wonder the working of Government is in a state of collapse. It has one of the most venal and corrupt regimes on the face of the earth. It is dumbing down education to the extent that degrees from South Africa are rapidly becoming unacceptable anywhere else in the world. Mugabe led the world in dragging his country back into the primitive savagery of his forefathers with one of the most racist regimes on earth. No wonder unemployment in South Africa is soaring. And Moeletsi Mbeki has described South Africa as having a culture of "entitlement". If you are black, you don't have to work. You are entitled to be rich. Having struggled to create projects with black empowerment partners, I have had the first-hand experience of having a perfectly good project wrecked by this attitude. The Eskom affirmative action programme has wrecked one of the great hopes for industrial future in South Africa. Endowed with great resources of chrome, manganese and iron, the prospects of a great future for these industries has been wrecked forever. And unfortunately, because of the momentum of the country, because of the large white remnants running companies, the decline will not be as visible as it was in Zimbabwe and Mozambique, so the decline will be slow and the penny will not drop in the basically illiterate and ill-educated electorate, who nevertheless can see a black elite swanning around with vast wealth which they have done little to create, but have largely extorted from the whites by the BEE policy. So there is little point in trying to create anything of value in South Africa. In doing so, you are forced to carry a heavy burden of passengers who can bring nothing but political connections.

On the other hand, there are signs of hope. Zambia and Botswana are examples of countries going forward at pace. The penny has dropped. That's where I intend spending the last of my productive days.

FARMER HILL

During the course of business one had to lead a private life. Having four children, it was natural that we should look to Plettenberg Bay, the east coast's most popular holiday playground, for our summer holidays. We rented a very nice house on what was commonly called "millionaires' row" or, more accurately, Beachy Head Road. It was a perfect place for the children as the beach was right below the house. After a few years, having some spare cash, we bought a house on the same road for R85,000.

Nowadays, it is de *rigeur* to have a house on the front on Beachy Head Road. We sold our home there a couple of years ago for R15.5 million, only to see it planked by the buyer (I believe the head of a local bank) and a R18 million mansion erected. It was a reasonable return after 30 years of bliss for our family. Over this period the town council had a field day – our rates were R10,000 per month! R120,000 for a month's holiday! For two people! *Sic transit Gloria.*

In Plet we took to a lot of exploring. We were shown a house built by Basil Read (one of the contracting moguls) on the coast to the south. It was built as a pseudo-castle with a spectacular view of the wild coast between Plet and Knysna. During our forays we found an unlocked gate through forestry and came upon some spectacular coast. Later, we found out from a local agent that there was a farm which had some 7 kilometres of coast which included the portions we had chanced upon. He told me that it was in the estate of Jock

Farm near Plettenberg

Marr, a well-known Cape Town surgeon. On further investigation I found that one of his children, Heather Marr, had been my dancing partner at Mrs Irvine's dancing classes at St Thomas's Church in Rondebosch! One of his sons (Sandy Marr) lived on the farm and I paid him a visit.

He told me that he was looking after the farm for his mother and siblings. He told me that the farm could only carry one sheep per 100 acres and was not really a farming proposition. He ran an earthmoving business and really wanted shot of the farm. He thought it was worth R300,000. Well, this sum was way beyond my resources, being nearly four times the price we had paid for our beach house. I had a horrible holiday trying to think of a way to buy it. Then Neill Andrew, the estate agent who had introduced me to the farm, told me that the Marr estate could easily afford to sanction a bond of R240,000. I figured I could put together R60,000 and so we became the happy owners of 700 hectares of farm with a 7km seafront! We kept the name of the farm – Cairnbrogie – a small town in Aberdeenshire in Scotland.

One of Dominique's great friends was a member of the Thesen family, one of the founding families of Knysna, and we talked to her. She said we should plant trees, and gave us some valuable contacts. So, over the next couple of years we established 150 hectares of trees, and acquired an ex-forester to manage the place. By this time we were in full swing in the fertiliser industry, so I talked to our marketing manager, Abel Botha, who was a top agronomist. I told him I had bought the farm because of the coast, but it would be a sin not to try to farm it properly. So Abel went off to Plet to do some investigations. On his return, and after he had had soil samples analysed, we sat down to discuss what was to be done.

He said to me: "Have you ever put your finger in the soil?" I said "No", and his answer was: "Well, don't. You don't have an acid soil, you have a corrosive soil, which is saturated with salt. You have a heavy clay subsoil which is impenetrable to water, so your farm is a desert which no water will penetrate. You have no nutrients at all in your soil!" I asked him what I had to do.

In the first instance, he prescribed 30 tons of lime per hectare to remove the acidity, 5 tons of gypsum per hectare to remove the salt, and to deep plough to 18 inches to increase the organic content (which was zero). We concluded the only way to achieve this was to take a cash crop off and to spread the liming over three years. By ploughing back the wheat stalks into the ground every year with deep ploughing and liming 10 tons each year, he concluded that we could then have a satisfactory soil structure. As far as nutrients were concerned, he told me it was the first soil he had ever seen with zero phosphate! Fortunately, we had a big stock of di-ammonium phosphate which was badly caked, and I was able to buy it cheaply.

However, planting wheat had its problems. Although we were supposed to get 1,100mm of rain per year, nothing was said about its erratic nature. We suffered from drought during critical planting times. I sat one year in December and watched a bumper crop rot as the ground was so water-logged we couldn't get in to harvest it. My Rhodesian ex-farm manager then concluded that the only solution was to farm animals. So eventually, after fits and starts, we went dairy farming.

We had one small benefit. When I bought the farm from Sandy Marr, as part of the package he built a large dam, so during the drought months we were able to irrigate – all of which took a lot of trial and error and many years.

At the same time, we had been spending some time in the eastern Free State on some friends' farm. I fell in love with the stone buildings being built. Our host was an architect, Brian De La Harpe, who had done some work for us in Johannesburg, and he explained that prisoners in jail in Lesotho were put to work cutting the sandstone of the eastern Free State. As a consequence, you could buy cut stone for 50 cents a cubic foot – cheaper than brick!

Then he phoned me to tell me that the farm next door was for sale for R60,000. It was spectacular, being on a mountain top. It was only suitable for grazing cattle, but had the most incredible views. I suggested to Brian that I would buy it if he would run the farm and build a castle on top of a spectacular cliff. So Hilltop Estates was born. As part of the castle building plan, Brian and I did a tour of those famous Welsh castles: Harlech, Caernarvon, Conway, Beaumaris, Pembroke and Caerphilly.

And castle-building started. Whilst a rough track had been built up to the top, it could hardly serve as a construction road. So we got Brian's neighbour, Robbie Boswell, to build a road to the top. His problem was that he required quite a lot of blasting. I talked to our sales manager for explosives, Steve Middleton, who told me we had a special right, called the swimming pool dispensation, whereby he could put some explosives in the boot of his car, and put the detonators in the cubby hole in order to do small blasting jobs.

So we got Robbie to drill all the holes he needed, and Steve and I drove down to the farm and Steve set about doing the blasting. He got the shock of his life when, out of the blue, the local police drove past on their way to their TV aerial, which they had set up on the mountain top. Steve told me the site was littered with boxes marked HIGH EXPLOSIVE with a red "explosives" printed on them, detonating cord was festooned all over the site, and people were stuffing explosives down the holes. The policemen waved cheerily at him, and did the same on their return. He watched them disappear back to Fouriesburg, and then set the lot off. There was a massive explosion, and the police car was seen heading at a high speed towards the farm at the foot of the mountain. Their enquiries met with a bland denial that there had been an explosion there.

Incidentally, the swimming pool dispensation allowed for half a box of explosives in the boot. Steve had transported more like ten boxes! The police put it down to an explosion in Lesotho.

So Robbie got on with building a concrete road up the pass, which enabled big trucks to reach the castle site. And we got on with building the castle. It remains one of the spectacular sights in the eastern Free State. Brian quit farming and I bought Bestersvlei, his farm at the foot of the mountain. However, we were never able to get satisfactory farm management, and I sold first Hilltop and then Bestersvlei to a Michael Fogg, who turned the castle into an up-market hotel. He never finished the castle to its original design.

We had an amusing comment from one of our friends who visited it. He looked at the cut stone lying all over the site, and said that for the first time he now understood Greek ruins. Everyone thought that they had fallen down. His new thesis was that they had never been completed!

At least we got our money back when we sold.

Back to Cairnbrogie. Everyone thought we were mad to buy 12km from Plet centre. But our longest boundary was with the Harkerville forest, and we had a plentiful flow of wildlife out of there, the most exciting being leopards, who helped keep some 300 baboons in check. And one of the farm manager's dogs got gored by a bushbuck he tackled!

The price of this lot was R25 million for 100 hectares – rather more than. The farm has now been developed into a model dairy with 60 hectares under irrigation, to be expanded to 120 hectares under irrigation to make it one of the finest properties on the Garden Route. Of course, its market value now exceeds by many times its value as a farm. Every year we get approaches from developers. Jack Nicklaus, who visited the farm with one of them, felt he could build one of the world's top 100 golf courses on the site as a sort of spectacular Pebble Beach course.

We decided to build a Cape Dutch centre as the main concourse to the farm. Included was a copy of the Groot Constantia barn some 1,600 square metres in extent. This has become a popular wedding venue.

My youngest son Andrew now runs the farm as a model dairy farm, milking 600 cows. We have continued to run a forestry section, but we had to close down our timber-treatment plant. We were told we could not sell our popular post and rail fencing unless we had an SABS stamp on the timber. The price that SABS wanted in order to give us the stamp was enormous for a small operation, which made the whole thing uneconomic.

Because of the huge value which has now accrued to the farm, it is clear that farming alone can never make an adequate return on its market value. So we now just soldier on farming, with little hope of ever turning to account the great value in the farm, unless we sell it. Having put half my life into the property, all I can do is just enjoy the place.

I remember sitting up on the cliffs with the late Sydney Press (the chain store mogul) and talking about my plans for the farm. He, of course, had developed one of the country's most spectacular farms at Lydenburg – Coromandel Estates.

As I was telling Sydney what I visualised for the property, he said to me, very gently: "It really gets to you, doesn't it?" I suppose he was one of the few people around who really understood what drove me. After a four-hour tour of the farm, Sydney sat down and wrote down all his comments! It was quite a *tour de force* and gave some insight into what it took to be a chain store magnate!

It was only after Andrew started to run the farm that we had the necessary commitment to really turn the estate into a proper farming venture.

Cairnbrogie remains the apple of my eye and gives me great pleasure in my old age.

FAMILY MAN: Hill reads to his grandsons Dylan (left) an Gwylim, from the tales of his favourite character from childrens's literature, Barbar. The Hills have a few close friends – not even Johan Hahn, Hill's partner of 20 years, is to be seen in the family photo archive. Instead, Oliver and Dominique happily enclosed their lives within a close family. It may explain, says Dominique, why they have found themselves so alone in their troubles.

www.ingramcontent.com/pod-product-compliance
Lightning Source LLC
Chambersburg PA
CBHW071216080526
44587CB00013BA/1393